Neo-Feminist Cinema

What lies behind current feminist discontent with contemporary cinema?

Through a combination of cultural and industry analysis, Hilary Radner's *Neo-Feminist Cinema: Girly Films, Chick Flicks and Consumer Culture* shows how the needs of Conglomerate Hollywood have encouraged an emphasis on consumer culture within films made for women. By exploring a number of representative "girly films," including *Pretty Woman, Legally Blonde, Maid in Manhattan, The Devil Wears Prada* and *Sex and the City: The Movie*, Radner proposes that rather than being "post-feminist," as is usually assumed, such films are better described as "neo-feminist." Examining their narrative format, which revolves around the story of an ambitious unmarried woman who defines herself through consumer culture as much as through work or romance, Radner argues that these films exemplify neo-liberalist values rather than those of feminism.

As such, *Neo-Feminist Cinema* offers a new explanation as to why feminist-oriented scholars and audiences who are seeking more than "labels and love" from their film experience have viewed recent "girly films" as a betrayal of second-wave feminism, and why, on the other hand, such films have proven to be so successful at the box office.

Hilary Radner is Professor and Foundation Chair of Film and Media Studies at the University of Otago in New Zealand. She is author of *Shopping Around: Feminine Culture and the Pursuit of Pleasure* and co-editor of several books including *New Zealand Cinema: Interpreting History* (forthcoming); *Jane Campion: Cinema, Nation, Identity*; *Swinging Single: Representing Sexuality in the 1960s*; *Constructing the New Consumer Society*; and *Film Theory Goes to the Movies*, also published by Routledge.

Neo-Feminist Cinema

Girly Films, Chick Flicks and Consumer Culture

Hilary Radner

 Routledge
Taylor & Francis Group

NEW YORK AND LONDON

First published 2011
by Routledge
270 Madison Avenue, New York, NY 10016

Simultaneously published in the UK
by Routledge
2 Park Square, Milton Park, Abingdon, Oxon OX14 4RN

Routledge is an imprint of the Taylor & Francis Group, an informa business

Typeset in Perpetua by Taylor & Francis Books
Printed and bound in the United States of America on acid-free paper by
Sheridan Books, Inc.

Library of Congress Cataloging in Publication Data
Radner, Hilary.
Neo-feminist cinema : girly films, chick flicks and consumer culture / Hilary
Radner.
p. cm.
Includes bibliographical references and index.
1. Feminism and motion pictures. 2. Women in motion pictures.
3. Motion pictures for women—United States. I. Title.
PN1995.9.W6R335 2010
791.43'6522—dc22
2010009654

ISBN13: 978-0-415-87773-2 (hbk)
ISBN13: 978-0-415-87774-9 (pbk)
ISBN13: 978-0-203-85521-8 (ebk)

For Alistair, without whom this book would not have been written.

Contents

Figures

Acknowledgments

I wish to acknowledge the generous assistance I received from the University of Otago in the form of a University of Otago Research Grant and a one semester Research and Study Leave. I would particularly like to thank Geoffrey White, former Deputy Vice-Chancellor of Research at the University of Otago. He was an unfailing friend to researchers throughout his term. Without his support, this project would not have seen the light. Additional assistance was provided by the Department of Media, Film and Communication and the Division of Humanities; in particular the general staff have helped to progress this book through its various stages over the past three years. Karen McLean, Lisa Marr and Peter Stapleton provided much appreciated editorial assistance in preparing the manuscript, while Ellen Pullar in her capacity as research-assistant worked on the project in its initial stages. The Margaret Herrick Library of the Academy of Motion Picture Arts and Sciences generously allowed me to use its resources; staff were ever friendly and accommodating, while my fellow researchers, Sally, Eric and especially Raymond and Ellen, supplied congenial company and camaraderie throughout my time at the library. I am especially grateful to Alistair, Ashleigh and Hannah who have forgiven me the many lost weekends I spent working on this book rather than with them.

Numerous friends and colleagues have offered support and encouragement, sharing their insights about popular culture for women. Janet Staiger cheered me on during the project's early stages. My colleagues at the University of Otago, among them Len Andersen, Barbara Brookes, Annabel Cooper, Natalie Smith and Rebecca Stringer, as well as Ewa Ziarek and Kathy Psomiades, former colleagues from the University of Notre Dame, were generous with their kind words and sound advice. Celestino Deleyto included me in a panel organized for the Society for Cinema and Media Studies 2008 conference, which provided me with an opportunity to discuss my developing ideas in a congenial and informed atmosphere; similarly, Rosalind Gill's invitation to present at "New Femininities: An International Conference" (LSE and the

British Library) in 2007 was crucial to the project's evolution. Raphaëlle Moine, a model of industry and academic rigor, has, through her example and her friendship, been an inspiration to me. Finally, I would like to thank the Film and Media Studies PhD students here at Otago who have shared their work and their thoughts with me: Pam Fossen, Clément Da Gama, Gabrielle Hine, Bronwyn Polaschek, Ellen Pullar and Erica Todd. Their feedback and enthusiasm has been a primary motivation for me, a sign that research on women's issues remains a vital and important area in Film and Gender Studies.

Note on sources: all box office figures and release dates, unless otherwise indicated, are provided by Box Office Mojo, available online at boxofficemojo.com.

Earlier versions of some material included in this book appeared in *Film Theory Goes to the Movies* (Routledge, 1993), *Swinging Single: Representing Sexuality in the 1960s* (University of Minnesota Press, 1999) and *Falling in Love Again: Romantic Comedy in Contemporary Cinema* (I.B. Tauris, 2009).

Introduction

Reassessing Feminism and Popular Culture

Growing up in a feminist household, in my youth I was largely protected from popular culture by my earnest Californian parents. As a result, American popular culture held a distinct fascination for me as a terrain that was strangely familiar and alien at the same time. It is probably not surprising, then, that eventually popular culture became, for me, an object of intellectual and scholarly curiosity, the focus of an almost anthropological sense of inquiry on my part as I attempted to understand the dominant cultural trends of the historical period into which I had been born, and through which I came of age. In the course of researching popular culture for women as part of my doctoral thesis in the 1980s, I was shocked to discover not the downtrodden housewives that I had been led to expect by feminism, but a group of lusty, independent females determined to have fun, to succeed and to develop a healthy bank account, while masquerading behind a girlish demeanor.

Popular culture generally, and women's magazines in particular, were not lamenting woman's fate—rather, there was a mood of celebration and heated anticipation about what the present offered and what the future might bring. This discovery prompted me to begin a reassessment of the place and function of second-wave feminism, in the course of which I took a number of wrong turns, attributing, as did many scholars, the confidence of succeeding generations of women to the hard work of feminists in the 1960s and 1970s; however, the divide between the "can-do" woman and the feminist continued to sharpen. While the 2008 US Presidential Campaign left a bad taste in the mouths of many because of the scrutiny and abuse to which Hillary Clinton and Sarah Palin were subjected— of a type reserved only for women—their respective candidacies also reflected a general sentiment that women should not limit their aspirations, and that the possibility of having, perhaps not "it all," but "most of it," remained very real for many women. Feminists, in contrast, viewed the developments of contemporary culture with understandable dismay. In a recent book, feminist scholar Diane Negra asks, "Why does this period feel so punishing and anxious to many?"[1]

More recently, I have concluded that this division is not the result of feminism-gone-awry, or of women more generally abandoning feminism, but of the influences of other templates for feminine behavior and aspirations for women—provided most notably by a generation of women who, though contemporaneous with feminist figures such as Betty Friedan, had a very different set of goals that centered around expediency and personal fulfillment. This point of view was expressed by popular novelists such as Grace Metalious, Rona Jaffe, Jacqueline Suzanne, Erica Jong and Judith Krantz, and also in magazines for women, most notably *Cosmopolitan Magazine*, edited by Helen Gurley Brown, as well as in self-help books that ranged from *Coffee, Tea or Me*, by Trudy Baker and Rachel Jones (1967), to *The Beautiful People's Beauty Book: How to Achieve the Look and Manner of the World's Most Attractive Women*, by Princess Luciana Pignatelli (1973).

This volume is the result of my reassessment of second-wave feminism and its consequences, a process that has inspired me to conclude that the conditions that produced second-wave feminism also produced another movement among women, one as yet unnamed, that shared some of its aspirations (but not all), while adding a few others. I will argue that this other unnamed movement, which I will dub, for want of a better term, "neo-feminism," has been the primary influence in developing what is now casually referred to as "post-feminist" culture, which, as I shall demonstrate, has very little to do with feminism. Neo-feminism, in fact, is only very tangentially a consequence of feminism; while it was quick to incorporate catch-phrases, such as "empowerment," and "self-fulfillment," which it used to its own ends, the major thrust of its perspective coincided very neatly with neo-liberalism as the prevailing philosophy and ethos of the late twentieth century, with which it was eminently compatible.

In order to elucidate the terms of contemporary neo-feminism, I have chosen to examine a group of related films, directed towards a female audience, that highlight its significant traits and tenets. While to some degree the choice to examine cinema may seem arbitrary and idiosyncratic, as a film scholar I had a particular interest in attempting to elucidate the influences of neo-feminism on cinema as a cultural form that both included women, and also systematically attempted to reach a broader audience than niche-marketed cultural forms such as magazines. In many ways, cinema is perhaps the most logical arena in which to analyze dominant trends in popular thought, because feature-length films provide a dense articulation of the contemporaneous discursive formations in which a film participates—formations that it may reproduce, modify and critique. As a lynchpin element in a system of media synergies, films often include highly schematic representations of contemporary discourses in which the tensions and controversies of an era are writ large.

Because the neo-feminist paradigm encourages and reinforces consumer culture practices as one of the primary means through which a woman can confirm her identity and express herself, it constitutes a very attractive version of feminine culture in terms of the needs and designs of the media conglomerates that dominate the contemporary scene. Current interest in fashion and style, strongly encouraged by neo-feminism, may, for example, contribute to the "unaided awareness" that a hit movie is judged to require, even before it opens.

This collection of essays examines, then, what I call "post-Pretty Woman" films—or "girly films," referring to the spate of female-oriented films, culminating with *Sex and the City: The Movie* (Michael Patrick King, 2008), that rely on the international success of the format initiated by *Pretty Woman* (Garry Marshall, 1990). My goal is not to describe exhaustively women's films produced during the last decade of the twentieth century and the first decade of the twenty-first century, but, rather, to highlight a selection of films that, in my view, most aptly embody what I am calling neo-feminism, as understood by a mainstream audience that embraces its belief-system without naming it as such. In so doing, I draw upon a number of previous studies that have described the general lineaments of contemporary culture and its representation of gender, such as Rosalind Gill's *Gender and the Media*[2] and Imelda Whelehan's *Overloaded: Popular Culture and the Future of Feminism*.[3] While I fundamentally agree with these authors in terms of how they characterize contemporary feminine culture, I also diverge from them by showing, through my analysis of the girly film, how the perspective offered by these films suggests not a reaction against feminism, but the continuation and dominance of what I am calling neo-feminism.

In contrast with the broader perspectives of these previous works, this volume focuses on a set of case studies involving films that unite a significant number of traits: a charismatic female star embodying a character at the center of her universe who is a "working woman"; an emphasis on fashion and consumer culture; the disappearance of chastity as a "feminine virtue"; romance as a significant theme (if not always necessarily the primary plot); the privileging of the "do-over" as the resolution to seemingly insurmountable problems, among others. Quite a few films, such as the seminal *Bridget Jones's Diary* (Sharon Maguire, 2001) or the box office hits, *My Big Fat Greek Wedding* (Joel Zwick, 2002) and *Mamma Mia!* (Phyllida Lloyd, 2008), which I discuss briefly,[4] mobilize some traits but not others, testifying to the broad, if uneven, influence of the neo-feminist paradigm. I have chosen to focus on films, such as *Maid in Manhattan* (Wayne Wang, 2002),[5] that unite a maximum number of traits that could be said to constitute expressions of neo-feminism (not to be confused with feminism)—a strand in feminine culture which, I argue, develops out the 1960s with a set of ideas and practices that are not a consequence of feminism (as many post-feminist scholars claim) but, rather, constitute another (ultimately much more influential) reaction to the same conditions that produced second-wave feminism.

I have dubbed these films "girly" films in order to underline their relations to a feminine ideal that is represented though "girlishness" as a mode of appearance and set of character traits that are not necessarily linked to biological age. The analysis proceeds by isolating a number of key texts that exhibit the significant traits of the girly film and its evolution over a 20-year period, beginning with *Pretty Woman*. Each film was chosen not only because it represents a particular dimension of the girly film and its relations to women, but also because of the way it illuminates the state of cinema today in the era of Conglomerate Hollywood. By combining cultural and industry analysis, as well as drawing upon contemporary work in star studies, I attempt to explore why Hollywood makes so few films for women, and why the few that are made have such a limited scope and perspective.

I begin the volume, in chapter one, with a discussion of the relations between feminism and neo-feminism. In particular, I discuss the inception and the development of the neo-feminist paradigm as exemplified through the life and writing of Helen Gurley Brown. Chapter two develops the concept of the girly film as an example of how the neo-feminist paradigm comes belatedly to influence successful popular films for women, as in *Pretty Woman*, which, arguably, defines the terms for subsequent Hollywood films that seek to address the female audience. Chapter three, focusing on *Romy and Michele's High School Reunion* (David Mirkin, 1997), adumbrates and explores the characteristics of the female friendship film as it evolves to adjust to the format of the girly film. Chapter four investigates *Legally Blonde* (Robert Luketic, 2001) as an example of the "career woman" formula, modified to fit the format of the girly film, in particular with a view to the earlier *Working Girl* (Mike Nichols, 1988). Chapters five and six address the shifting terms of the neo-feminist paradigm in its attempts to appeal to a "raced" subject. Chapter five describes the star narrative and persona of Jennifer Lopez as an expression of contemporary Latinidad and its relations to the neo-feminist paradigm, while chapter six assesses *Maid in Manhattan* as a Jennifer Lopez-vehicle, offering a new fairy tale for second-generation Latinas. Chapter seven discusses how recent developments in Hollywood Cinema, grouped under the rubric of "Conglomerate Hollywood" by scholars such as Thomas Schatz,[6] have affected films directed at the female audience. Chapter eight continues this theme by looking at the increasing synergies between the fashion industry and cinema, and its effects on the development of the fashion film as another facet of the girly film, of which *The Devil Wears Prada* (David Frankel, 2006) provides an exemplary instance. Chapter nine, focusing on *Sex and the City: The Movie*

(Michael Patrick King, 2008), offers an analysis of the female event film as the ultimate incarnation of the girly film, one that is particularly compatible with neo-feminism because of its emphasis on consumer culture. Finally, chapter ten looks at how an auteur director, Nancy Meyers, while pursuing a personal vision, also reproduces the neo-feminist paradigm in *Something's Gotta Give* (Nancy Meyers, 2003), accommodating the older woman as a variation on the girly ideal, demonstrating how girlishness and age are not correlated.

While the films that I highlight have been largely described in terms of post-feminism by previous film scholars, I argue that far from representing a turning away from feminism, these films represent the ways in which neo-feminism proved more successful in providing models for women seeking to confront the complexities of contemporary culture—in particular, changing expectations about gender-defined roles—than feminism itself. The more utopian vision promoted by feminists failed to offer solutions to individuals who sought to preserve their identity as "feminine" while aspiring to the kind of material comforts and achievements that define success in the terms of neo-liberalism. In the following chapter, I explore in greater detail the distinctions between feminism and neo-feminism as well as the specific tenets, as they come to be defined in the 1960s and 1970s, of neo-feminism itself.

Chapter 1

Neo-Feminism and the Rise of the Single Girl

Explicitly and implicitly, women are instructed by their environment (from the school room to the women's magazine) in how to "become" a woman—a task that is never completed and is subject to constant revision.[1] This concept of identity as a process of "becoming" has been understood as offering emancipatory possibilities to the individual who is invited, not to take up a stable, untested and fixed position, but, rather, to see her "self," or even "selves," as subject to a multiple and on-going process of revision, reform and choices.[2] The development of contemporary culture, however, beginning with the rise of consumerism and the concomitant cultivation of the body and self-presentation, exploits the idea of the "becoming woman" for the purposes of consumer industries. As a result, it is difficult to maintain an entirely optimistic view of this system of unstable identities, which capitalism encourages, rather than discourages.[3]

In 1992, sociologist Robert Goldman used the terms "neo-feminism" and "commodity feminism" to describe the ways in which advertisers suggested, in the 1970s and 1980s, that "control and ownership over one's body/face/self, accomplished through the *right* acquisitions, can maximize one's value at both work and home." He maintains that "[a]s far as corporate marketers are now concerned, this new 'freedom' has become essential to the accumulation of capital—to reproducing the commodity form."[4] Following upon analyses like that of Goldman, I propose to use the term "neo-feminism" to refer to the tendency in feminine culture to evoke choice and the development of individual agency as the defining tenets of feminine identity—best realized through an engagement with consumer culture in which the woman is encouraged to achieve self-fulfillment by purchasing, adorning or surrounding herself with the goods that this culture can offer. Choice, particularly in the form of "shopping," as a process of weighing and evaluating alternatives with a view to making a decision that optimizes the individual's own position, is the fundamental principle that governs neo-feminist behavior.[5]

Neo-feminism, then, can be understood as a set of practices and discourses that define a certain position or "identities" (that women may or may not take up) that have developed in the post-World War II period in the United States and in Western Europe. The topic that I wish to explore here is the discursive formation that arises out of this development in the evolution of feminine subjectivity, particularly in the way it informs a spate of films that I call "girly" films, using the term girly for two distinct reasons.[6] The first is to suggest how "girlishness" and "girl" have been reclaimed by feminine culture as a new ideal promising continual change and self-improvement as a sign of individual agency (a girl is always in the process of "becoming"). Second, the term underlines ways in which the sexual availability of women, represented by images initially addressing a male viewer, as in the girly magazines of the 1940s or 1950s, has been rewritten as a form of personal empowerment. The girly films form a distinct class of cinematic narratives, regularly released over the last 20 years, that reproduce a neo-feminist paradigm aimed at women audiences, falling into the category "chick flick," without exhausting it. While all girly films sit comfortably within the category "chick flick," not all "chick flicks" are girly films, nor do all "chick flicks" reproduce a neo-feminist paradigm. It would be difficult, however, to find a single popular film made after 1965 that has not been influenced by this neo-feminist position—or rather, the sets of discourses and practices that inform it.

The various discursive practices involved all concern contemporary feminine identity—in Stuart Hall's terms, "not 'who we are' or 'where we come from,' so much as what we might become, how we have been represented and how that bears on how we might represent ourselves."[7] For Hall and other cultural-studies scholars, "identity" in the form or a "self" or "selves" is a necessary heuristic device—not simply for scholars, but also for the subject, who must fashion a "self" in order to perceive, understand and act.[8] This does not mean, however, as Hall explained in an oft-quoted article, that the self is an invention by a particular individual; rather, "selves" have a "discursive, material, or political effectivity."[9]

My interest in the girly film as a particular representation of neo-feminism stems from the manner in which this cycle of films underlines the inherently fissured and contradictory nature of the discursive formation that it invokes. In a 1974 article commenting on classical Hollywood cinema, film scholar and theorist Dana Polan remarks: "[b]ourgeois existence is often little more than a continual succession of disappointments, of subversions, all of which fissure our self unity and social unity as acting subjects." For Polan, popular art-forms hold a privileged relationship with the "self-unity and social unity" of a given subject—which is not to say that this unity is homogeneous, but rather that it is itself a facet of identity as a process of self-revision. In the same article, he comments that "texts ... are contracts in which spectators or readers willingly agree to relate to codes in a certain way ... with knowledge usually of the workings of many of these codes." Polan also underlines the fact that transgressions of the code—the production of contradiction and critique—are "inherent in the system."[10] The girly film, being a discursive form that depends upon both shared codes and their transgression, displays the inherently vexed nature of femininity that both feminism and neo-feminism imply for the feminine subject in contemporary culture.

Fundamental to this analysis is an assumption that feature-length films provide a particularly dense articulation of the contemporaneous discursive formations in which the film participates—formations that it may reproduce, modify and critique.[11] In contrast with television programming, women's magazines, blogs, or other popular-culture forms, the feature-length Hollywood film characteristically condenses the terms that define a given formation in order to amalgamate them into a single representation of a finite duration. While film and television (as opposed to the blog) share a mode of production depending upon a deep division of labor, the feature-length film, as a lynchpin element in a system of media synergies, constitutes a privileged cultural form in terms of capital investment as well as labor. Consequently, these films offer highly schematic representations of both the codes, and the transgressions of these codes, that define neo-feminism. Scrutinized by marketing experts, the popular Hollywood film may well provide a "royal road" to the collective drives, conscious and unconscious, of its audiences, its desires and fears, in so far as these can be made to coincide with the tenets of the consumer-culture orientation of the medium itself. Because the neo-feminist paradigm encourages and reinforces consumer culture practices, it constitutes a very attractive—and hence often exploited—version of feminine identity, from the perspective of Hollywood.

The term "neo-feminism" has been used sporadically and somewhat impressionistically in a variety of ways since the 1970s, having in common the assumption that neo-feminism is a reaction to feminism, in particular second-wave feminism. A 1998 manifesto claimed "neo-feminism" as the antidote to post-feminism, focusing on "choice" and individual fulfillment. These self-proclaimed "neo-feminists" reject certain forms of consumer culture, as did third-wave feminist Naomi Wolf, but share her focus on the individual and individual fulfillment. "Neo-feminism" is a term also used in opposition to "state feminism" in the discussion of Soviet bloc countries. Again, the term suggests a turning away from political reform. Similarly, neo-feminism also appears from time to time to characterize any kind of wrong turn in feminist thought, as in the case of Margaret A. Simons, who describes as "neo-feminist" the trend in French feminist thought that sought to replace Simone de Beauvoir's rationalist (and hence masculinist) feminism (moving towards the erasure of gender difference) with a glorification of the feminine, frequently referred to as essentialism. These perspectives have in common the assumption that neo-feminism is a reaction to feminism, in particular second-wave feminism.[12]

Most notable are feminist literary critics, who have tended to locate "neo-feminism" as an outgrowth of feminism, manifested most clearly in novels in which the heroine, in the words of Ellen Morgan, writing in 1978, "is a creature in the process of becoming ... struggling to throw off her conditioning and the whole psychology of oppression."[13] Kim Loudermilk, for example, writing in 2004, associates "neo-feminism" with third-wave feminists such as Naomi Wolf, because of Wolf's emphasis on individual choice as the solution to women's oppression, in particular through her critique of the feminist position-ing of women as "victims."[14] Loudermilk traces the development of "fictional feminism," a form of feminism propagated by novels, and to a lesser degree cinema, which she claims "recuperates feminist politics, containing any threat that feminism poses to the dominant culture."[15] The novels and films that she considers, such as *The Handmaid's Tale*, or *The Witches of Eastwick*,[16] engage explicitly with the representation of feminism in ways that undermine a con-temporary understanding of the goals of second-wave feminism. Where I take issue with scholars such as Morgan and Loudermilk is the manner in which they see second-wave feminism itself as the origin of these neo-feminist ten-dencies in contemporary culture. I argue that neo-feminism, while arising out of the same social conditions as feminism, and sharing some ambitions of second-wave feminism, such as affirming the need for financial autonomy for women, had significantly different goals—goals that coincide not with the reformist agenda of second-wave feminism, but with the individualist and rationalistic agenda of neo-liberalism.[17] In part, what provokes Morgan's and later Loudermilk's reactions to what Loudermilk calls "fictional feminism" is not simply the co-option of feminism, but also the rise of neo-feminism, which did indeed deftly turn many of feminism's reforms to its advantage, while being motivated by principles of self-interest.

Second-wave feminism is represented by activists like Bella Abzug (1920–98) or Betty Friedan (1921–2006), middle-class educated women, as a whole "white"; these last were inspired by ethical imperatives to take up the cause of women and become her political voice, with the aim of achieving political and institutional reform within a traditional definition of a civil society, which they sought to enlarge (see Figure 1.1). While second-wave feminism did advocate a program of self-fulfillment, it did so within a climate of social responsibility and state intervention. Individual fulfillment was meaningless outside the policy of larger social and institutional change. Characteristic of this position (which remains a crucial dimension of contemporary feminism) is that of Barbara

Figure 1.1 Betty Friedan, second-wave feminist. Courtesy of Photofest.

Ehrenreich (b. 1941), feminist activist and writer, who, in 2002, exhorts her readers to seek "activist solutions" to the plight of "migrant women engaged in illegal occupations such as nannies and maids." Ehrenreich and her co-author Arlie Hochschild (b. 1940), another longstanding feminist, urge their readers "to consider these women as full human beings. They are strivers as well as victims, wives and mothers as well as workers—sisters, in other words, with whom we in the First World may someday define a common agenda."[18]

In contrast, the preoccupation of neo-feminism is the individual woman acting on her own, in her best interest, in which her fulfillment can be understood as independent of her social milieu and the predicament of other women as a class that crosses international boundaries. As a largely pragmatic set of behaviors and principles, neo-feminism seeks to provide a means of survival and success for the woman who, without family or other sources of material support, counts her own body and the work that it performs as her principle resource. Though neo-feminism can be said to challenge patriarchal structures, it does so in the name of capitalism, in which allegiance to family, for example, has little significance within an economic field. The subject is a free agent working in his or her own interests with a view to optimizing his or her position outside of the confines of family and hereditary status, but within a profit-driven society.

Crucial to the establishment of the neo-feminist paradigm in the 1960s and 1970s was the emergence of the single girl as a feminine ideal, exemplified by Helen Gurley Brown (b. 1922) as a media icon, as well as through her various publications, beginning with *Sex and the Single Girl* in 1962 (see Figure 1.2).[19] The single girl achieves her identity outside marriage and, significantly, does not define herself in terms of maternity. Both in appearance (waif-like and adolescent) and in goals (to be glamorous, adored by men and financially independent), the single girl, for whom sexual pleasure is a right, defines femininity outside the reigning patriarchal construction based on marriage and motherhood. At the same time, the single girl is defined through consumerism—in particular, her capacity to function as a knowledgeable acolyte of feminine consumer culture. One of the significant traits of the neo-feminist paradigm is the way in which consumer-culture glamor replaces the maternal as the defining trait of femininity. While the neo-feminist paradigm does not preclude maternity, as the recent vogue for "yummy mummies" demonstrates, it displaces the centrality that it held, for example, in the early twentieth-century and nineteenth-century accounts of feminine self-fulfillment.[20]

Fueled by the ever-increasing need of consumer industries for new markets, popular culture encouraged the emergence of discourses presupposing that fulfillment of an individual's needs and desires is an expression of good citizenship and, paradoxically, the sharing of a common culture. This discourse

Figure 1.2 Helen Gurley Brown in 1965. Courtesy of Photofest.

encourages the individual to realize his or her self in the pursuit of pleasure—
a pleasure that is first and foremost sexual—with individual gratification being
the final expression of the citizen's inalienable right to the pursuit of happiness.
In this articulation, popular culture posited the personal rather than the political
as the primary arena of experience and citizenship. Although the formula "the
personal is political" came to characterize the new feminist values of the 1970s
and 1980s, this neo-feminist position, far from challenging consumer culture,

affirmed its continued attempts to collapse the public and the private, to eliminate the public sphere as the forum of a specifically political engagement.[21] This is not to negate the feminists' legitimate contention that private space has a political dimension, but rather to point out how feminist concerns came to be confused in the public mind with a neo-feminist perspective that justified itself exclusively in terms of self-gratification as a sign of individual fulfillment.

Helen Gurley Brown and Betty Friedan, each writing a best seller that defines her perspective, if divided in their sense of how best to achieve this objective, had in common their conviction that each woman has the right to fulfillment defined in her own terms (as opposed to those of patriarchy). As feminist scholar Imelda Whelehan underlines: "Both emphasize individual transformation over and above social transformation."[22] This sense of the individual as the site of fulfillment became the basis for a discussion of parity between man and woman, and also for the assessment of equality across the lines of class, race and sexual identity. The establishment of the autonomous individual who must apprehend her pleasure for herself, whose health (psychological and physiological) can be measured by the body's capacity to experience itself as pleasurable, permeated discourses on child psychology, sexology, marriage and legal rights. Less obviously, this discourse of autonomy and fulfillment established the terms of debates about politics, citizenship and identity that led to a fragmentation of the feminist voice in the 1980s and 1990s, culminating in the construction of the queer constituency as the surviving authentic voice of the 1980s and 1990s for a politics of gender that included the concept of community. This discourse of autonomy ultimately generated, in consonance with neo-liberalism, a new cultural arena that evolved around an assumption that individual fulfillment was the goal of human experience.

This cultural arena contests the heterosexual paradigm founded on a reproductive model of gender and sexuality. Specifically, reproduction is supplemented, and even superseded, by the production of other sexualities in which the self, rather than the family, becomes the primary unit of social construction. In the words of ethnologist and zoologist Desmond Morris (b. 1928), author of the 1967 best seller *The Naked Ape*: "It could even be said that we now perform the mating act, not so much to fertilize an egg as to fertilize a relationship."[23] The position described by Morris encourages an expanded conceptualization of sexuality that nonetheless supports a hetero-centric view of eroticism; heterosexuality remains the norm, affirming a culturally inscribed sexual dimorphism in which masculine and feminine remain distinct categories. The challenge to reproductive sexuality represented by the figure of the single girl is contained by the femininity of her body, marked as such through her participation in consumer culture.

The Playboy of the 1950s and the single girl of the 1960s were cultural icons that underlined that a new consumer ideology of "singleness" was not synonymous with homosexuality. At the same time, these two figures represented a departure from previous norms defined by kinship and family. If the political agenda of the 1960s did not produce the utopia it promised, the sexual revolution resulted in a reconfiguration of identity with significant political and economic implications. Among these is the advent of "the New Girl Order"—young women who marry later in life, or not at all, while holding salaried positions, and who have become fundamental agents (as workers and consumers) in the global economic system at the end of the twentieth century and the beginning of the twenty-first century.[24] This new economy depends upon a mobile workforce, including women, with significant discretionary income.

The effects of the "sexual revolution" might be termed liberating in the sense that this public discourse produced new norms of behavior. Chastity was no longer the gauge of a woman's value. These new norms, however, also produced the foundation of new forms of social regulation grounded in "the sexual fix," to borrow from Stephen Heath, in which "sexual fulfillment" legitimated the individual as such.[25] The rights and duties of citizenship came to revolve paradoxically around the pursuit of pleasure, in which sexual pleasure provided the model for all other pleasures, producing an environment in which sexuality itself became compulsory, the sine qua non of human existence.[26] The sexual revolution, unlike the civil rights movement and the anti-war movement, encouraged the feminine subject to construct herself as individual qua individual. The social became primarily a pretext, the site of opportunities to develop one's self.

From this perspective, the sexual revolution was hardly a revolution at all; it signified the triumph of bourgeois pragmatism over counterculture idealism, albeit while expanding the category of the bourgeois to include women, gays, lesbians, with the individual in all her multicultural variations paving the way for the rise of neo-liberalism more generally. Sharon Ullman contends that the seed of current controversies around sexuality are found in late-nineteenth and early-twentieth-century American culture, at which point, she argues, sexuality was redefined "as a means of self-realization rooted in pleasure and unconnected to reproduction," emerging as "central to personal identity and even to a definition of a successful life."[27] This shift in the place of sexuality had important consequences for women. Paul Robinson argues that "modern" sex can be understood as a reaction against the Victorian. In particular, he concluded that "where the Victorians had all but denied woman a sexual existence, the modernists argued her sexual parity with the male, even at the risk of transforming her into an exclusively sexual being."[28] More abstractly, he sees modernist theories as an attempt to reconcile the romantic ideal of transcendent union with the material reality of "human sexual response," defined in empirical terms.[29] Critical in defining this tension was the research of zoologist Alfred Kinsey (1894–1956), published in the late 1940s and early 1950s, which substantiated the view that sexual practice in the mid-twentieth century did not conform to either romantic or Victorian ideals, and that women as well as men actively sought sexual fulfillment both within and outside traditional heterosexual relations.[30] Kinsey's work was crucial to the ways in which the search for sexual pleasure, in all its variations, was redefined as an essential motivator and driver for all human behavior.

These new theories of sexuality pre-dating the sexual revolution suggest the complicated nexus of cultural forces that led to the emergence of the sexually active single girl in the 1960s. Benjamin Spock's cognitively stimulated child, the libidinous sex kitten incarnated by Brigitte Bardot, as well as Hugh Hefner's ever-available and ever-eager Playboy in the 1950s, prepared the way for the swinging adult of the 1960s.[31] If, at the end of the nineteenth century, Krafft-Ebing commented, "The man who avoids women, and the woman who seeks men are sheer anomalies," by the mid twentieth century, attitudes had changed.[32] Typically, in the novel *Marnie* (which was the basis for the 1964 film of the same name, directed by Alfred Hitchcock and starring Sean Connery), the hero explains to his reluctant wife: "Sex is a fundamental instinct that you can't compare to love of music. If it isn't there in some form, something is wrong."[33]

The Bond girl, originally appearing in the novels of Ian Fleming (1908–64) in the 1950s, was an early incarnation of the sexually liberated single girl that reached full maturity as an icon in the Bond films of the 1960s, beginning with *Dr. No* (Terence Young, 1962).[34] Her trajectory, from hardback to paperback novel and finally to the post-classical Hollywood cinema screens, points to the way in which the sexual revolution was hardly a revolution at all. The changes in sexual mores associated with the 1960s were the product of a slow evolution toward an economic and social structure in which the individual rather than the family became the primary locus of identity and economic responsibility. The Bond girl represents a change in the woman's position, in which family and kinship no longer necessarily determine her fate. Economic status, her ability to negotiate consumer culture as both agent and object of exchange, become the prime determinant of her social expectations. The Bond girl had in common with her subsequent popular incarnations, such as the single girl, that she was a free agent, operating in her own interests, which she came to understand under the guidance of Bond himself.

In general, the Bond girl has been dismissed as an atavistic representation of the feminine, a woman who is out of place, who brings chaos—an unruly woman who must be tamed by Bond as "an agent of patriarchal order."[35] Scholars who promote this view fail to acknowledge that Bond's recognition of feminine pleasure as something that the woman has a right to expect marks a new position in the formulation of feminine identity. His attention to her pleasure and his own is offset by the indifference that the cycle of films exhibits towards the fate of women. Women in general, throughout the Bond films, lead a dangerous life. As a rule, only the Bond girl, exceptional in appearance, physical performance and intelligence, escapes with her life, if she is lucky (ultimately only Bond himself is invincible). The exceedingly stringent standards, in terms of appearance, to which the Bond girl must adhere indicate the importance of consumer culture in regulating the new feminine modes of behavior; the Bond girl is emblematic of a representational mode that supports the subordination and oppression of women through consumer culture (if not patriarchy), demonstrating how the path of "liberation" was not "free." This redefinition of femininity, and of sexual identity more generally, served the purposes of consumer culture and its industries. While the Bond girl preceded the single girl as a popular icon, she did not disappear, but, rather, endured and developed as an example of the new independent woman for whom love, if not chastity, remained an important goal.

In contrast, the single girl, unlike the Bond girl, was not by nature exceptional. Rather, she was an ordinary girl who strove successfully to become exceptional. As such, she presented a utopian fantasy of a woman freed from the social and sexual constraints that appeared to have limited her mother. Her girlishness also responded to, and contained, the anxieties that a woman no longer under the yoke of patriarchy (if still subject to the whims of capital) might evoke. She was a girl in a state of perpetual immaturity. She ultimately could not challenge an order grounded in the primacy of masculinity. Crucial to the single girl's autonomy is her efficacy in the workplace. The single girl did not reject marriage or heterosexuality but, rather, understood both in terms of her own needs and desires. Marriage remained an important avenue to self-fulfillment for the single girl; however, it was neither a necessity nor a solution to her situation.

During the 1960s, best-selling women writers such as Helen Gurley Brown and the notorious "J" sought to evolve a technology of feminine sexual practice outside marriage in which nubility (as marriage-ability) is reproduced through the articulation of the woman as a consumer of goods and sexual pleasure. As Nora Ephron (b. 1941), journalist, novelist screenwriter, producer, director and, more recently, blogger, commented, Helen Gurley Brown advocated "that the Single Girl with no other man in her life must somehow make the men that are there serve a purpose."[36] Barbara Ehrenreich pointed out that, in some ways, Brown's position in *Sex and the Single Girl* (1962) was more radical than Betty Friedan's in *The Feminine Mystique* (1963), a volume often seen as inaugurating second-wave feminism in the United States.[37] What Ehrenreich did not predict, writing in 1986, was the way in which the ethos promoted by Brown—what I am calling neo-feminism—would reject "the feminist mystique" (a term coined by Linda Gray Sexton, daughter of the poet Anne Sexton, writing in 1979) and come to dominate feminine culture as a whole.

Sexton commented that: "My grandmother taught me that the only fulfilled woman was a devoted wife and mother. My mother had countered that the only fulfilled woman was a career woman."[38] She continued: "the femin*ist* mystique force-fed us a dose of liberation and promoted the ideal of the independent professional woman."[39] Friedan, one of the second wave's most visible proponents, assumed marriage and motherhood as the sine qua non of a woman's life; she claimed, however, that woman could *also* work, that "it is not as difficult as the feminine mystique implies, to combine marriage and motherhood and even the kind of lifelong personal purpose that was once called 'career.'"[40] In contrast, Brown "announced that marriage was unnecessary and that a new life was already possible, the life of the single, urban working 'girl.'"[41]

This "new life" predates the feminist movement, arising in response to a new socio-economic system in which the home was not longer a site of production, with the family no longer functioning as an economic unit. More pointedly, in an era in which a woman could no longer expect to be supported by a father or a husband, women were motivated to seek financial security outside marriage. Similarly, the skills needed for the service industries could increasingly be acquired by women. The greater physical strength of men was no longer necessarily an asset to his employer; a woman could do the same work, as in the case of secretarial support. If she were paid less than her male counterpart, she could, nonetheless, acquire economic independence and autonomy, which continued to be advantageous to her even if she did, ultimately, choose to marry.

Brown herself was a married woman by the time she became the guru of the single girl, her husband, whom she wed in 1959, being the famous film producer David Brown, long-time partner of Richard D. Zanuck, and responsible for hits like *Jaws* (Steven Spielberg, 1975). Like Victoria Beckham 40 years later, Brown had a pragmatic view of her position as wife, in which she continued to work and present herself as a glamorous and desirable woman in the media eye. In this sense, the "yummy mummy" of the twenty-first century represents a continuation of the neo-feminist ideal and its rewriting of the feminist mystique. Like the single girl, the yummy mummy must devote herself to reproducing herself as an image of perfected femininity that depends upon the exploitation of consumer culture to achieve its effect. The yummy mummy may be married (though not necessarily); however, she acts and looks like a "single girl" who must work for her living within a media-oriented environment.

Instructional handbooks for single women, such as *Live Alone and Like It* (1936), pre-date the 1960s.[42] Indeed, the development of what is known as "the Modern Girl"—young women "identified" through "their use of specific commodities and their explicit eroticism"—was "a global phenomenon in the 1920s and 1930s," according to the members of the Modern Girl Around the World Research Group.[43] They further note: "U.S. corporations emerge as a major source and the most important international distributor of imagery associated with the Modern Girl, especially because of U.S. preeminence in the international distribution of advertising and film."[44] They elaborate:

> Our research has shown that during the 1920 and 1930s "girl" and its equivalent translations appeared around the globe. In these decades, "girl" denoted young women with the wherewithal and desire to define themselves in excess of conventional female roles and as transgressive of national, imperial and racial boundaries. Indeed, our research strongly suggests the historical emergence of "girl" as a modern social and representational category and as a style of self-expression largely delinked from biological age.[45]

The Research Group emphasizes the fundamental role of advertising in producing the "style" that characterized the Modern Girl.[46] While she is associated with the use of cosmetics, particularly with American products, she is also linked to "dating, romantic love and premarital sex."[47] Her full impact, however, in terms of redefining femininity across class lines could not be realized without effective, easily available and relatively inexpensive forms of birth control that would allow an ethics of self-fulfillment, as one of the founding principles of neo-feminism, to be fully developed and democratized. Hence, the ethos of the sexual revolution and its technologies, which emphasized birth control as well as multiple pathways to sexual pleasure, was crucial to the redefinition of femininity represented in the single girl of the 1960s as the final incarnation of the Modern Girl.

The guides to modern feminine behavior of the 1960s, including Brown's *Sex and the Single Girl* (1962), as well as *Sex and the Office* (1964) and *The Way to Become the Sensuous Woman* by "J" (1969),[48] distinguish themselves from earlier volumes through their franker discussion of sexuality, and, more importantly, through their status as best sellers within the new paperback industry which made their views available on a national and global scale. These volumes were not directed at an elite, but at the burgeoning urban populations that were coming to characterize Middle America. In *Sex and the Single Girl*, Brown emphasized her modest beginnings: "My family was, and is, desperately poor and I have always helped support them."[49] Her mother was widowed when Helen was 10: she supported an invalid sister throughout her life.[50] Beginning as a secretary, she worked her way up the ladder in advertising. Without a college education or family connections, she, through dedication and perseverance, became a national celebrity in her own right; however, her major successes were achieved in collaboration with her husband, David Brown, whom she wed at the age of 37. In her words: "It *could* be construed something of a miracle considering how old *I* was and how eligible *he* was."[51] And yet, she described herself in the following terms: "I am not beautiful, or even pretty. I once had the world's worst case of acne. I am not bosomy or brilliant."[52] Financial management skills are of more significance than beauty to the single girl's success, whether this includes marriage, or not.

At the heart of the single girl ethos is a chapter titled "Money, Money, Money."[53] Brown advocates the virtues of thrift and self-restraint as integral to the single girl's economic and emotional fulfillment, inevitably linked in Brown's philosophy. Though the single girl is a consumer, she is a smart consumer who invests in stocks as well as fashion. Finally, then, the volume is about how a woman might best manage her life given that she and she alone is responsible for her situation. Ironically, Brown is almost never critical of men; rather, she advocates a pragmatic approach in which men constitute neither allies nor enemies, but a series of opportunities and obstacles that a woman encounters in her attempts to achieve economic stability. Her instrumental approach, which stands in stark contrast to the ethical concerns voiced by feminists of her generation, foreshadowed the neo-liberalism of the 1970s, suggesting how and why neo-feminism, in tandem with neo-liberalism, was destined to become the dominant ethos of Western culture. In this context, "work" is not a "right" for Brown—it is a necessity.

It would be a mistake, however, to see Helen Gurley Brown's position as anti-marriage, or to see "singleness" as in and of itself a source of pleasure. The married state, according to Brown, is the ideal position for a woman, but it is not a sinecure. Furthermore, singleness is not necessarily synonymous with spinsterhood. The unmarried woman can lead a fulfilling life, perhaps more fulfilling than that of many of her married counterparts, if she is careful. The innovation in Brown's position, echoing the earlier *Live Alone and Like It* of the 1930s, is that marriage or its absence is not the measure of a woman's success; however, this perspective does not rely on ethical absolutism, but derives from the increasing instability of marriage itself as a social institution.

With her own mother's example before her, Brown advocated that a woman should be prepared to face life on her own, and that singleness was not in and of itself a catastrophe. Brown claimed in *Sex and the Single Girl*: "[T]he Single woman, far from being a creature to be pitied and patronized, is emerging as the newest glamour girl of our times."[54] She further stated in the less successful *Sex and the Office* that "I believe most women—married or single, mothers or childless, grandmothers or ingénues—are better off working at least *some* of the time."[55] For Brown, if work was ultimately a financial necessity, it was also, as it was for Friedan, a source of personal fulfillment. Beyond self-realization, work was also practical. Women who work (whether married or unmarried) retain their mobility as part of a paid labor force; they are also in a position to spend money on dieting, exercise, fashion and grooming, and in so doing remain attractive to men.

Helen Gurley Brown's enormously successful transformation of the ailing *Cosmopolitan* in 1965 into a publication that spoke to and legitimated the working woman testifies to the cultural importance of the new single girl ideal. Considered one of the most successful women's magazines in the history of publishing, in 2008 *Cosmo* (as it came to be known) was published in over 30 languages and over 50 international editions.[56] Helen Gurley Brown held the position of editor-in-chief for 32 years.[57] When she left, her successor "made few substantial changes" because "focus groups with readers reveal that they liked the magazine the way it was," adhering to "the basic Helen Gurley Brown formula, which included four pillars: relationship issues, emotional issues, career issues and sexual issues."[58] Her initial reformulation of the magazine (based on a proposal developed by her and her husband for a new magazine)[59] proved not only successful but influential in pioneering developments in women's publishing as a means of targeting working women with their disposable incomes, resulting in new magazines such as *New Woman* (1971–99), *Self* (1979) and *Working Woman* (1977–2002), as well as the reorientation of existing magazines such as the now defunct *Mademoiselle* (1935–2001) and the still thriving *Glamour* (1939). The terms according to which the women's magazine was reconceived are laid out in *Sex and the Single Girl*.

Brown's formulas, which emphasized consumerism and sexual practice, encouraged and supported a feminine subject who functioned within heterosexuality; however, by focusing on women's right and capacity to choose, Brown's advice also ultimately granted women permission to explore other identities. Within Brown's discourse, although the woman's pleasure functions as part of her marriageability, it is still signaled as her "own." Less obviously, her sexuality is ancillary rather than fundamental to her identity. Helen Gurley Brown is a woman's woman. The goal of her magazine is conversation among women. Ultimately, other women are the single girl's most stable resource. Brown explained this explicitly in a later volume:

> A mouseburger's friends are, in some respects, like her lungs or liver—she can't get through life without them. Friends are almost a bigger deal than lover or husband. Those you get though life without, at least for long periods, but friends—they are a staple of every functional mouseburger.[60]

She added:

> We've spent pages piloting you through the love affair—which probably won't survive the year—we're only going to spend a paragraph or two on girlfriends who may last your lifetime. Why? Because girlfriends don't need explaining or piloting; they don't bring problems or traumas; they bring solutions and peace.[61]

The term "mouseburger," an epithet coined by her critics, is taken up ironically by Brown. It serves as a metaphor for the disenfranchised state of the single girl. The single girl is by definition not exceptionally beautiful, rich, or even talented; if she is intelligent, it is the result of hard work and discipline rather than nature or nurture. Brown's message is that every "girl" must make the best of what she has in a world that is neither hostile nor inviting, but rather largely indifferent to her fate. It is this indifference that the single girl must combat by making herself attractive and accomplished according to the norms of 1960s culture and the sexual revolution.

Within a paradigm in which a woman bartered her participation in the sexual act for material goods of one sort or another, her pleasure was irrelevant to the act itself. A different system of exchange was inaugurated by the sexual revolution in which the woman was the agent rather than the object of exchange, in which she exchanged orgasms as pleasure in a system of equivalence in which her pleasure was measured against his pleasure, or against her pleasure, as the case may be. The erotic possibilities of "free" sex constitute a crucial element in the package of rights to which the single girl gained access through her willingness to work and her capacity for labor. Sexuality, then, constitutes a paradox at the center of the single girl's ethos. On the one hand, sexuality is part of her capital, her expertise (performance), rather than her chastity, enhancing her value; on the other hand, there is no price on pleasure. By extension, if pleasure replaces reproduction as the goal of sexuality, then the "sex" of either partner is significant only to the extent that it increases or decreases pleasure. This tendency towards rationalization and optimization of human activity is an important dimension of the developing neo-liberal subject, here applied to what might be considered the most intimate and private dimensions of human activity.

Similarly, homosexuality, both male and female, does not in and of itself threaten the social hierarchies generated by neo-liberal practices, in which status and class supersede gender and race in determining a subject's position within that hierarchy. In a system in which the individual works for him or her "self," Helen Gurley Brown's advice to women "works" for men or women. She describes a system, an erotics of power, in which sexuality is defined by position within a specific power structure, regardless of the gendered identity of the subject occupying that position. The "girl" is a position that is defined not by gender but by the relations between employer and employee, between eligible bachelor and suppliant single girl. In this sense, the single girl is the prototype of a new model of citizenship within consumer culture, in which the individual is always at risk, never secure, in the struggle to ensure his or her personal fulfillment in an environment in which each seeks to optimize his or her position. Inherent in the term *girl* is an attempt to feminize the position of the suppliant—to naturalize it and to retain a notion of eligibility and, by extension, citizenship as inherently masculine. Hence, gender returns as a socially inscribed category in which the masculine is aligned with eligibility and the feminine defined in terms of patterns of consumption, of the cultivation of a certain self that affords pleasure to the subject while rendering her desirable and enviable in the eyes of others.

Important to the new terms of parity, in which either member of the couple could play the role of the "girl," was the conceptualization of feminine pleasure in terms of the female orgasm as a form of pleasure that could be measured and understood as comparable to the male orgasm. Thus, in the 1960s, the research team of William Masters and Virginia Johnson convinced the American public that the vaginal orgasm was a myth and that clitorial orgasm could be understood as the equivalent to the male orgasm.[62] The social and scientific recognition of female pleasure within a context in which sexuality was a matter of individual choice opened up erotic practice as an interaction between independent entrepreneurs seeking equal returns on their investments. In this sense, Brown's single girl represents a certain practice, a construction of "self" that ultimately authorizes gay and lesbian identity. "Queer" identity is the logical result of a self that is represented through the individual right to pleasure and the consequent right to choose the form (and practice) that this pleasure might take. This new sexual self was defined by institutions as disparate as pornography, feminism and popular television programming for women.[63]

In the case of the single girl, however, it is difficult to read these transformations as utopian. As a popular icon, the single girl testifies to the fact that the Enlightenment's promise of universal emancipation did not resolve the problems of women. As feminist theorist Camilla Griggers argues: "The call-to-being proffered to women as their share of an Enlightenment legacy of individual identity brings with it a politics of shifting seductions and investments."[64] If an ethos of self-fulfillment appears to be in women's interest, the terms whereby this self-fulfillment is defined as a practice within consumer culture suggests something quite different. The feminine subject must construct herself in a manner (through the wearing of clothing, make-up, hair styles, but also dieting, exercise and surgical intervention) that will define her "self" as feminine within contemporary culture. Recent films such as *Gray Matters* (Sue Kramer, 2006), starring Heather Graham as "Gray," a young woman who belatedly comes "out" as gay in the course of the movie, or television programming such as *The L Word* (Showtime, 2004–09), highlight how the homosexual female subject is accepted to the degree that she conforms to consumer culture standards of femininity. The lesbian subject is visible to the degree that she looks like any other starlet—she must be "girlishly" pretty, sexy and perky—as such indistinguishable from all other feminine icons attached to the New Girl Order, the culmination of the trends that initially defined the Modern Girl.[65]

The rules that Brown lays out for the single girl are relatively simple: a woman must be fiscally independent and responsible; a woman must bow to the codes of consumer culture by developing and maintaining a style that is both personal and fashionable; she must have her own well-appointed apartment; she must have an interesting job and, less importantly, be both an entertaining host and accomplished cook. Finally, she must be thin as well as physically fit, because in Brown's words, "you need to look glamorous every minute."[66] The most enduring imperative of Brown's discourse is one that requires a life-long process of self-surveillance in which the woman constantly monitors her "looks" as well as her bank account. Only by this process of self-monitoring, in terms of her fiscal position as well as her physical state, may a woman become a worthy subject who is in a position to realize her self and attain fulfillment.

While the fundamentals of the neo-feminist paradigm are laid out in the 1960s through publications such as *Sex and the Single Girl* and later *Cosmopolitan Magazine*, the rise of neo-feminism continued through the 1970s and 1980s, increasingly in conflict with the reformist stance of feminism. While Brown considered herself to be a feminist, in particular because of her support of women's right to abortion, she was frequently under attack—most notoriously when she published an article about AIDS. As reported on *The New York Post's* infamous "Page Six":

> She ran a piece titled "Reassuring News About AIDS" reporting that women whose lovers were neither homosexual, bisexual or intravenous drug users faced little risk. Brown said, "We spent such a long time getting sexual equality for women, and just when we're beginning to enjoy ourselves, somebody's got to come along and say sex kills." AIDS activists howled, but Brown has since been proven right.[67]

Brown's position on AIDS was typical of her refusal to negotiate the ethical complexities of the feminist consciousness, which is characteristic of the development of what I am calling neo-feminism, grounded in the principles of neo-liberal pragmatism. As Charlotte Hays, journalist and writer, points out, citing the 1970 occupation of *Cosmopolitan's* offices by Kate Millett and a group of "militant feminists," while not hostile, Brown's relationship with "the feminist movement has always been, at best, ambiguous."[68] In fact, her position is much more closely allied with a developing neo-liberalist discourse in which all decisions were made in terms of the optimization of self-interest. Symptomatic of this affinity with neo-liberalism was the creation, most notably through ad campaigns, of an archetypal Cosmo Girl—one who changed very little in the course of Brown's tenure at the magazine.[69] In Brown's own words: "She is still the one who loves men and loves children but doesn't want to live through other people—she wants to achieve on her own—to be known for what she does."[70]

Brown's consistent stance on issues like money-management, as well as abortion (at times at odds with her readers), earned her the approbation of scholars such as Jennifer Scanlon, who asserts that Brown has a "rightful place as a feminist trailblazer."[71] Similarly, media scholar Laurie Ouellette, quoting a 1966 issue of *Newsweek*, describes Brown as the "working girl's Simone de Beauvoir," because "she articulated a girl-style American Dream that promised transcendence over class roles as well as sexual ones."[72] To the degree that Brown emphasized an ethics of a woman's personal responsibility for her "self," she in some ways merited this appraisal. Significantly, however, for the neo-feminist, like Brown, moral choice revolves exclusively around her sense of her own fulfillment, and is completely in keeping with the general neo-liberal trends in American culture. The feminists, in contrast, were in search of a moral universe in which the need for individual fulfillment was compatible with a desire for the larger social good, and for a civil society. Understanding this crucial distinction between neo-feminism and feminism underlines the reason why twenty-first-century feminists deplore what they deem to be the increasing gap between the promises of second-wave feminism and the reality of twenty-first-century gender politics, in which pragmatism prevails.

While Brown's legacy remains a vital element of twenty-first-century feminine culture, neo-feminism in the 1980s and 1990s moved significantly beyond the Cosmo Girl. The first sign that Brown was out of step with the times was a 1980s survey about the content of *Cosmopolitan Magazine*. While Brown insisted upon including articles about money and career, "readers favored the emotional-content material, the pieces about men and friendships and love and loss."[73] While neo-feminist discourses continued to revel in strategies of self-gratification, the work ethic promoted by Brown waned, evidence of a culture in which production and consumption seemingly bear no connection to each other. Thus, for example, neo-feminist cinema frequently offers its viewers a consumer Green World in which the protagonist engages in a shopping orgy—most famously, in the Rodeo Drive sequence in *Pretty Woman* (Garry Marshall, 1990)—without significant financial consequence.

Typically, then, through popular genre films, neo-feminist cinema extends the logic of the neo-feminist position, resolving its contradictions through fantasy sequences, while simultaneously probing its inconsistencies. As such, the series of "girly" films, of which *Pretty Woman* is one of the first important examples, covering the period, roughly, of the late 1980s through the first decade of the twenty-first century, offers significant insight into the further cultural production of the neo-feminist paradigm as defined through a set of contradictory discourses. One of the most significant shifts in the neo-feminist paradigm that these films underline is the way in which Brown's insistence on responsibility, particularly fiscal responsibility, has been replaced by a culture of unabashed self-gratification in which fantasy prevails over notions of professionalism and work. The next chapter isolates and explores the consequence of these developments as expressed though the themes and characteristics of the girly film.

Chapter 2

Pretty Woman (1990) and the Girly Film

Defining the Format

In the previous chapter, I explored how a competing set of discourses, which I call the neo-feminist paradigm, developed alongside second-wave feminism in the 1960s and 1970s, most clearly expressed through the writings of Helen Gurley Brown. Two defining strands of thought in neo-feminist discourse emerge: the emphasis on economic and fiscal responsibility achieved through work outside the home, and the importance of constantly improving the self through cultivation of the body and its appearance in accordance with norms dictated by consumer culture. Subtending these two strands was the social trend whereby chastity was replaced by sexual expertise as a sign of a woman's value on the marriage market. I have suggested, furthermore, that starting in the 1980s, Gurley Brown's readership moved away from desiring the hard-headed, at times cynical, financial advice that she offered readers, preferring instead a more sentimental fantasy-perspective focusing on romance and emotions rather than fiscal responsibility. Finally, I have proposed that popular Hollywood "girly films" in the 1990s offer an especially rich site for investigating how the "Cosmo Girl" icon is modified and adjusted, and the neo-feminist paradigm subsequently refined.

In this chapter, I shall briefly suggest why the consequences of the sexual revolution took so long to attain representation in mainstream cinema, and will then delineate the main features of the new genre that successive filmmakers elaborated, showing how the sentimental romantic comedy *Pretty Woman* inaugurates the girly genre. Shot in 1989, directed by Garry Marshall, and released in 1990,[1] this film documents an important shift in neo-feminist sensibility, while at the same time it "mainstreams" many elements of the neo-feminist discourse for a broad popular audience that included husbands, wives, grandparents and teenagers, as well as single working women. While appealing to women, *Pretty Woman*, produced by Touchstone Pictures, a subsidiary of Disney, contrives also to be family fare: Marshall concludes his Director's Commentary with the remark that this film will "help your kids understand love ... what love is all about," signaling the ways in which Helen Gurley Brown's shocking innovations a mere 25 years earlier had become widely accepted. In spite of the success of *Pretty Woman*, it took more than 20 years for the neo-feminist paradigm, even in its more sentimental incarnation, to become a significant influence on popular film.

The relative lateness with which the neo-feminist paradigm reached the big screen is the result of changes in the movie industry itself. With the demise of the studio system following the Paramount decree in post-World War II Hollywood, American cinema sought to retain its economic stability through the production of mega-hits geared towards a family audience (examples range from *The Sound of Music* (Robert Wise, 1965) to *Jaws* (Steven Spielberg, 1975)) and youth-oriented exploitation films (such as those produced by American International Pictures that targeted the 19-year-old male). The rise of young European-influenced directors, with films like *The Graduate* (Mike Nichols, 1967), was another offshoot of the reorganization of the movie industry; such directors had little interest in topics and stories that might address a specifically female audience. Within the male-dominated arena of independent film, there was little room for the consideration of mainstream women's issues outside of the context of the family. While the festival circuit, heavily influenced by feminism, produced such films as *Daughter Rite* (Michelle Citron, 1979), female audiences, young working women in particular, were not considered important movie-going audiences. And indeed, cinema attendance in these years dropped to an all-time low.[2]

Nonetheless, examples of media images that anticipate the "Cosmo Girl" icon of the 1970s in post-World War II culture are too numerous to list; however, these are usually presented either as de-eroticized, offering a heavily sanitized version of single life during the sexual revolution, as was the case with the popular television program *That Girl* (ABC, 1966–71), or as tragic. Typically, in *Written on the Wind* (Douglas Sirk, 1956), Lauren Bacall played a career woman who married impulsively with tragic results; *The Best of Everything* (Jean Negulesco, 1959) explored the lives of glamorous working women in New York, again fraught with tragedy and loss. Similarly, *Peyton Place* (1957) and *Valley of the Dolls* (1967), both directed by Mark Robson, offered lurid and sensationalized accounts of the pitfalls that single women risk in American society. While *The Avengers* (1961–69) brought the Bond girl image to television in the form of the character of Emma Peel (played by Diana Rigg), her relations with the male lead were chaste and professional.[3] "Romantic comedies" presented an unrealistic view of courtship practices in the form of "sex comedies," "a sub-genre depending on sex being talked about, plotted and lied for, but never actually enacted," as in the 1959 film *Pillow Talk* (Michael Gordon) starring Doris Day and Rock Hudson.[4]

While the single girl image jubilantly dominated the magazine stands in the 1970s, cinema viewed this persona more cautiously. The 1970s post-sexual revolution cinema gave spectators such films as *Looking for Mr. Goodbar* (Richard Brooks, 1977), in which the heroine is duly punished for her promiscuity, or *Girlfriends* (Claudia Weill, 1978), a small independent production that portrayed the single woman's life as difficult and lonely—certainly not glamorous. Indeed, the pioneer feminist film critic Molly Haskell claimed that cinema had actually regressed in terms of its portrayal of women, in particular sexually active women, during this period.[5] In contrast, television programming, more sensitive to demographics and to female audiences as potential consumers, portrayed active, glamorous women who were the equals of most men, as in *Charlie's Angels* (1976–81), a program revolving around a group of beautiful, sexually alluring, competent detectives who nonetheless knew how to please the boss, the eponymous Charlie—but whose sexual encounters (if there were any) remained off-screen.

Possibly because aging baby boomers who had grown up with the sexual revolution were increasingly influential both as decision makers and as consumers, the 1980s brought a shift in the representation of women onscreen, routinely producing films that took a neo-feminist perspective on women's sexuality. The success of independent films like *Annie Hall* (Woody Allen, 1977) among demographically desirable audiences, such as the "yuppy" (young urban professional), was a contributing factor, as well as the increasing emphasis on niche marketing that encouraged the industry to target women viewers along with other well-defined demographics, such as teenagers. The rise of pay television (in the form of cable and pay-per-view) and the home theater (through the proliferation of VHS and later DVD rental services) also supported the marketing trend that considered the tastes of women viewers, who were avid home viewers and a stable part of the buy-through audience.

One genre to emerge in recognition of the women's market was the female friendship film—films such as *Nine to Five* (Colin Higgins, 1980), *Beaches* (Garry Marshall, 1988), *Steel Magnolias* (Herbert Ross, 1989), *Fried Green Tomatoes* (Jon Avnet, 1991) and *Thelma & Louise* (Ridley Scott, 1991);[6] however, even more important, as far as production numbers were concerned, was the return of the romantic comedy, often hybridized to incorporate elements of the female friendship film. The success of *When Harry Met Sally* (Rob Reiner, 1989) marked the rise of the neo-romantic comedy, with its heroine, Sally (played by Meg Ryan) representing a new version of the "Cosmo Girl," who, unlike Helen Gurley Brown, puts affairs of the heart before fiscal responsibility, while nevertheless remaining gainfully employed.

The female friendship film, the new romantic comedy, as well as earlier films like *Alice Doesn't Live Here Anymore* (Martin Scorsese, 1974), or *An*

Unmarried Woman (Paul Mazursky, 1978), or "the new woman's film,"[7] which offered more personal views on women's predicaments, have much in common with the types of "fictional feminism" discussed by Loudermilk. Karen Hollinger postulates that the female friendship film is "an attempt to assimilate into mainstream cultural representations ideas from the women's movement such as female autonomy and sisterhood"; as such, these films "might be best approached neither as progressive ... nor as reactionary propositions ... but rather as complex products of an intricate process of negotiation."[8] While the female friendship film offers a highly ambiguous perspective on women's place in contemporary society, with its emphasis on female bonding, and its unconventional heroines—most notably in films such as *Thelma & Louise*—these films have in common with neo-feminism a focus on the individual and on personal solutions to the problems of social inequity. More importantly, this genre, or, more properly, cycle of films was overshadowed in the 1990s by the more prolific and popular neo-romantic comedy, beginning arguably with *When Harry Met Sally*, with its pro-social message and emphasis on heterosexuality.

As with the female friendship film and the neo-romantic comedy, the development of the girly film, which grew out of these two genres, attests to the recognition of a new kind of female audience. While girly films may underline the importance of female friendship, and may borrow, as convenient, slogans and ideas from feminism, these films offer an updated version of the neo-feminist paradigm as represented by the "Cosmo Girl." What sets the girly film apart from other films geared towards a female audience is its focus on consumer culture; this can be seen in girly female friendship films and girly neo-romantic comedies such as *Romy and Michele's High School Reunion* (David Mirkin, 1997) and *13 Going on 30* (Gary Winick, 2004). While united through their concern with feminine subjectivity, manifest in a heroine at the center of her universe who motivates and drives the narrative, stylistically girly films do not offer a cohesive body of work bound by the specific formal permutations that are associated with a specific genre or a specific narrative formula. In the girly film—a diverse set of films that include: *Pretty Woman*; *Sabrina* (Sydney Pollack, 1995); *Romy and Michele's High School Reunion*; *Legally Blonde* (Robert Luketic, 2001); *Maid in Manhattan* (Wayne Wang, 2002); *Something's Gotta Give* (Nancy Meyers, 2003); *Le Divorce* (James Ivory, 2003); *13 Going on 30*; *Sex and the City: The Movie* (Michael Patrick King, 2008); *Confessions of a Shopaholic* (P.J. Hogan, 2009)—the generic conventions of the romance may provide a significant narrative structure (usually the defining narrative structure). Nevertheless, only a few of these films are romantic comedies in the strict sense of the term. The aspects of these films that unite them revolve around: (1) the way in which the heroine herself is defined; (2) a shift away from melodrama to romantic comedy as the primary structural vehicle for the feminine narrative, resulting in the predominance of hybridized narrative forms; (3) the creation of a set of narrative tropes that function for thematic purposes like the medieval "commonplaces," being repeated from film to film, more or less obviously.[9]

These "commonplaces," associated with the neo-feminist paradigm, are tied to social developments surrounding the feminine subject and the heterosexual couple that arise in response to the larger technological and economic environment of the late twentieth and early twenty-first centuries. Such commonplaces include: an engagement with the image and representation as a technological process of production and reproduction; a preoccupation with consumer culture; the use of the makeover to represent the process of education and transformation; the deployment of a double heroine and a double ending that often translate into a "do-over"; the wedding as a set of images and narrative expectations; finally, a continued concern with maternity and the maternal bond associated with a "disappearing father." In general, girly films tend to emphasize familial bonds—but as a process of constant rearticulation as opposed to stasis—in which, within either intimate or public culture, the Father no longer incarnates the Law. As a rule, the girly film, ignoring feminism, portrays women as seeking to achieve parity in the workplace, while maintaining "difference" within intimate culture through relations with men, and by preserving the maternal bond in feminine culture.

I use the term "girl" because an important aspect of these films is the way in which they demonstrate how, for better or for worse, the term "girl" and something like "girlishness" has been retrieved and reinstated as defining a particular ideal of femininity associated with neo-feminism and the development of individual agency. The term "girl" evokes the idea of a woman in a continuous state of becoming, who is empowered by her ability to sexualize herself for her own pleasure. The notion of the girl also underlines the ambivalence of her position, one in which she must call upon codes of heterosexuality to construct herself as pleasurable, and in which she retains a weaker role vis-à-vis the more powerful masculine position, and the world of mature, stable identities. Girly films appear at the end of the twentieth century and at the beginning of the twenty-first century. As such, they are an extension of a phenomenon that began in the twentieth century, reaching its full flowering in the 1960s with the sexual revolution, during which the concerns of women come to solidify around concepts of personal fulfillment in which sexuality and consumer culture play principal roles.

Within a popular arena, certain aspects of second-wave feminism were assimilated into the neo-feminist paradigm, notably those that emphasized individual rights and individual choice; however these were translated into a language that found its most obvious expression in the development of feminine consumer culture. Examples would be the growth of magazines, advertising and television programming specifically directed at the economically independent woman.[10] Clearly these are not the only examples: women's importance as a demographic constituency is manifest across an array of areas from health care to insurance policies. This study singles out film narrative as an area in which economics and culture marry to produce a symbolically fecund field for the cultural analyst; importantly, these films serve to give expression to underlying desires and tensions produced by the neo-feminist paradigm as it is developed across a number of different media from "chick lit" to "self-help" programming for television, all of which inflect the films' presentation of femininity.

The girly film illustrates how popular culture for women may constitute a way of thinking about issues that might be called women's issues outside the context of academic or political debate. The girly film in popular culture parallels the development of feminist theory in academia as a means of expressing and interrogating the terms of an evolving feminine identity in contemporary culture with, however, significantly more conservative outcomes. In putting forth this argument, I do not wish to celebrate feminine culture as necessarily "feminist" or politically progressive. Often, on the contrary, the meditations of popular culture are conservative and even reactionary; these are, nonetheless, serious propositions that express the concerns of women in indirect ways, as a means of making them seem less urgent and threatening. The often "silly" or "implausible" pretexts of the girly film enable women to consider radical shifts in the conception of femininity in an apparently safe environment that does not alienate the still dominant class of heterosexual men.

Importantly, as part of this process of negotiation, neo-feminism in the 1980s frequently took a nostalgic turn—a significant shift away from the Cosmo Girl ideal promoted by Brown that was very future oriented. This is reflected in these films in what might be described as a "do-over," in which the heroine (very obviously in *13 Going on 30*) is given a second chance. Beginning with *Pretty Woman* itself, the heroine, and sometimes the hero, seeks to correct what might appear to be an irrevocable error, often one that is the result of pursuing a purely instrumental view of the world. These films are not, however, cautionary tales, but fantasies that invite the viewer to believe in the possibility of happy endings, while simultaneously recognizing the implausibility of these endings.

While elements of the girly film may be found throughout popular film and television narrative, harking back at least as far as the 1927 Clara Bow vehicle *It* (Clarence G. Badger), *Pretty Woman* represents a significant moment in the translation of the neo-feminist paradigm to cinema, both in terms of the number of characteristics that it brings together, and also because of the iconic status that it acquired in terms of subsequent iterations of the genre. Improbably, given the film's popularity and its essentially conservative world-view, *Pretty Woman* recounts the story of a prostitute, Vivian (played by Julia Roberts in her breakthrough role), who wins the love of a successful businessman, Edward, played by Richard Gere. The film follows the traditional marriage or romance plot which depends upon the heroine "finding validation of one's uniqueness and importance by being singled out among all other woman by a man";[11] however, it also signals a significant variation in this structure whereby it is the woman herself who takes charge of the process. *Pretty Woman* emphasizes that the role of woman is no longer a possession to be exchanged between men, from father to husband. Rather, in the words of the film's heroine, Vivian, who begins the narrative as a lowly "hooker," "We say who. We say when. We say how much." In contrast, the eighteenth-century novel, according to feminist critics like Nancy Miller, promulgated the ideal of the chaste virgin who though she "must marry … must remain within the family, chaste and willing to circulate, but only and necessarily in accordance with the law of the father."[12] Here, sexual knowledge, and by extension knowledge in general, was the sign not of value but of "damaged goods." Crucial to this system of value was the ideal of two separate spheres, the public and the private, with the good woman confined to the latter. *Pretty Woman* breaks down these distinctions, promoting a fantasy world in which the private and public merge to be regulated by an idealized notion of the family.

This theme is realized through the film's subplot, which focuses on Edward's plans to take over a family shipping business. Edward is successful in his strategy; however, he has a change of heart, signaling his education. Edward realizes that corporate raiding is evil, because he does not "build anything." Instead of ripping apart the family business that he proposes to acquire at the film's conclusion, he decides to join the family, finding in James (Ralph Bellamy), the head of the ship building clan, the father that he never had. Director Garry Marshall comments: "This is a moment when he finally sees an image of his father that he likes."[13] In James, Edward finds the father who is missing in both Edward's and Vivian's lives. Vivian herself grew up with her mother, with both having been abandoned by her father; while earlier in the film, Edward's admission that "I'm very angry with my father," in spite of $10,000 worth of therapy, highlights the absence of an adequate father in the childhood of both hero and heroine. Vivian proposes her "self," with her legs wrapped around him in an 88-inch embrace, as a more effective substitute to counseling. And, indeed, from their first meeting, Vivian likes James and his son—the fact that they are a family—and begins supporting them against Edward's lawyer, Philip Stuckey (Jason Alexander), who represents profit for its own sake. The film gives us to understand that it is Vivian who enables Edward to comprehend what James might have to offer, and to discover the "good father" in himself, the man who wants to build rather than destroy. In this particular film, the finding of a father in James—as someone who creates things (in this case ships, with all that this might imply metaphorically) and maintains relationship between generations—is important to the film's resolution, which offers a fantasy to the viewer: not only that a prostitute can marry a CEO, but also that the problems of childhood can be repaired in adulthood, that the individual can change and ameliorate his or her situation in a form of prolonged adolescence in which education is a continuing process.

Vivian, as the heroine of *Pretty Woman*, also undergoes an education, one that mimics the one offered by Helen Gurley Brown in *Sex and the Single Girl*.[14] In the course of the film, Vivian learns both how to cultivate her appearance, and also the proper place of love and sex for the single girl, and, by so doing, redeems herself. While the film condemns prostitution, it does not do so in moral terms, but, rather, because as a form of work, it fails to provide the self-fulfillment to which all single girls must aspire. Paradoxically, then, the film also offers prostitution as the model for all human behavior, including intimate life, in which the "deal," and in particular the optimization of the deal (getting the best deal possible), offers the logic by which decisions are made. Prostitution is not a very "good deal"—Vivian's education leads her to see that "she can do better," both personally and financially. Marshall emphasizes how, from the beginning, the couple have in common an investment in money and "one-upmanship." "They are both interested in money … it's a whole new kind of game playing, based on money."[15] Edward himself explains to Vivian, in a widely quoted line, that "[y]ou and I are such similar creatures, Vivian. We both screw people for money."

Indeed, the first line of the film underlines the importance of money. A magician, who appears only briefly as he performs his tricks for a group of wealthy "Los Angelenos," gathered for Edward's benefit, announces: "No matter what they say, it's all about money." The film's production notes highlight that "[i]nitially it appears to be a case of opposites attracting, when in fact these people are very much alike."[16] Significantly, near the film's conclusion, Edward offers to set Vivian up in an apartment. She refuses, saying: "You made me a really nice offer. … I want more." In essence, she holds out for a better deal, what she calls "the fairy tale," or what Edward refers to as "impossible relationships"—his "special gift." While the film seems to say that the impossible will work out, Marshall, the film's director, emphasizes the fantasy dimension: "The audience really wanted to make believe that this was a real, real story."[17] An ability to believe in the impossible, at least temporarily, comes to be one of the strong characteristics of the girly film, emphasizing as it does both fantasy and sentiment; however, these elements are accompanied by a strong visual investment in the pleasures of consumer culture.

The focus on pleasure distinguishes the girly film from earlier films that revolve around similar issues to those raised by *Pretty Woman*. For example, in *Working Girl* (Mike Nichols, 1988), Tess (played by Melanie Griffith) undergoes a makeover for the purposes of advancing her career, underlining the importance of a level of feminine competence in the modification and regulation of

Figure 2.1 Vivian (Julia Roberts), a "lady." Courtesy of Photofest.

her appearance. Vivian, while also motivated by ambition in the sense that Edward required that she look like a "lady," takes pleasure in her transformation that is in excess of the effect on others that she achieves (see Figure 2.1). Though many of her outfits in the film were echoed again and again by the

Figure 2.2 Vivian in her "Pretty Woman" boots. Courtesy of Photofest.

fashion industry and in other films such as *She's All That* (Robert Iscove, 1999), it is her initial appearance as a hooker (before her transformation) that would have the most significant impact. Bloomingdale's catalogue advertised "Pretty Women boots" shortly after the film's release, while eBay, in 2009, offered "New and 100% authentic Christian Louboutin 'PRETTY WOMAN' boots"[18] (see Figure 2.2). The pleasure and power in Vivian's transformation derives as much from the fact of transformation as the end that it achieves. Her capacity to incarnate different looks, to play the lady as well as the hooker, expresses her consumer culture expertise and pleasure.[19]

In general terms, girly films mobilize a number of significant traits that constitute the "commonplaces" of the genre, and which are linked to the neo-feminist paradigm. Most of them are clearly marked in *Pretty Woman*, and can be summarized as follows.

1. Through the creation of a story world in which the heroine is at the center of her universe, these films address a female audience, but at the same time underline appearance as a crucial aspect of feminine identity, thus appealing to the masculine viewer incidentally. As "chick flicks," neo-feminist films are considered ones that women especially enjoy watching with other women. Female bonding is often a theme in the films, which routinely feature friendship (as in the case of Kit and Vivian in *Pretty Woman*), amplifying the "female" address of the film as a film "for women."

2. Though chastity rarely figures in these films, structurally they rely heavily on what in literature is called the "marriage plot"[20]—in which a girl succeeds in life by marrying the man of her choice—linking these films to the tradition of romance while exploring anxieties about the role of sexuality in contemporary life. *Pretty Woman*, by depicting a prostitute who wins her prince in the form of an extremely wealthy suitor who promises her a fairy-tale ending, exemplifies both the genre's reliance on the traditional marriage plot and its significant modifications.

3. The protagonist is usually a single woman who works for a living, and whose work in some way defines her (in *Pretty Woman*, Vivian is initially identified through her work as a prostitute); however, at the same time, regardless of the role that she plays, she is distinguished by her girlish personality and looks. The place of the family, which seeks to contain the girl by marking her as a woman and mother, while almost always significant, is often ambivalent and fraught as a result. While the woman is no longer defined by her role within the family, she does not escape it entirely, often investing the image of the family with nostalgic regret. In particular, the role of the father is increasingly vexed, or often simply absent. In *Pretty Woman*, both the hero and the heroine have difficult relations with their

families who have ultimately failed them. In particular, Vivian's father abandoned her and her mother, while Edward's father failed to provide him with an adequate and productive role model, both emotionally and professionally.

4. Consumer culture and consumer-culture competence are crucial elements in the setting, as well as often providing tools that enable the heroine to resolve her conflict; at the same time, unlike the "mouseburger," an unexceptional single girl, the girly heroine is always exceptional in some way, while retaining demotic connections. Vivian's stunning good looks set her apart, but these are not sufficient until she learns to shop. In *Pretty Woman*, Vivian's ability to learn to dress convincingly like a "lady" is a significant step not only in her education and in reaching her goal of the "fairy tale," but also in helping the viewer to understand her interior transformation. Marshall explains: "The point of the whole picture was ... she wasn't going back to prostitution, she was going to go to school." That Vivian's education is represented by her coming to know how to shop and how to spend money was, for many reviewers, a contradiction that the film seemed unable to resolve. Dennis Delrogh of the *LA Weekly* wrote: "Director Garry Marshall projects his *My Fair Lady* concept as a derisive male fantasy: whore regenerated as ideal woman, one who shops."[21] Henry Sheehan, in *The Reader*, objects to "the infantile pleasure of unfettered materialism."[22] Notwithstanding these reservations, reviewers tended to find the film convincing because of Roberts' star charisma and other attributes, none of which are available in even the most exclusive of shops. "Nothing works, except perhaps the sight of Julia Roberts' lean, well-tempered midsection and her roughly eight yards of legs," claims Sheila Benson in the *Los Angeles Times*.[23] The "shopping" dimension of the girly film continued to gain in importance, in spite of reviewers' largely negative comments; similarly the star's charisma, underlining the double nature of the female protagonist as both exceptional and ordinary, is crucial to a girly film's success, signaling that while consumer-culture competence is necessary, it is never sufficient.

5. Consumer culture, either as a central aspect of the plot, or as an incidental detour, offers the protagonist a kind of "Green World"—a term used by literary critic Northrop Frye[24]—a magical place in which everything goes right, as in *Legally Blonde*, or completely awry, as in *13 Going on 30*, or both, as in *Pretty Woman* (as exemplified in the famous Rodeo Drive sequence). Paris and Frenchness may often offer an additional magical location usually associated with both consumer culture and femininity, as in *Sabrina*.

6. Thematically, the films often exhibit a profound ambivalence about certain issues—in particular, the role of romance, marriage and work in a woman's

life—made manifest through the doubling of characters and/or the use of double narratives. In *Pretty Woman*, Verdi's opera *La Traviata,* which the hero and heroine attend, suggests an alternative ending to the romance between a prostitute and her upper-class lover, in which Violetta (Vivian's counterpart within the opera) is accepted by his family only in death. The presence of the opera reminds us that while love ennobles those who experience it, it does not guarantee a happy ending. Significantly, the musical theme from the opera associated with Violetta's heartbreaking decision to sacrifice the happiness she has found by renouncing her lover ("Amami Alfredo") is played in a swelling orchestral reprise during the couple's final triumphant reunion at the film's conclusion, providing an ironic counterpoint that reminds the viewer of an alternative possibility.

7. The primary events of these films take place in well-defined geographic locations that are urban in nature, usually New York, but sometimes LA, and less often some other urban metropolis such as London, Chicago, or Washington, DC. Paris may be featured, but usually represents an alternative universe for the heroine, even if the majority of the action takes place in Paris, as in *Le Divorce.* The countryside rarely appears, even as an idyllic interlude, in the way it does, for example, in the romantic comedies of auteur directors such as Eric Rohmer and Woody Allen. The characters' lives are thus ultimately and irrevocably constrained by the ethos of a modernity expressed through a pervasive urban culture for which there is no antidote. In *Pretty Woman*, the film emphasized its urban setting as well as notable Los Angeles landmarks and locations, such as Rodeo Drive and Hollywood Boulevard. The Green World is not recreated through bucolic or nostalgic images of the countryside, as, for example, in the classic screwball comedy *It Happened One Night* (Frank Capra, 1934), but through the invocation of consumer culture and shopping as the acme of urban life.

8. These films are concerned with the theme of transformation, often represented as a magical makeover, the purpose of which is to give expression to an internal process of education, which, through the makeover trope, is linked to consumer culture. *Pretty Woman*'s director, Garry Marshall, avers that "every picture has a makeover or a love montage … or some have both."[25] Vivian's education, whereby she comes to behave and look like a lady, and takes the decision to abandon prostitution and return to school, is represented through a radical change in her appearance and her clothing. Importantly, part of her deal with Edward is that, in return for her services as a "beck and call girl" during the period of a week, she will not only receive three thousand dollars, but also be able to keep the clothing he purchases for her (or, rather, that she purchases for herself with his money). Her new clothing and look are thus, within the film, considered

significant assets that will enable her to further her education. In contrast with her friend Kit, who cannot follow her into a different kind of life, Vivian's ability to wear clothes well, to "look good," becomes a significant sign of her worthiness and virtue.

9. The education that both hero and heroine undergo often entails a "do-over," in which a past mistake is rectified. In *Pretty Woman*, Garry Marshall explains that "[t]hrough him and through her, they both grew. That's what a love relationship is." Both are redeemed. "So what happened after he rescues her? She rescues him right back," claims Marshall. "They finally, finally go to where they can love."[26] Notably, Edward finds the father he never had and comes to understand that the point of life is to make things, rather than to destroy them—to be productive! Both can start life again, Vivian as a "lady" and Edward as a builder, their past mistakes as prostitute and corporate raider forgiven. The "do-over" aspect of the film is emphasized by its double ending. In a first ending, Vivian and Edward agree to part because Vivian has realized that she can no longer continue to work as a prostitute or even as a "kept woman" which would merely be, in her terms, a "change in real estate"; however, Edward quickly realizes his mistake and rectifies it by seeking Vivian out in her apartment in order to modify his original offer to set Vivian up as his mistress. We assume, then, that he is now ready to offer her the fairy tale she requested—in other words, love and marriage—though those words are never spoken and remain implicit.

10. These films are marked by a significant intertextuality and a preoccupation with citation that often produces a nostalgic perspective on the past. Another equally important strand is the constant references to consumer culture more generally, as well as specific fashion labels and lines. In the case of *Pretty Woman*, the film not only cites the opera *La Traviata*, which recounts the ill-fated relationship of Violetta and her young aristocratic lover, but also the romantic comedy *Charade* (Stanley Donen, 1963), starring Audrey Hepburn, in which a similarly seemingly ill-fated romance turns out well, and the television show *I Love Lucy* (CBS, 1951–60), which references Marshall's own beginnings on television. While the film does not highlight particular lines of clothing, as do later girly films obsessed with labels such as Prada and Gucci, it does underline various upscale stores located on Rodeo Drive.

These films can be set in contradistinction to Hollywood films that draw upon and incorporate aspects of European art house film. This is reflected in the fact that though "style" in terms of consumer culture may be important to the protagonists, film "style" is not developed as a meaningful aspect of the filmic experience. As Marshall points out, "Shots are very important but the story is more important."[27] Though cutting becomes faster and MTV and advertising styles may be appropriated, by and large these films reproduce the codes of psychological editing defined by classical Hollywood film. In some ways, these films are much more heavily tied to TV culture than to film culture, and have distinct parallels in television programming, most notably with shows like *Sex and the City* (HBO, 1998–2004), which generated one of the most successful girly films at the box office, the theme of which is "love and labels" (as in designer fashion labels). In a sense, this genre offers what might be called a "zero degree" of style, in so far as the film focuses on plot and character (the appearance of the character), and does not draw attention to itself as such, sharing with certain traditional women's melodramas—such as *Now Voyager* (Irving Rapper, 1942), and classical Hollywood film more generally—an emphasis on the relationship between appearance, femininity and transformation. (See, for example, the use of the makeover in *Vertigo* (Alfred Hitchcock, 1958); or in *Rebecca* (Alfred Hitchcock, 1940).)

While *Pretty Woman* defines the lineaments of the new girly film that successive examples of the genre would progressively elaborate, a number of other films, such as *Desperately Seeking Susan* (Susan Seidelman, 1985), or *Working Girl*, suggest the beginning of a girly trend that pre-dates *Pretty Woman*. In significant ways, however, these films do not reproduce the neo-feminist paradigm as it will come to dominate the chick flick productions of the 1990s. While neither of these two earlier films gives much credence to the importance of chastity, and both include makeover motifs, each departs from the girly paradigm in significant ways, with consumer culture playing a less significant role than in later films. *Desperately Seeking Susan* evokes the neo-feminist paradigm most clearly by giving Madonna as the Material Girl a co-starring role in the film;[28] however, the film itself does not subscribe to the "striver," pro-social values that mark later girly films, opting for a more bohemian, counterculture perspective in its conclusion. *Working Girl*, while close to the point of view offered by Helen Gurley Brown in its emphasis on ambition, offers a cynical view of relations between women by presenting a heroine who gets ahead by impersonating another woman and sleeping with her boyfriend. In both films the heroine offers viewers an independent "single girl" who must assume responsibility for her own decisions and life. Neither film, however, has achieved the canonical status accorded *Pretty Woman* in contemporary feminine culture, within which it has become the touchstone for a particular kind of viewing pleasure, one that is repeated and shared with other women.[29] Thus, Barbara Klinger, in a survey conducted in 2000 among university undergraduates, found that *Pretty Woman* ranked number three among "most rewatched films." Klinger surmises that "for some college age women, chick flicks such as *Pretty Woman* provide them with shining examples of heroines ... while also operating as 'a security blanket you carry with you through the years'—a known quantity that furnishes satisfying and uplifting effect."[30]

Pretty Woman, then, offers a fairy tale that often, in Klinger's terms, "becomes a template for feminine dreams of achievement"[31] while incarnating a number of significant principles associated with neo-feminism. The film departs from the principles articulated by Helen Gurley Brown by retreating from a pragmatic perspective in which actions always have consequences. Brown's instrumentalism is overwhelmed and negated by the fantasy—the impossible happy endings that the film offers its eager audiences, producing a soft, sentimental version of neo-feminism that is legitimated through an appeal to traditional notions of romance. The melodramatic dimensions of the film are similarly softened through its borrowings from the tradition of romantic comedy, with its characteristically pro-social, hence essentially conservative, conclusions. The fantasy dimension of the girly film constitutes the significant contribution of the genre to neo-feminism: the girly film takes the more radical attributes of neo-feminism and makes these palatable to a general audience by incorporating them into the cinematic tradition of romance, fantasy and happy endings. In so doing the films underline a contradiction in neo-feminist discourse, the instrumentalist perspective of which leaves no room for romance. In the girly film, instrumentalism may indeed lead to romance: a relationship that begins with fellatio can conclude with a kiss. The girlishness of the heroine, representing an identity that is not yet fixed or determined, permits her to regain her innocence even when she is marked by experiences, such as prostitution, that might have destroyed this in earlier women's narratives. In *Pretty Woman*, the actual youth of Julia Roberts, in comparison to the comparative age of Richard Gere, underlines the girlishness that she portrays; however, as the genre develops, its stars are often increasingly older. The most famous "girly" heroines, such as the four friends in *Sex and the City*, range in age from 30 to 40 at the show's beginning and 40 to 50 in *Sex and the City: The Movie*, suggesting how girlishness in this genre becomes a mode of being—as advocated by Brown well into her eighties.[32] As the genre develops, the emphasis on fantasy and on girlishness as a mode of being (independent of age) become increasingly important features, while the obvious self-conscious centrality of "money" exhibited by *Pretty Woman* becomes less visible in later films, but without any diminution of the importance of wealth to the neo-feminist ideal. In the chapters that follow, I will explore the development of this ideal as the girly film itself becomes more clearly defined and gains momentum as a genre.

Chapter 3

Romy and Michele's High School Reunion (1997)

Female Friendship in the Girly Film

The previous chapter explored ways in which Garry Marshall's *Pretty Woman* (1990) set the terms by which the romantic heroine is reinvented in the girly film. My analysis of the film emphasized how chastity no longer functions as a defining element that signals the heroine's virtue and exceptional status. Instead, I argue, appearance, especially "looking good in clothes," comes not simply to represent more abstract qualities such as "virtue," but to constitute an attribute that is perceived as desirable in itself. The "single girl" as defined by Helen Gurley Brown becomes, paradoxically, the new ideal wife. This focus on a consumer-constructed self as well as sexual availability underlines the film's relationship to the neo-feminist paradigm, as does a focus on friendship, especially between women.

This chapter will narrow the focus to the neo-feminist friendship film, examining *Romy and Michele's High School Reunion* (David Mirkin, 1997) as a specific example of this sub-genre. While *Pretty Woman* is not a female friendship film, it incorporates some of the elements of the genre by foregrounding the relationship between Vivian and Kit. Though Kit is not able to follow Vivian into the new world that she creates for herself, their separation is not an easy one. Marshall comments on lovers' partings, adding that "to part with a great friendship is just as hard." He continues: "Friendship is always a part of life ... and if you are lucky enough to have a friend, your life is far more better and if your friend can be your wife, your husband, well that's even good or your lover ... all good ways [*sic*]."[1] For Vivian and Edward to come together, both must part with their best friends, Kit and "Stuckey" respectively, who perhaps with the best of intentions have led them down the wrong path (corporate speculation in Edward's case, and prostitution in Vivian's case)—a wrong path that is perhaps necessary to finding the right path, each other, the restoration of the heterosexual couple, but also their own moral equilibrium and family values. Marshall remarks, citing Bertolt Brecht: "First food, then morals. ... Later in the picture, the morals come," delineating, in particular, Vivian's journey from a point at which she moves from fearing for her survival to considering the kind of life she wishes to lead.[2]

While Vivian seems to abandon female friendship to pursue a better life, subsequent girly films will place increasing emphasis on friendship, sometimes with disastrous results, as in *13 Going on 30* (Gary Winick, 2004), sometimes as the primary sustaining relations of the heroine(s), existing alongside heterosexuality, marriage and family (not necessarily in that order), as in *Sex and the City: The Movie* (Michael Patrick King, 2008). The significance of *Romy and Michele's High School Reunion* is the manner in which it explores the nature of female friendship as defined within the neo-feminist paradigm—incarnating a "girly" version of the female friendship film described by Hollinger in the 1980s and early 1990s.[3]

Romy and Michele's High School Reunion takes the prototype offered by *Pretty Woman* and reverses it—so that the feminine couple, Kit and Vivian, with which *Pretty Woman* begins, but which Vivian must abandon in order to achieve the film's conclusion, becomes its focus. While this film was significantly less successful than a number of other girly films, it was a modest surprise hit, with "$22 million at the box office in 25 days of release."[4] Another Touchstone release, like *Pretty Woman*, the film testified to the importance of the female audience as an audience that was not interested in the more dominant action films and event films targeting older (over 25) and younger males, and, thus, could be relied upon to support films that offered an alternative to these pictures. In recognition of its success, the film received an award for "Excellence in Film Marketing." In particular, the two stars, Mira Sorvino and Lisa Kudrow, were cited as being "helpful in promoting the film by appearing on many talk shows around the country," testifying to the tendency of the girly genre to rely upon the draw of charismatic stars, for whom the film would serve as a vehicle.[5]

The film itself recounts the story of two young women in their late twenties (played by Mira Sorvino as Romy, and Lisa Kudrow as Michele) who decide to attend their 10-year high school reunion. Their problem, they realize, is that they are "failures," "slackerly misfits" or "Beavis and Butt-head with breasts," in the words of reviewers.[6] "They are not really doing much with their lives. But because they are truly happy, this never really occurs to them—until that moment," explains screenwriter Robin Schiff.[7] Their attempts to construct themselves as "images of success" at the reunion lead them from disaster to disaster until they are unmasked as fakes when they attempt to pass themselves off as the inventors of "post-its." Michele resolves the situation by proclaiming that until Romy announced that they were failures, she, Michele, had always thought that they were immensely successful, because "they always had so much fun."[8] They reappear at the reunion as "themselves" in outfits that they have designed and that Michele herself has sewn. Judged on their own accomplishments, as represented by their outfits, in which they "look good," they are pronounced a "success." The movie concludes with a view of their future as owners of a successful boutique on Rodeo Drive.

Unlike *Pretty Woman*, this film evolves out of an ironic, critical perspective, in particular through a comic character developed by Kudrow with a view to ridiculing and undermining the values and perspectives that this character represents. The "Michele" character was initially developed for a stage play, *The Ladies Room* (1988–89), written by Robin Schiff. Sorvino characterizes Schiff as a satirical author: "Her writing is seductively subversive and edgy. It's social commentary, incisive and moving, but presented in a highly entertaining, very funny way."[9] Schiff, in her first screenplay, created *Romy and Michele* by elaborating a new narrative about two secondary characters from the original play, a process in which Kudrow was intimately involved.[10] Indeed, the success of Kudrow's persona, one which she reprised for the hit television show *Friends* (NBC, 1994–2004) during the same time-frame, was crucial to the development of the project and the successful film that resulted from it. Director David Mirkin affirms that "Lisa was always Michele. ... She had been Michele from the very beginning." Kudrow herself has a very negative view of the character, commenting that "[i]t's a portrait of abject idiocy and obnoxiousness."[11] Indeed, much of the humor of the film derives from its mobilization of the blonde dolly bird, bimbo stereotype initially associated with stars such as Marilyn Monroe and Jayne Mansfield, and exemplified in such tag lines as "The Blonde Leading the Blonde," used to characterize the film on a widely disseminated poster.[12]

The use of irony and satire, however, is a common and marked strategy in "chick lit." In girly films, even though as a rule it is less visible, it nevertheless still tends to be present. Important chick lit volumes, such as the original *Sex and the City* (1997), as well as Candace Bushnell's subsequent novels, or the Shopaholic series by Sophie Kinsella beginning with *Confessions of Shopaholic* (2003), both of which have been adapted into girly films, offer satirical and seemingly critical perspectives on neo-feminist culture.[13] A defining characteristic of the girly narrative is, thus, its ability to mock itself while at the same time, paradoxically, sustaining and reproducing the objects of its derision. *Romy and Michele* offers a particularly striking example of this deep contradiction at the heart of the girly film and neo-feminism more generally, which holds a deeply ambivalent perspective on the ideals that it represents that does not deflect from the appeal of this position. The film, then, concludes, not with a rejection of a girly life, but with its glorification and acceptance as "fun." Executive Producer Barry Kemp opines, "If there is a moral in 'Romy and Michele's High School Reunion' ... it's that the only person you ultimately have to impress is yourself. Having a dear friend, a best friend, an *only* friend is much more important than having the best job in the world. Romy and Michele are incredibly lucky to have each other. ... that they've been able to sustain their friendship for so long makes it all the more special. Somewhere for every Romy there is a Michele. And if they can only somehow find each other how fortunate they will be." Schiff also emphasizes the attractive dimension of the characters: "I love that they say what's on their mind and how much fun they have with each other. But I especially love how much their friendship means to them. Even though characters are sort of these airheads, I can totally relate to that aspect of them."[14]

The two characters return to the city, in this instance LA, and to the Edenic life that it seemingly provides, with a future now in front of them and a career of which they can be proud. The film reverses the usual place accorded consumer culture as a Green World in which magical things can happen. Unlike the consumer-culture Green World of many films, in this film it becomes the characters' permanent abode: at the film's conclusion the two women are safely back in Los Angeles, installed on Rodeo Drive in their own boutique, selling their own creations. From the very beginning, the urban world provides a refuge for Romy and Michele; it is the everyday world of Tucson, Arizona, where the two women attended high school, that proves to be a topsy-turvy universe in which nothing holds—in which the two girls are are tormented by their outsider status in spite of the fact that they remain "Barbie-like stars"[15] (see Figure 3.1). This is not the only reversal that the film performs: the characters' position in life is also at odds with the girly prototype, with Romy and Michele incarnating the lower rungs of the female workforce, stuck in unrewarding routines, or, even worse, unemployed.

In the typical "girly film," the protagonist (in contrast with Vivian in *Pretty Woman*) is a successful career woman, usually within professions such as fashion or public relations that are considered glamorous and media-worthy. For example, the heroine is a magazine editor in *13 Going on 30*, and also in *How to Lose a Guy in 10 Days* (Donald Petrie, 2003); in *Raising Helen* (Garry Marshall, 2004), she works for "a top modeling agency," an executive assistant to its head, and so forth.[16] In contrast, Romy and Michele represent the lowly "working girl" who struggles to make ends meet, surviving on a limited budget while admiring, and attempting to emulate, the lives of the "It Girls," whose career profile resembles that of the chick flick heroine as described in magazines such as *InStyle* or *Vogue*. While this type of disenfranchised feminine subject who survives with difficulty is often the subject of serious dramas, such as *The Good Girl* (Miguel Arteta, 2002), or independent films, such as *Hysterical Blindness* (Mira Nair, 2002) or *Friends with Money* (Nicole Holofcener, 2006), the girly film rarely addresses the financially precarious situation of young women who do not hold a position of relative financial privilege.

Figure 3.1 Romy (Mira Sorvino, left) and Michele (Lisa Kudrow, right) as "Barbie dolls." Courtesy of Photofest.

In *Bridget Jones's Diary* even Bridget Jones with her university degree, as the prototypical chick lit heroine or Singleton, marginally brighter and significantly less Barbie-like than Romy and Michele, enjoyed a more privileged, if equally precarious, economic status; however, a more recent branch of "chick lit," such as the novels of Plum Sykes, herself a member of British aristocracy, revolve around an obsession with the lives and habits of the very wealthy as icons of fashion, while at the same time satirizing the superficiality and insecurities of these same young women.[17] While the working-girl protagonist in these novels usually proves herself more worthy than her wealthy and idle counterparts, she is also often magically transported, usually through marriage, into the world of the fabulously wealthy for whom success and money are not a concern. In this way, an impossible dream is presented as the resolution of her problems—one in which she is allowed to thrive in a world in which inherited wealth is the norm and the ideal.

Romy and Michele follows a similar narrative arc, but one which is located within the more modest arena of everyday America, reprising the high school experience as the common ground of adolescence. Their failure to find adequate employment, and husbands, can only be reversed by a *deus ex machina* intervention in the form of Michele's long-standing high school admirer, Sandy Frink (Alan Cumming), now a millionaire, who miraculously reappears at the reunion, lowered from a helicopter out of the sky. He is, thus, a literalization of the term, *deus ex machina* (god from the machine), typically used to refer to the contrived endings in classical theater, in which the actor playing the "god" who arrives to resolve the characters' dilemmas was literally lowered mechanically onto the stage. The term is still commonly used to describe implausible and unconvincing plot devices employed to provide some sort of conclusion to a story. This kind of tongue-in-cheek reference is typical of girly films, which often attempt to redeem their debased status through highly developed systems of citations.[18]

In the case of *Romy and Michele*, a system of citation (here exemplified through the reference to the *deus ex machina* strategy of classical drama) serves to underline the film's ambivalent status as both participating in and critiquing neo-feminist culture and the girly film: the resolution of the heroine's dilemma usually depends upon a magical component that functions like the *deus ex machina* of the past, a fact upon which *Romy and Michele's High School Reunion* playfully comments, pointing to the conclusion's implausibility. This ironical stance highlights in this film the fact that the girly heroine(s)'s problems may not be as easily solved as the formula ending tends to imply.

This contrived ending in *Romy and Michele* is offset by another possible ending, repeating the strategy of multiple endings that is such a marked feature in *Pretty Woman*. In the middle of the film, the viewer is offered a counter narrative—which later proves to be Michele's dream—in which a traditional heterosexual conclusion is explored. The dream is provoked by a contentious argument between the two friends about which of them is "cuter"—or, rather, which of them is the "Rhoda," the neurotic but plain and chubby friend, and which the "Mary," the neurotic but attractive and thin heroine in the hit television show *The Mary Tyler Moore Show* (CBS, 1970–77), which gave star status to Mary Tyler Moore and social status to the 30-something single woman, or career "girl." In her dream, Michele is married to Sandy Frink, and is now an old woman at the end of her life, which was "happy" but "lonely," because she had "no one to talk to." She attempts to effect a reconciliation with Romy, with whom she has not spoken in years, since in fact their high school reunion. This attempt fails, however, because Romy, on her deathbed, refuses to relinquish her claim to being "the Mary," which terminates the dream.

Michele is shaken by the experience of her dream, and of the subsequent return to the "real" world, which seems no more "real," in the sense of being plausible, than the dream sequence; however, the dream becomes a vehicle for Michele's education. In the dream, she and Romy have achieved everything that escapes them in their current lives. They are both married and wealthy, Romy to the football hero whom she idolized in high school, whose children she bears. Yet, Michele is stricken by the barren fate that appears to await her in which she will have "no one to talk to," a vicious indictment of heterosexuality and marriage within the world of Romy and Michele. Such is her terror that her subsequent actions in the film are driven by her desire to repair the friendship—and the viewer is encouraged to believe that, in part, it is the dream, with its dystopian depiction of the future, that leads Michele finally to defend Romy and stand up for her when she is ridiculed by her former classmates—an act that eventually effects a reconciliation.

The dream sequence suggests that the characters' interest in romance, having a boyfriend and potentially entering into a marriage is ambivalent at best, given that that these attachments are conceived in terms of an accessory, a symbol of "success"—something that the successful woman "owns" rather than the fulfillment of a desire or need. Thus, another significant dimension of the education of these heroines is the discovery that they enjoy the life they have with each other. At the end of the film, Romy, at Michele's insistence, is obliged to concede that their life is indeed "successful" in its own terms because of—as Michele puts it—their "life style."

Their values, however, though articulated or expressed though consumer culture, are not material. Like Vivian and Kit, Romy and Michele are not wealthy, and appear to lack visible means of support. Michele is unemployed, and Romy is a cashier at a car dealership. They live in a dingy apartment in

Venice of very modest proportions; on the other hand, they also appear to be immune from the kinds of material concerns that plague, for example, the protagonists of *Hysterical Blindness*. They are undaunted by poverty—the laundromat, which in a film like *Midnight Cowboy* (John Schlesinger, 1969) underlines the destitution and desperation of the protagonists, is "fun" for them. The nightmare of urban life is transformed into a fantasy world of infinite possibilities. Such romanticization of urban life as offering the terrain on which "girls" can pursue a life devoted to fun illustrates the neo-feminist dimension of the film and its emphasis on a self-fulfillment that can be procured through consumer culture.

The importance of consumer culture is underlined by the way in which *Romy and Michele* invokes *Pretty Woman* by including footage of the movie—indicating its status as an iconic "chick flick" in 1997—in its initial sequence. This scene in which the two women watch the film on TV, lying on their twin beds, characterizes the way in which "cinema" has been transformed, particularly for the "feminine" viewer. The VCR (later DVD and VOD) brought cinema literally into the bedroom, integrating it into what Angela McRobbie has called "bedroom culture."[19] The VCR and DVD as well as the downloaded computer file also allow for repeat viewings, enabling the viewer to isolate and watch specific segments over and over again. The *Pretty Woman* sequence, a Touchstone production embedded in another Touchstone film, points to a number of developments in feminine culture, including the increasing importance of female viewers as a target demographic.

Scholars like Henry Jenkins have examined how the VCR has empowered a certain kind of fandom; similarly, the cinematic apparatus has transformed or perhaps inter-penetrated bedroom culture.[20] In a parallel vein, scholars have explored the importance of urban consumer culture and the ways in which consumer culture has empowered the young feminine consumer to move out of the bedroom into public spaces, albeit in a limited context;[21] conversely, new media, including now the internet, have also encouraged women to remain within the home while continuing to wield influence as consumers.[22] Women are thus a major factor in the "sell-through market," and the women's film typically targets the home as well as the theater—not only through television (always an important market for women's films), but also through, initially, the sale of VHS tapes, later replaced by DVD and VOD technologies.[23] Here, in this sequence, the film invites the viewer to reflect upon the reconfiguration of cinema and its importance for female viewers as an object of consumption that supports and enhances the centrality of consumer culture more generally.

The film also suggests the ways in which viewers remake a film—or perhaps view it in the context of their own understanding. We see this in the interpretation that Romy and Michele give to the sequence they watch toge-ther, which is the shopping sequence. The "happy ending" that they comment upon is one that occurs early in the film—in which Vivian, after several saleswomen refuse to serve her, returns the next day in a state of triumph as a successful shopper. Michele exclaims, "I just get really happy when they finally let her shop." The two women focus on Vivian's shopping experiences, rather on than on the development of the heterosexual romance to which the bulk of the film is devoted. Shopping and the transformative potential of fashion are what hold the interests of Romy and of Michele as viewers. These are the sequences that activate their emotions most strongly and that provide the "happy ending" to their viewing experience.[24]

This moment of re-reading contests the assertions of scholars like Barbara Klinger, who claims that repeat viewing of "chick flicks" "amounts to a kind of ritual anchoring of female subjectivity in normative standards of gender," in particular, with regards to their emphasis on the "fairy tale romance (complete with the rescue of a damsel in distress)."[25] Romy and Michele's re-reading of *Pretty Woman* privileges consumer culture, which, while affirming "shopping" as an activity that supports the dominant economic structure, undercuts the importance of romance and heterosexuality. Re-reading films, this sequence implies, allows viewers to privilege those strands or themes most important to them as well as allowing them to question the film's implicit social hierarchies. Thus, when initially Vivian is ignored by the Rodeo Drive saleswomen, Romy remarks: "Aw, look, poor thing—they won't let her shop. Yeah—like those salesgirls in Beverly Hills aren't bigger whores than she is." Romy and Michele's reinterpretation of the film points to the importance of consumer culture to the neo-feminist paradigm and the ways in which the obvious emphasis on heterosexual romance in films like *Pretty Woman* serves to create "cover stories" that authorize other kinds of value systems, including an emphasis on fashion and female friendship and the rejection of a social hierarchy that places arrogant saleswomen above prostitutes.[26]

Significantly, it is also Romy and Michele's engagement in feminine consumer culture that allows the film to produce a happy ending for its characters, much as they construct their own "fashionable" garments. If Romy and Michele's success is not entirely implausible, it is because they are undeniably talented within their very limited range of expertise—in "girl culture," which, the film leads them to understand in the course of their education, is valuable. Their engagement with fashion allows them to continue their girlish pursuits into what promises to be a fulfilling adulthood within the consumer culture indus-tries. These industries encourage a prolonged adolescence, not solely in terms of consumption, but also in terms of production. Thus, the ideal "chick flick" career, such as that of fashion designer, magazine editor or celebrity public relations representative, is one that permits the subject to engage in "girlish" activities as a life-long pursuit.

The style promoted by the characters is similarly youthful—cheap and tongue-in-cheek in terms of its relationship to high fashion. Romy and Michele represent the allure of Vivian in her high "fuck-me" boots, rather than that of the understated elegance of Vivian in a silk dress, hat and gloves when she attends the polo match. When Romy and Michele reveal themselves as themselves, they wear short skirts and snappy colors, low cut with a fluffy trim— apparel that would not look out of place on a Las Vegas stage or in a Busby Berkeley musical. While they are pronounced fashionable by one of their old classmates, now an Associate Editor at *Vogue*, it is difficult to see her pronouncement as signaling the triumph of good taste over bad taste. The editor herself stands out in her man-tailored suit and slicked-back hair against the backdrop of aging prom queens and cheerleaders, now pregnant, with their "big" hair, over-done tans and pastel, sequined gowns. More accurately, this moment represents the apparent triumph of do-it-yourself fashion over a style that supports conformity, taking up a common trope in "teen films" such as *Sixteen Candles* (John Hughes, 1984).

Another significant element, pointing to a tradition that emphasizes apparent non-conformity, is the nostalgic references to the "girl power" pop singers of the 1980s: Cyndi Lauper, Pat Benatar and, most of all, Madonna, in terms of fashion and appearance, as is reflected in the sound track, which includes such hits as "I Want Candy" (Bow Wow Wow), "Time after Time" (Cyndi Lauper) and "Don't Get Me Wrong" (Chrissie Hynde). In the words of *Boxoffice Magazine*, the film offers "a soundtrack jam-packed with '80s hits."[27] The fashion choices of the two protagonists continue to cite Madonna in her various guises, with the sound track evoking a visual panoply of continuing, now conventionalized, unconventional girlish stars. In this context, one might say that the style represented by Romy and Michele reiterates the triumph of a disposable "youth oriented" style inaugurated by stars such as Brigitte Bardot in the 1950s, and highlighted by the girl singers of the 1980s, over the expensive elitist elegance of the old haute couture.[28]

This youth culture style refutes the notion of "classic" style. It sees no advantage in the investment in expensive "timeless" items, nor in the exploration of craft and technological innovation. Youth culture style favors an ever-changing array of mass-produced items. There is a sleight of hand here in terms of exactly what the film's relationship might be to the world of fashion: in highlighting the cheap disposable clothing of youth, the film subscribes to fashion on a mass scale while seemingly supporting concepts of individual style. This mass style has continued to erode and displace elegance in high fashion magazines, to the extent that in the first decade of the twenty-first century celebrity "girls," such as Paris Hilton, take the place of fashion models on the covers of high fashion magazines, often promoting their own ready-to-wear lines. Again and again, fashion magazines explore the seemingly insignificant differences between the cheaper "high street" styles and runway styles, which serve as publicity for mass-produced lines owned by the same conglomerate without obviating the need for the higher-priced model that authenticates the "budget" version. High fashion, no longer dependent on craft or taste, seems to exist only to legitimate less expensive clothing directed at a youth market, often diffusion lines owned by the same conglomerate supporting the couture line.

Secondly, Romy and Michele's style graphically demonstrates that youth culture is not the prerogative of youth. *Romy and Michele* represents an ideal echoed in television shows like *Seinfeld* (NBC, 1989–98) and *Friends*,[29] in which characters continue to live out both the dramas and the clothing tastes of adolescents over a prolonged period of time, well into their thirties. Scholars and concerned parents have noted how adolescence, in terms of viewing habits and tastes, stretches further and further down into childhood.[30] Equally true is the manner in which adolescence extends increasingly into adulthood, in particular when it comes to matters of taste in dress, music and media. Media scholar Mary Celeste Kearney asserts: "The extension of adolescence backward into childhood and forward into adulthood has, in turn, affected what has been known as the 'youth market,' which today might be more accurately described as the 'youthful market.'"[31]

If, musically, *Romy and Michele* is a film that is nostalgic for the 1980s, in terms of fashion it anticipates the sense of style propagated most forcefully in the late 1990s and the first decade of the twenty-first century, with programs like *Sex and the City* (HBO, 1998–2004) and films like *The Devil Wears Prada* (David Frankel, 2006), with their broadly based, multi-generational female audiences.[32] In *Sex and the City*, the heroine Carrie Bradshaw would be far more likely to turn up in a revamped version of Vivian's hooker look, than in her red evening dress, rejecting the maturity evoked by the evening dress for the irreverent girlish "fun" of trash style.

What is the appeal of girlhood? In the girlhood ideal, older single women may find a model for identity that is not available in more traditional icons of mature femininity. Kearney goes so far as to claim that "feminists have comprised the largest and oldest group of Americans who reject traditional forms of adulthood, primarily through critiques of the patriarchal structure of the family and society, and by refusing to be confined to the domestic role of wife and mother."[33] Second-wave feminists like Betty Friedan, who were associated with marriage and motherhood, would disagree; however, Kearney's characterization of feminists points to the ways in which the tenets of neo-feminists, such as Helen Gurley Brown, who promoted a "girlish" image and actively rejected motherhood,[34] came to be confused with second-wave feminism. Kearney's characterization also highlights the appeal of girlishness and, by extension, neo-feminism: girlhood represents a version of femininity that is neither that of the spinster nor that of the mother, offering a notion of agency, in particular the capacity for change, that is specifically feminine but not yet aligned with the normative behaviors associated with womanly roles.

Girlhood is typically depicted as a period of flux and development, in contrast with the fixity of womanhood, in which the female subject finds her place most notably through marriage. The notion of the perpetually youthful "girl" is already present in Helen Gurley Brown's definition of the single girl in the 1960s. The girl remains an important figure in feminine culture in the 1980s—but she may be an unruly girl, even at times a bad girl, as in the case of certain pop figures such as Courtney Love in the 1990s.[35] Romy and Michele as characters and as style icons represent subdued versions of the unruly girls of the 1980s, such as Cyndi Lauper and Madonna, whom they imitate. The rough edges of the latter, however, are smoothed in a haze of nostalgia—creating an unruliness that is rooted in style rather than actions, serving to reinvigorate consumer culture norms, rather than undermining them.

Prolonging adolescence has significant implications for consumer culture—since girlhood at any age requires high maintenance, which increases with age. Though Romy and Michele seemingly maintain their status as girls while leading a relatively impoverished existence, viewers are well aware of the money and time that two stars of the caliber of Kudrow and Sorvino expend on appearance. In this sense the earlier *Clueless* (1995, Amy Heckerling), which exhibits many of the characteristics of the girly film and shares the same costume designer, Mona May, with *Romy and Michele*, offers a far more realistic view of the consumer girl's economic place by confining its story to the predicaments of the very wealthy. It is no accident that the style icons of the twenty-first century, such as the Hilton sisters, Jade Jagger, Stella McCartney, etc., are from wealthy families and have mothers who would have encouraged their daughters to acquire consumer expertise. The world of Romy and Michele is, thus, as much a fantasy as that of *Pretty Woman*—it is, however, clearly a consumer fantasy in which, for once, sexuality plays a relatively insignificant role.

The role of sexuality in this film can also be understood as one that deliberately presupposes and suppresses the representation of a lesbian relationship, thus categorizing the film as a version of the female friendship film, widely referred to as "the ambiguous lesbian film"[36] or "the hypothetical lesbian heroine film."[37] Indeed, Sorvino deliberately attempts to interject a masculine dimension to her character, initiating an undercurrent of sexual ambiguity by giving Romy what she describes as a "weirdly masculine walk. ... [I]t gave me a chance to have her sort of impersonate male movie heroes from TV and film from the '70s and early '80s."[38] (See Figure 3.2.) While the film allows viewers to imagine a version that includes a lesbian relationship, it also explicitly underlines that Romy and Michele are not lesbians, as is illustrated by a conversation that takes place near the beginning of the film, in which they deplore their lack of male partners:

Romy: Swear to God, sometimes I wish I was a lesbian.
Michele: Do you want to try to have sex sometime just to see if we are?
Romy: What? Yeah, right, Michele. Just the idea of having sex with another woman creeps me out. But if we're not married by the time we're 30, ask me again.
Michele: Okay.

The girly film permits an expression of same-sex partnership largely as a means of articulating its undesirability as a "second-best" choice, which is acceptable as such. While this view is rarely voiced as explicitly as it is in this film, a distinctive feature of *Romy and Michele's High School Reunion* is that it does not avoid exploring the social conventions that subtend the girly film as a category. As such, while it is not typical and did not enjoy the box office revenues of other films discussed in this volume, the film constitutes a useful object of analysis in so far as it highlights through exaggeration the traits of the girly film in particular, and "chick flicks" more generally.

Equally important to its treatment of female friendship is the way the film also invites the possibility of thinking about a consumer culture that is divorced from sexuality, in order to offer itself as pleasurable on its own terms. Consumer culture is, here, not necessarily a means of achieving something—such as transforming oneself into a romantic heroine (as in the case of *Pretty Woman*), or rising in class and economic status—as in the case of *Working Girl* (Mike Nichols, 1988). For Romy and Michele, consumer culture in general, and fashion in particular, need no justification beyond the immediate pleasures of sensations and self-realization. These pleasures are two-fold: one that is tactile, of the senses, and a second that is narcissistic, based on the pleasure of seeing one's "self" realized in a certain image. The opening of the film offers instances of both. Initially, during the credits, we see a series of fabrics smoothed lovingly by carefully manicured hands with red fingernails. This follows a series of detailed shots of collars suggesting the destiny of these fabrics as clothing. Later Romy and Michele dress for a night out and admire themselves with great pleasure—not only in the mirror, but, equally importantly, in each other's gaze, invoking the trope of the sister, or even the twin.

Figure 3.2 One of Romy's masculine postures (right). Courtesy of Photofest.

The trope of the sister finds its most poignant expression in the twin. The twin represents the dream of perfect symmetry—a fantasy in which the self is reaffirmed through doubling.[39] The look exchanged between twins differs from an identificatory or voyeuristic gaze, in which an image is possessed by that gaze, because it functions in terms of reflection, the returning of the gaze by an Other that is paradoxically the Self. The self is, thus, affirmed in its autonomy, while also being healed from, or compensated for, the initial separation from the mother. The problem of the double in literature and film for the masculine subject has been explored at length, being associated with fear and anxiety, particularly surrounding the threat of castration.[40] Doubling in feminine culture serves a very different function because the relationship of the feminine subject to the mother is, by definition, different from that of the masculine. In particular, as the influential feminist psychoanalytic theorist Nancy Chodorow has discussed in a widely cited volume, the separation between mother and daughter remains unstable and poorly resolved, because the daughter's destiny is linked with her ability to identify with the mother.[41] The twin is not the mother—and we note here coincidentally that this film depicts motherhood in a very negative light through its association with a punitive and normative femininity, represented by the vindictive and sadistic "A" list beauty queens who tormented Romy during high school, and now, in a state of advanced pregnancy, are offered up for ridicule.

In contrast, the twin represents a release from motherhood—not only from the original mother, but also from the need to reproduce a daughter in order, in turn, to reproduce the intimacy of the mother/daughter relationship. The relationship between twins may be unstable in that it also runs the risk of being torn apart by envy and rivalry, by the desire of the daughter to win the ultimate approval of the father and take the place of the mother. Michele's dream miraculously convinces her to refuse the role of rival. And, thus, when Sandy Frink, who ultimately saves both Romy and Michele by loaning them money, asks Michele to dance, she responds: "Only if Romy can dance too," completing the process of reconciliation. The symmetry of Romy and Michele's relationship is characterized by the phrase "me too"—a phrase that recurs repeatedly in the film, especially in the opening scenes, to signify the closeness of the two women.

Both protagonists, then, undergo a process of transformation or maturation, proper to the *Bildungsroman*, which ennobles their relationship. In the case of Michele, she learns to value others and to care for and about others. She is transformed from the unacceptable saleswoman at the film's beginning who is brutal to others and, as a consequence, loses her job, to the motherly, affirming saleswoman in her own shop who attempts to assist others to express them-selves through fashion. Indeed, she claims that she feels like a "mother," without undermining the general negative view of motherhood to which the film subscribes. She explains her relationship with Heather Mooney (Janeane Garofalo), a former high school classmate, now a customer in her boutique: "For me, it's like I've just given birth to my own baby girl, except she's like a big giant girl who smokes and says 'shit' a lot. You know?"

Most of all, Michele learns to value her relationship with Romy as the source of "fun" in her life. Romy, in turn, must come to esteem Michele and to see her as an equal partner in their lives. Their education is represented in the resolution over their conflict about who plays the role of "Mary" (the star) as opposed to "Rhoda" (the supporting friend). Michele concedes that while Romy is "the Mary," they can both be "Mary," offering an "and/and" rather than an "either/or" logic that invokes their twinned status. They are both separate and one and the same, representing the paradox of a femininity that is "neither one nor two."[42] Romy, in turn, recognizes that Michele not only sews but designs with her "fifty-fifty." Michele, who is subservient to Romy at the film's beginning, by the film's end comes to take an equal, and even at times dominant, role. Though it remains Romy's task to check the reality of their situation—it will take two years to pay back the loan that they received to set up their boutique, for example—Michele's *joie de vivre* takes the lead in defining the terms of their lives. "Let's fold scarves," she says to Romy in the film's final sequence, and fold scarves they do. The endless tidying, folding and refolding that is part of retail culture, and which falls to the "salesgirl" as a sign of the triviality of her life (as in *The Good Girl*, for example) is reclaimed as a joyful rhapsody of color and texture in this film through the happy acceptance of a couple joined in parity. Janet Maslin comments in the *New York Times*: "Romy and Michele have to confront their self-doubts. As a consequence of this crisis, they wind up as improved and empowered as anyone wearing a pink, fluff-trimmed mini-dress and platform wedges can be. Their final mantra—'"Let's fold scarves!'—can be seen as a cry of affirmation and an inspiring fulfillment of their retail destiny."[43]

Romy and Michele's High School Reunion represents a fantasy in which consumer culture might come to fulfill the needs of women in a world that undermines traditional models for femininity without offering new possibilities. This fantasy is regressive in the sense that it fixes subjectivity in a prolonged adolescence, refusing adult sexuality and parenthood in order to preserve the autonomy and integrity of the feminine subject. Hence, its vision of femininity is essentially pessimistic, in that the utopian world that it depicts is one that excludes the family, replacing it with a surrogate family of "singles." Heterosexuality is represented as undesirable, as resulting in the divorce of self from self, of Romy from Michele; however, the alternative of a chaste friendship celebrated through consumer culture is one that seems curiously devoid of the stuff of human experience, one in which the cultivation of the self remains arrested in its development. Yet within the context of this film, this choice of friendship over romance and over motherhood remains the noble and moral choice, hence the desirable choice, in which the petty and ignoble sin of envy is overcome.

The film seems to suggest that within contemporary culture the prudent and noble woman may find a space in which to cultivate herself for herself, but that this is a small and confined space at best. In this sense, the film's celebration of consumer culture and fashion is also ultimately a condemnation in that it requires an antiseptic and protected arena cut off from the political and economic upheavals and inequities that mark the contemporary world. The film implies that the traumas of adolescence can only be surmounted through the creation of a perpetual adolescence that holds the demon forces of heterosexuality and maternity at bay. For all its charm and style, the Green World of consumer culture is bleak in terms of the possibilities that its offers those content within its confines.

The film, then, depicts an example of how consumer culture and self-fashioning play a central role in the production of femininity and how the term "woman" is displaced by a sense of "girlishness" in which the adolescent girl, rather than the mature woman, incarnates the feminine ideal. Within this film "girlishness" offers an alternative, albeit a limited one, to the heteronormativity implied in marriage, while precluding the kinds of political speculations that might lead to social change or engaging with the possibility of sexual identities that exceed the bounds of heteronormativity. Yet, one of the powerful attractions of neo-feminism may indeed be the manner in which it seems to hold out the promise of a certain kind of utopian experience, if limited in scope, for women.

This utopian vision is undermined by a number of factors, falling into two larger categories. The first category revolves around the magical retail solution to Romy and Michele's dilemma, that of two good-hearted but not necessarily very bright women, who enjoy "good looks" (as did Vivian). Janet Maslin points out, in the *New York Times*, that their outsider status both in high school and in later years is not entirely plausible because, as she notes, "[T]hey could stop traffic anywhere."[44] Mona May, costume designer for the film, remarks: "They can wear anything. ... They're like Barbie dolls." If not particularly intelligent, the two women are exceptional in terms of their appearance, close to that of the Barbie doll as the symbol of an unattainable (and routinely vilified by feminists) ideal.

Should the viewer forget the exceptional status that Sorvino and Kudrow enjoy, the film offers a point of comparison in the character of Heather Mooney, a smart, if chubby and short, brunette. Bitter and neurotic, she represents a cautionary figure, the fate of a woman who cannot accommodate the "me too" culture of Romy and Michele, who, at the film's conclusion, is "mothered" by Michele as she assists her in her fashion choices. Heather incarnates a prototypical character of the girly film: she is the "wrong" woman, often, as with Zoe (Frances McDormand) in *Something's Gotta Give* (Nancy Meyers, 2003) or Enid (Meredith Scott Lynn) in *Legally Blonde* (Robert Luketic, 2001), a woman who is a feminist, intellectual, unconventional in looks, tolerated but ultimately excluded from the happy community that the girly film offers its heroine. While *Pretty Woman's* Kit (Laura San Giacomo) is left behind because of her inability to understand the import of Vivian's education and to abandon her way of life, Heather Mooney is condemned, the film gives us to understand, because of her intelligence and her appearance—in the words of the character, "the genetic legacy that is my betrayal." Yet Heather's position is viewed with benign goodwill by Michele, who reserves her venom for the now pregnant former prom queen and her entourage, thus, perhaps, avoiding any real interrogation of the film's position on intelligent women (or feminism), whose achievements (Heather, like Sandy Frink, is a successful entrepreneur) move them outside the narrow realm of feminine culture (see Figure 3.3). *Romy and Michele* imply that being blonde and beautiful is, for a woman, more important than intelligence and education. Kudrow is a graduate of Vassar and Sorvino of Harvard, a fact repeated frequently by the press, giving lie to their screen personas, and underlining the film's fantasy world.[45]

Figure 3.3 Former classmates in an advanced state of pregnancy. Courtesy of Photofest.

A second category of factors that similarly contributes to undermining the plausibility of the heroines' happy conclusion derives from the fact that, to anyone familiar with the fashion world, Romy and Michele did not create their own clothing; at the very best, they produced clever copies. Carla Hall from the *Los Angeles Times* comments: "In the movie, the eccentric and under-employed Romy and Michele sew their own clothes, but in real life, half of Sorvino's outfit is from Versace."[46] Mona May, costume designer, explains:

> A few designer labels do appear, including Michele's short red Dolce & Gabbana jacket worn with a flowery Jill Stuart skirt, and her window-shopping ensemble of a yellow gingham-trimmed suit by Moschino. Romy's skinny papaya-colored halter dress is by Herve Leger. Still, much of the wardrobe came from Melrose Avenue.[47]

The movie, then, suggests that the purchasing of already "fashionable" clothing (from "high" fashion to the (then) fashionable mid-range clothing represented by Melrose) and the ability to create a style using available (and largely expensive) items is what distinguishes Romy and Michele from their unhappy provincial counterparts, whose location in Arizona would not have afforded them the same opportunities. Betty Goodwin, fashion writer, advises: "Sorvino and Kudrow have fabulous bodies, but even they depend upon special under-garments for help with body-revealing clothes. Each wore G-strings and Wonderbra-style bras—meaning, padded, under-wire models." Costume designer, Mona May avers: "It's so important to have a very good under-wire bra. ... That's what makes a beautiful cleavage."[48]

Finally, then, the film advises young women to hone their shopping skills, signaling that Romy and Michele's happy ending depends not upon their ability to produce new creations, but on their ability to use what is already available (including effective undergarments) to them at a price, a price that two young women on meager incomes could never afford. The film, then, ends up sup-porting a broader system of feminine culture that is determined and regulated by the mega-corporations that control the high-fashion lines.[49] While some women, often with family connections to the corporation, will prove successful and rise to positions of power and influence, they do so by adapting to already recognized criteria of taste and distinction that, in turn, serve to support an already existing industry—as did Romy and Michele (or Mona May) by relying on established designers. There is little room for the outsider in this system, underlining the fantasy nature of the film's conclusion in which two unknowns, with one connection at *Vogue*, are immediately successful on Rodeo Drive. The Green World of consumer culture may not prove as safe a retreat as the film appears to imply for, while seeming to support non-conformity, the film offers a highly regulated vision of appropriate and successful femininity, governed by the rigid rules that moderate female appearance according to the neo-feminist paradigm.

Romy and Michele's High School Reunion did not enjoy the financial success of later films like *Legally Blonde*, or even *Maid in Manhattan* (Wayne Wang, 2002); however, its more modest achievements (and greater critical approbation) may derive from its ambivalence and the ways in which it often undermines the fantasy world that it purports to support, producing a level of discomfort for viewers seeking affirmation of their own choices, as well as deterring promotional partners, increasingly important to a film's box office take.[50] Subsequent girly films would lack the acerbic edge that Robin Schiff brought to the subject, and tended unabashedly to support a vision of the world in which the heroine's destiny would be one of unrequited self-striving and consumer gratification, in which the reality of work and fiscal responsibility would go largely unaddressed.

Chapter 4

Legally Blonde (2001)

"A Pink Girl in a Brown World"[1]

While recalling many of the themes of *Romy and Michele's High School Reunion* (David Mirkin, 1997), the even more popular *Legally Blonde* (Robert Luketic, 2001) thrusts the neo-feminist subject into the world of men, recounting the story of a young woman, Elle (Reese Witherspoon), who follows her boyfriend to Harvard Law School, where she proves more successful than he.[2] In many ways, though continuing the preoccupation with fashion that characterizes *Pretty Woman* (Garry Marshall, 1990), *Legally Blonde* has more in common with *Working Girl* (Mike Nichols, 1988), in which a secretary from Staten Island successfully proves herself in the world of high finance, finally acquiring an office and a secretary of her own at the film's conclusion (see Figure 4.1). Unlike *Working Girl*, *Legally Blonde*, however, softens and sentimentalizes the predicament of a woman in a man's world, while emphasizing the importance and pleasures of feminine consumer culture; this places it much more clearly in the girly category than the earlier film.

Legally Blonde takes some of themes of the 1980s explored in the film *Working Girl* and resituates them within a benign world in which the young woman's ambitions overshadow romance, with male characters being relegated to a secondary status. In *Working Girl*, Tess (Melanie Griffith) succeeds by allying herself with an already successful man (Harrison Ford), who also happens to be her boss's boyfriend. Tess is a woman who moves into the world of men in which she strives according to the terms set out by men—which means competing with other women. The marked animosity between the two main female characters led reviewers like Theta Pavis-Weil to point out that "despite critics' references to the movie's feminist themes, the relationships between the characters told a different story."[3] Both films rely on the well-honed Hollywood formula of a fish-out-of-water, suggesting, perhaps, the place of women at the time, newly emerging into certain areas still considered a male preserve, such as the upper echelons of business or prestigious law schools. Melanie Griffith explained about her character:

Figure 4.1 Tess (Melanie Griffith) transformed from "Working Girl" into "Career Woman." Courtesy of Photofest.

I'm never going to get away from having some kind of sexuality. ... And I don't have any desire to get away from it. That's me. What I am inside. But I think that women who have a sexuality are judged. "Oh you're blond. You've got breasts and a behind so you're stupid." And that makes me really angry.[4]

The problem of exclusion was further specified and emphasized in *Working Girl* by raising the issue of gender in the context of "class." The film was not simply about women, but about recognizing an underpaid, feminized segment of the workforce, contributing to a larger social sensibility that has resulted in banning the word secretary from contemporary vocabulary. Whether the term is "secretary," or "assistant," women continue to fill these positions, which remain less well paid than typically masculinized trades, such as electrician. Taking into account this dimension of the film, 20th Century Fox, the distributor, devolved a marketing strategy that targeted secretaries. *Hollywood Reporter* describes the campaign:

> Secretaries across the country, including George Bush's secretary and others in 30 major cities, have been receiving gifts in the mail for the past two weeks. No it's not national secretary's month—just 20th Century Fox's way of promoting its upcoming film "Working Girl."
>
> The five-point mailer, begun three weeks before the film's release, kicked off with "Working Girl" pencils, going out to approximately 15,000 secretaries across the country. This was followed by a button that read "Working Girl—There's more to life than smiling, filing and dialing," "Working Girl" Post-It note pads, a "Working Girl" coffee mug and paper clip holder, and finally an invitation to a screening of the film to be held for secretaries in each participating city.[5]

In contrast, *Legally Blonde* elides a possible political dimension to the film by removing any economic or class dimension to the character's battle to gain respect and, thus, paradoxically offers a more inclusive vision of femininity. The heroine acts only out of concern for her personal satisfaction, independently of economic consideration—a perspective that she extends to include a concern for other women defined in the same terms. "Work," then, in this film is understood in terms of individual satisfaction and self-fashioning rather than as part of a larger social structure fuelled by an economic imperative.

Like *Working Girl*, *Legally Blonde* also mobilizes the image of the blonde bimbo or dumb blonde that was treated affectionately, if not respectfully, in *Romy and Michele*, within its plot, for the purpose of reclaiming her as a symbol

Figure 4.2 Reese Witherspoon as "Elle," an archetypal "Blonde." Courtesy of Photofest.

of feminine empowerment that reaches across class lines (see Figure 4.2). In so doing, the film articulates a vision that has more in common with Romy and Michele's ethos of "fun," than it does with Tess's ambition and determination to rise above the rank of secretary. Not coincidentally, the film's release was accompanied by a marketing strategy that emphasized "blondeness" as a pleasurable fashion choice that empowered women, exemplified in the film's poster by-line, "This summer, go blonde."[6] These included Vidal Sassoon (a national hair salon franchise) "offering free blond dye jobs from 8:30 to 4:30, and free screening tickets,"[7] as well as a "Cosmo Blonde Contest," in which 10 young women received scholarships "based on a 300-word essay about 'Why blondes are as brilliant as brunettes.'"[8] The film's writers, Karen McCullah and Kirsten

Smith, described the film as "an ultimate exhibition of girl power," while feminist writer and columnist B. Ruby Rich applauded the film: "The scenes of female bonding across class in the beauty parlor would be enough to make it worthwhile even if it weren't the best empowerment movie for teenage girls to come along in ages."[9]

In spite of these gestures towards female solidarity, the film's focus remains on the individual. The actress, Jessica Cauffiel, who plays a sorority sister, comments: "This is a comedy about the idea that a person's worth can't be judged one way or the other by what they look like, how they dress, what their vocabulary is, whatever, and that's really interesting."[10] Here the film rejoins *Romy and Michele*—as seen in Lisa Kudrow's comments about her character "I love the character of Michele. ... I think that what I like best about her is that she doesn't judge herself. She doesn't judge her life or what she is doing. She is just having fun living."[11] These comments underline that way that the girly film encourages a myopic focus on the individual and her status within the confined circumference of an existence in which her pleasure and her happiness dominate her concerns.

One of the film's writers, Kirsten Smith, describes the heroine, Elle Woods (Reese Witherspoon): "She is such a pure and vibrant character. ... She's outgoing and hilarious and she's the ultimate in 'girl power.'"[12] "Girl power" within this film can be defined, in the words of Ali Larter (who plays Brooke Taylor, a fitness queen accused of murder and defended by Elle) as "about women getting what they want using what they've been given. This is what Brooke is about and that's what Elle comes to discover about herself."[13] The strength of this message produced not only a successful book by Amanda Brown, but also a Broadway musical that *Variety* characterizes as "girl-empowerment aplenty,"[14] emphasizing the inter-media nature of the girly film, the narrative of which usually circulates through a number of media, most notably as novels and television programming.[15]

The film's focus on "the familiar, all-American messages of determination to succeed against all odds and never judging people by their physical appearance" is undermined by its ambivalent perspective on the notion of education.[16] The film's heroine undergoes a transformation introduced most enduringly to film audiences with *Clueless* (Amy Heckerling, 1995), in which a young woman, Cher (Alicia Silverstone), learns to value education and in so doing finds herself a proper boyfriend and eventual husband. Reviewer Kenneth Turan, in the *Los Angeles Times*, remarks that "'Legally Blonde' is basically 'Clueless Goes to Harvard.'"[17] In the case of Elle, this education is undermined by her fidelity to feminine culture. As *Variety* film reviewer Todd McCarthy remarks: "[T]he means by which Elle triumphs remain entirely tied to her SoCal preoccupation with looks and fashion and are therefore far too coincidental and flimsy to prove anything about her real abilities."[18] Similarly, Witherspoon comments: "Some people might succeed because they know about Plato and Socrates and other people succeed because they know about Porsches and Clinique. The point is to use what you have and believe in yourself."[19] In the sense that Cher is obliged to consider issues outside her own world of fashion and conspicuous consumption, one might argue that her education was more significant; however, for both Cher and Elle, education is a luxury rather than a necessity.

Elle and Cher distinguish themselves from Romy and Michele, and from Tess, through the ways in which they represent the wealthy heiress—their wealth masking the precarious economic position occupied by single women more generally. The importance of this persona can be seen in the rising popularity of socialites such as Paris and Nicky Hilton who have come to occupy the fashion limelight alongside actresses such as Sarah Jessica Parker, displacing, or at the very least competing with, the super-model who was the privileged vehicle for feminine style in post-1960s youth culture until the late 1990s. The actress and the heiress, who may also be a singer or television star—at times united in a single individual, as in the case of Paris Hilton—dominate the images of femininity on display for the viewer, offering the possibility of developing significant media synergies in which the industries of fashion and cinema can cooperate to their mutual benefit.[20] Because of the privileged position that the heiress seems to enjoy within this evolving feminine iconography, education may seem optional, in particular education beyond the confines of feminine consumer culture, and is certainly clearly marked as such in *Legally Blonde*, in which Elle's parents, though supportive, attempt to explain to her that work, especially as a lawyer, is something that one does out of necessity, not choice.

There are other ways in which *Legally Blonde*, highlighting the specific traits of the girly film, departs from previous films directed at a female audience, in particular *Clueless*, though many reviewers noted the similarity between the two films.[21] In *Clueless*, while the heroine Cher must come to understand the value of education in opposition to popular culture, she does not give up popular culture so much as put it to the side in favor of the culture practiced by her father and stepbrother who becomes the surrogate father whom she chooses as her boyfriend, echoing the traditional marriage plot. The film openly acknowledges its debt to the nineteenth-century novel, and to Jane Austen's *Emma* in particular. Typically, in terms of the marriage plot, the heroine's goal is find an appropriate husband, or in this case boyfriend—though the film seems to suggest that in due course he will come to take up the role of spouse, as was the case in *Emma*. In order to do this, Cher must educate herself in the world of men, which within her family is that of work, charity and high culture.[22]

Ultimately, Cher's destiny is defined by her relations to men, initially to her father, and ultimately to her husband-to-be. She remains, in so far as this is possible, within the family, exchanged between father and surrogate son, whose filial ties are legally recognized, rendering marriage almost unnecessary. The apparent consanguinity of the relationship is offset by its legal and moral nature: the surrogate son is not Cher's biological brother, but the son of a previous wife by yet another husband. Because Cher's father informs her that whereas one can divorce a wife, a child is forever, she can find no better way to remain within the family than by tying herself to the man that her father has already chosen "forever." Through its emphasis on the family and the powerful patriarch as well as its heroine, who has no need to work outside the family, the film significantly departs from the neo-feminist paradigm, recalling earlier models of femininity, most clearly evoked through the linking of the film to the Jane Austen novel, *Emma*.[23]

The general popular revival of narratives based on Austen's novels in the forms of film and television adaptations, as well as "chick lit" that references her work—as in the case of *The Jane Austen Book Club*, also a film[24]—testifies to the fragmented nature of feminine identity and its articulation in contemporary culture. While *The Jane Austen Book Club* (Robin Swicord, 2007) had a domestic gross of $3,575,227, *Becoming Jane* (Julian Jarrold, 2007), a fictionalized account of Austen's early life, earned a domestic gross of $18,670,946, and *Pride and Prejudice* (Joe Wright, 2005) a very respectable $38,405,088. The ubiquity of the Austen-based narrative (even when it critiques the marriage plot, as in the case of *Becoming Jane*) points to the power of the traditional marriage plot as a residual paradigm influencing feminine identity. In contrast, *Legally Blonde* earned a domestic gross of $96,520,674 and a worldwide gross of $141,774,679, signalling the greater popularity of the film and perhaps its values.

Legally Blonde moves the heroine outside the typical marriage plot; while benign, Elle's family exerts little influence on her. More importantly, the film undermines the fundamental assumption of the marriage plot—that a woman may best fulfill her destiny by marrying. Though one reviewer describes the film as a "fish-out-of-water, believe-in-yourself romantic comedy,"[25] romance and marriage, while providing the pretext for the plot and Elle's quest for success, are soon superseded by Elle's desire to prove herself to her own satisfaction in the new and untried arena of Harvard Law School.

Dumped by her boyfriend, Elle decides to follow him to Harvard Law School in order to win him back. Against all expectations, she is not only admitted to Harvard, but succeeds brilliantly, moving on to a better and brighter version of her now surpassed boyfriend. The film thus optimistically charts Elle's successful journey outside the family and her ability to cross class boundaries. In contrast, Cher in *Clueless* must remain firmly within her own milieu, in a world that may include ethnic diversity, as exemplified by Cher's best friend, but does not transcend the lines of class and economic status. In *Clueless*, a girl's best friend is her father, though it should be recalled, as Cher reminds us at the film's conclusion, that she is only 16. Elle, on the other hand, has graduated from her four-year degree program when *Legally Blonde* commences. Her parents are distant but supportive, particularly when it comes to money. Money in and of itself is of little concern to Elle, though she depends for her survival on the powers with which it endows her. The reasons for this are obvious: her family is wealthy. Elle's transformation from blonde to legally blonde is not a matter of achieving financial autonomy—rather, it is a matter of defining her place in the world and, by extension, perhaps the place of femininity.

Elle's education is both literal (she acquires a diploma) and metaphorical (her journey enables her to emerge with a better knowledge of herself); however, unlike the typical heroine of the girly film, Elle does not undergo an obvious transformation or makeover, although her look changes throughout the film, and her clothes have a significant role in it. The costume designer Sophie de Rakoff Carbonell claims: "Robert [the director] basically wanted Elle's clothes to be another character in the movie. ... We wanted her to pop out no matter where she is, always combining classic style with a dash of the avant-garde."[26] Witherspoon, in the film, had "five major looks and nearly 40 outfit changes."[27] Carbonell describes these in greater detail:

> There was a color scheme that followed the arc in the narrative, which went from lighter pinks to the hotter pinks to the purples, and then at the law school there is very little color. At the law firm it's monochromatic, gray, white and black. ... There is also a silhouette arc ... I actually referenced different movies and actresses; that was my focal point. The stuff at Harvard when it's in the winter is much more of an Ali MacGraw in "Love Story" look. And when she's interning at the law school it's more like a Rosalind Russell '50s "His Girl Friday" type of thing.[28]

According to *Variety*, "Getting these looks was easy, since besides many original creations, designers—Prada, Moschino and Celine, to name a few—lined up to outfit the photogenic Witherspoon."[29] Should viewers fail to notice, the diffusion fashion magazine, *InStyle*, offers precise instructions. For Elle's "bright pink side," choose "Vivienne Tam" or "Moschino." For her "serious" side, "Prada cashmere cardigans" and "Celine pencil skirts."[30]

Though her look evolves, and the ability to change her look is an important weapon in her cultural arsenal, the big transformation comes as a result of the goals for which she puts this arsenal to work. In order to succeed within the field of law, Elle must call upon traditional attributes of the masculine hero: perseverance and self-reliance. Unlike the masculine hero, she also can rely upon resources that are traditionally associated with femininity, such as compassion and charm, as well as her deep and extensive knowledge of feminine culture itself. Elle proclaims: "The rules of hair care are simple and finite. Any Cosmo girl would've known." Elle's knowledge of these rules proves crucial to her successful defense of the exercise entrepreneur, Brooke Taylor. Should her own substantial abilities fail her, she also has the support and understanding of the Sisterhood—not only her sorority, but also women engaged (like Romy and Michele) in consumer culture as a feminine practice, such as hairdressers and exercise moguls.

In the courtroom, Elle opens up the world of feminine consumer culture to the public gaze and demonstrates the value of understanding its intricacies, particularly as it comes to define the behavior, practices and psychology of women. Elle wins her the case though her knowledge of *Cosmopolitan Magazine* (referred to as "the Bible" within the film), and the intricacies of a permanent wave, which enables her to pinpoint the guilty party. *New Yorker* film reviewer David Denby commented, "The movie is openly dedicated to the *Cosmopolitan* ethos, and, sure enough, Witherspoon turned up on the cover of the July issue in a Dolce & Gabbana dress."[31] While Denby is critical of this ethos; he claims that "[t]he magazine seems eager to trap women in a perpetual limbo of desire and fear."[32] He fails to recognize, however, that Elle represents a significant evolution of the Cosmo Girl. She is a rich, spoilt heiress, rather than a poor working girl, governed by sentiment rather than necessity. For Denby, "Witherspoon, a talented comedienne, both embodies and parodies on a kind of female ideal—the *Cosmo* girl, Lancômed to the hilt."[33] Denby's reaction underlines the film's schizophrenia: it values feminine culture, but confines its heroine to a ghetto of womanly pursuits. It supports the utility of traditionally feminine attributes, while confining them to ones whose "cuteness" distracts from the condescension with which she is treated.

Significantly, empathy takes place alongside rationality as important strands motivating and explaining human behavior. Elle's empathy is exemplified in her devotion to her dog, which the film goes to great length to ridicule, while at the same time highlighting his value to the heroine—in a move typical of the girly film, which consistently appears to undermine its own premises. The dog's presence suggests everything that a priori would be deemed tasteless and inappropriate within the context of Harvard University. He represents that intrusion of another world into the sanctity of the masculine preserve of the Law; at the same time, the dog serves as a kind of alibi or red-herring that disguises the deeply self-serving motivations that drive the heroine.

The film seems to suggest that focusing on appearances is inappropriate to someone who aspires to professional standing. In fact, "style" has become increasingly more important to contemporary culture, with expensive, fashionable garments, within the relatively constrained sartorial vocabulary, increasingly de rigueur for those aspiring to advance as a professional. *Working Girl*, through Tess's makeover, highlights the importance of "dressing the part" for an ambitious woman. Similarly, though Romy and Michele ultimately discover that "looking like businesswomen" is not sufficient, their initial strategy depended upon the accepted idea that "career women" had a look that could be imitated.[34] Elle is, somewhat deceptively, held up as an anomaly, the fish-out-of-water, within law school, while also the insider heroine of feminine culture. Her status as a fashion icon supersedes her position as a lawyer; the viewer is encouraged to see her investment in fashion as the secret to her success in law, encouraging the perception that appearance is crucial to a woman's career, while also implying that Elle's focus on style is somehow an anomaly. Fashion, however, is not the only dimension of a woman's looks to which the film draws attention.

The importance of Elle's hair, emphasized by the film's marketing campaign, is also a significant visual trope that lends continuity to the film, underlining the importance of appearance, especially for a woman. In *Working Girl*, Tess's blonde locks were initially ridiculed as the nadir of taste, but also festishized, lovingly cultivated and lit once she improbably manages to achieve the right hair length. Her gleaming locks set her apart from her follow secretaries and from rival, Katharine (Sigourney Weaver) whose dark tresses seem to absorb light in contrast with the aureole of radiance the surrounds her. Elle's hair enjoys an equally significant role in *Legally Blonde*. Joy Zapata created "40 unique hairstyles" for Elle, humorously referred to in the film as "The Hair That Ate Hollywood" (see Figure 4.3). Zapata explains:

> Elle's hair has a life of its own in the movie … Luckily Reese has the most amazing, heavy, thick, beautiful blonde hair. The more I worked with it, the more I loved it. I could try anything with it, and I did!. … Hair plays a major role. … Reese would come into the trailer as Reese, and I would give her this bouncy, Pamela Anderson, Gianni Versace, Beverley Hills-style, and she leaves as Elle. It snapped her right into the character.[35]

Underlining the production values of the film within the plot, *Legally Blonde* includes a beauty parlor, aptly called the "Beauty Oasis," that serves as an Edenic retreat for the heroine, bathed in blues and greens that recall the lighting and colors of Elle's native California, "a lush tropical garden in which tropical flowers bloom," in the words of Melissa ("Missy") Stewart, the production

Figure 4.3 Highlighting of Elle's luxuriant blonde hair. Courtesy of Photofest.

designer, literalizing the role of consumer culture as offering a haven and a source of solace to the girly heroine.[36]

Through its visual emphasis on its heroine and her appearance, *Legally Blonde* invites the viewer to participate in Elle's style as a source of empowerment and comfort, the do-it-yourself approach to clothing and fashion. This bricolage style, which encourages viewers to mix high fashion, diffusion lines and vintage pieces, was also highlighted to a lesser degree in *Romy and Michele*, and is associated by Ginette Vincendeau, film historian, with the rise of Brigitte Bardot as a star and the "decline in the hold of couture over the fashion business."[37] While Bardot is not the only youth-culture star to emerge at this point in film history, she represents this new icon of feminine style with particular aptness and, as a result, is frequently referenced in fashion magazines at the beginning of the twenty-first century. Vincendeau notes that though Bardot's style was planned, "the modest cost and easy availability of [Bardot's] basic ingredients meant that it could be widely copied."[38] She compares her to Madonna, whose style in the 1980s also depended upon bringing together "clothes from different contexts ... diverted from their original meaning."[39]

It would be incorrect to say that Bardot did not popularize designers; her designer pink and white gingham wedding dress, for example, was widely copied and significantly helped the career of the designer, Jacques Esterel. Rather, as a cultural icon, she represented a shift in how fashion was predominantly conceived—no longer directed at young consumers, who made up in quantity for what they lacked in quality. The role of the costume designer also evolved to that predominantly of a stylist, who chose from pre-existing clothing, facilitating product placement, rather than designing and constructing garments that might be subsequently copied by viewers.[40]

Legally Blonde offers an exemplary instance of both costume design and "styling." The costume designer for *Legally Blonde*, Sophie de Rakoff Carbonell, began her career as a "stylist" for commercials and music video. Her approach is closer to that of the stylist Patricia Field (*Sex and the City*), than that of the costume designer, exemplified by Edith Head, of classical Hollywood. Nonetheless, some "outfits" such as the pink leather suit worn by Elle when she arrives at Harvard are designed and made for the film (see Figure 4.4). Most "outfits," however, are put together using items gathered from a range of sources including "vintage" or "recycled" clothing, in a more obvious manner that was the case with *Romy and Michele*. An example of this is the "Good Times" outfit that Elle wears in the sequence that follows directly upon her arrival sequence (see Figure 4.5). Carbonell also customizes inexpensive clothing by adding ruffles, changing buttons, shortening or lengthening hems (as in the outfits of Paulette Bonafonte, Elle's nail technician, played by Jennifer Coolidge), illustrating how these "styled" outfits (as opposed to designed

Figure 4.4 Elle in a leather outfit designed for her by Sophie de Rakoff Carbonnel. Courtesy of Photofest.

costume) emphasize fashion as a process of bricolage. This style is accessible to viewers because it enables even those on a budget to combine inexpensive items with a designer piece and a vintage (second hand) item to achieve a fashionable appearance. If the viewers are not clad exclusively in designer items, they are, nonetheless, purchasing some items, expanding the market-base of the fashion industry.[41] With its focus on styling and the use of clothing

Figure 4.5 Elle in her "Good Times" outfit. Courtesy of Photofest.

from high fashion lines (such as Moschino), *Legally Blonde* continues a trend established with *Clueless*, in which fashion is seen to have an intrinsic interest for the viewer, independently of the manner in which it serves to illuminate and illustrate character.[42]

The use of clothing in *Legally Blonde* highlights the ways in which *Pretty Woman* was a transitional film, in that it set the terms of the girly film while leaving it to subsequent productions to develop these traits more fully. While the clothing worn by Julia Roberts as Vivian received marked attention from the press, it was largely in terms of her red dress, designed specifically for her role in the film by Marilyn Vance-Straker. *Hollywood Reporter* featured a full-page spread on the dress; however, it emphasized its transformations, engineered by Vance-Straker with a view to character. "[Costume designers] are not doing fashion—we're doing characters, building energy, portraying a slice of real life," asserts Vance-Straker. *Hollywood Reporter* comments: "Without the red dress, she [Vivian] wouldn't have been quite so pretty. A single costume decision helped transform Julia Roberts into a star. ... Ironically, it was an outfit that would be comfortable on a rack at Neiman-Marcus," underlining that accessibility was a dimension of the outfit's appeal.[43] (See Figure 4.6.) If Vance-Straker thought in terms of Vivian's character, viewers thought about what they might borrow for their own wardrobe, an attitude that the press and the fashion industry were quick to underline and exploit. *People* comments:

Figure 4.6 Vivian (Julia Roberts) in her red dress. Courtesy of Photofest.

Julia Roberts metamorphoses from lady of the night to fair lady in *Pretty Woman*. ... But when it comes to fashion trends, the movie gets things backward. The hip look isn't Julia's demure, Princess Di-like "after" clothes, but her "before" style of thigh-high boots, micro-minis and midriff tops. These and other "hooker" fashions—including spandex and hot pants—were the stars of the European runways.[44]

Notwithstanding European taste, the more conservative outfits also had an impact. In 1992, the *Los Angeles Times* asked, "How long will this be going on?" The newspaper reported,

Fashion manufacturers are reviving the brown and white polka-dotted dress Julia Roberts wore in the polo match scene for the 1990 film "Pretty Woman." Laura Ashley boutiques are offering a sleeveless, belted dress with a mid-calf, full skirt in rayon for $138. JC Penney's rendition in acetate and rayon sells for $45. And Charlotte Russe stores have reissued their year-old $40 "Pretty Woman" dress for spring.[45] [See Figure 4.7.]

Figure 4.7 Vivian in polka dots. Courtesy of Photofest.

If Vance-Straker was not thinking in terms of "fashion," subsequent designers such as Mona May (*Clueless*; *Romy and Michele*), Sophie de Rakoff Carbonell (*Legally Blonde*) and Patricia Field (*The Devil Wears Prada*, David Frankel, 2006; *Sex and the City: The Movie*, Michael Patrick King, 2008; *Confessions of a Shopaholic*, P.J. Hogan, 2009), to name but a few, certainly were. Cinema's invitation to consume, its function as "window dressing" for the fashion industry, was formally recognized through the increasing eagerness of designers to highlight their wares within films but also through red-carpet appearances and fashion editorials featuring the same stars. The *Los Angeles Times* notes with regards to *Legally Blonde* that "Clinique, Prada and OPI Nail Products are all prominently featured within the first five minutes of the film and *Cosmopolitan Magazine* is written into the script," further commenting that Witherspoon's face "appears simultaneously on the Covers of *Cosmo* and *CosmoGirl* this month." This intensity of product and fashion synergies increased with each decade, reaching its apotheosis with films like *The Devil Wears Prada* and *Sex and the City: The Movie*, recalling the studio-generated interest that fans exhibited in the clothing and make-up choices of the stars of classical Hollywood, pointing to another trait that the girly film shares with that era, the emphasis on women stars.[46]

Beginning with *Pretty Woman*, the plots (and to a lesser degree the dialogue) of the girly films are almost universally panned by the critics; however, they are almost always also unified in their praise of the charismatic qualities exhibited by the principal female star, usually compared to a series of Hollywood counterparts. For example, Amy Taubin in the *Village Voice* states that "indeed, it's Julia Roberts as a cross between Audrey Hepburn's Sabrina and Sue Lyon's Lolita who makes the film pleasureable."[47] Janet Maslin in the *New York Times* is similarly enthusiastic: "And the hooker is played by Julia Roberts, who is so enchantingly beautiful, so funny, so natural and such an absolute delight that it is hard to hold anything against the movie."[48] In *Legally Blonde*, Reese Witherspoon receives her share of praise. The *New York Times* remarks that she is "a sharp, quick-witted Doris Day for our drab age of screen comedy."[49] David Denby in *The New Yorker* concludes that "the movie is worth seeing only for Reese Witherspoon, a brilliant corsage bobbing in junk-strewn waters."[50] *Screen International* conjectures that Witherspoon might well prove to be "the Carole Lombard or Judy Holliday of her generation."[51]

While Roberts and Witherspoon were catapulted into stardom with *Pretty Woman* and *Legally Blonde*, Sorvino and Kudrow, equally praised for their performance, did not leave the same indelible impression on their viewers, perhaps because the film was a only a modest success.[52] Nonetheless, these three films make clear that one of the primary functions of the girly film is to provide a vehicle for a female star whose charisma, which always exceeds the role to which she is confined, is an important element in the film's success. Equally, the stars tend to exhibit demotic qualities, Roberts with her coltish awkwardness and unaffected "good looks," Witherspoon with her "Valley Girl" vocabulary and "Everywoman" tastes in clothing and dogs, Kudrow and Sorvino's "bubblehead" attitude towards life.

Elle represents a democratization of taste in a world in which consumer culture has overtaken high fashion as the ultimate arbitrator; however, as a successful lawyer, her purview is one that moves beyond fashion, beyond feminine culture itself, to indicate the importance of her concerns as a representative of neo-feminism to the new world order. This new world order is not, however, regulated by the mandates of feminism. Again, the film is deceptive, in that it promulgates an illusion that encourages the viewer to associate its story with values associated with feminism—in particular, through the trope of empowerment, but also of sisterhood, which the film frequently invokes. Elle does not have a "buddy" or a "double," but she has the Delta Nu Sorority who again and again come to her assistance, reproducing her "self" albeit imperfectly on a national level. Elle is never alone. Her sense of attachment, her ability to create a connection through the recognition and cultivation of symmetry enables her to cross class boundaries—as when she and her hairdresser embark upon a life-long friendship. In *Legally Blonde 2: Red, White & Blonde* (Charles Herman-Wurmfeld, 2003), in which Elle conquers Washington, DC, in an aggressive defense of animal rights, it is increasingly clear that the majority of Elle's significant relations are with other women, and that it is her relations with other women that enable her to survive and succeed in the world. As in the case of *Romy and Michele*, the film clearly suppresses the possibility of the lesbian couple, while taking a "liberal," if patronizing, stand on homosexuality. The world of the sisterhood cannot accommodate the lesbian couple, because it would throw into question the taken for granted nature of the attachment that these women generate among themselves.

As in *Romy and Michele*, "envy" is the attribute that must be expunged, here represented by the reconciliation between Elle and her former rival Vivian (Selma Blair). There can be no envy between women, as Michele learns when she foolishly asserts that she is the "Mary"—and thus finds herself in a happy heterosexual relationship, but "with no one to talk to," no one to mirror and thus affirm her identity in the relationship of symmetry so important to "girl culture." "Me too!" These are the two most important words that Romy and Michele utter.[53] Women who fail to understand their connection to other women will not enjoy success or happiness within the world of the girly film. In *Working Girl*, for example, the film attempts to offset Tess's negative relations with Katharine by highlighting her positive relations with her fellow secretaries, including her best friend, Cyn (Joan Cusack). *Legally Blonde* takes a more forceful stance, like *Romy and Michele*, issuing a warning against the woman who strikes out on her own. It is not patriarchy, however, that cautions the "unruly" woman; rather, it is feminine culture itself that serves to regulate and normalize the feminine subject, to persuade and bully her into conforming to the rigid modes of behavior and appearance required by neo-feminism. Envy implies the drama of acquisition and loss that puts the feminine culture of "me too" at risk and as such cannot be tolerated within the feminine culture of the girly film.

Fashion in both films becomes a way of expressing the complexity of these contradictory strands—the desire for self-fulfillment, and the need to maintain a "me too" culture in an aestheticized form that both recognizes autonomy and connection, thus solving one of the fundamental problems of relations between women. The fashionable woman is complete unto herself, but cannot recognize herself as such outside the common discourse of fashion based on "me too." Fashion within these films is not a topic for men. In fact, with the exception of gay men, men are "blind" to fashion, whether it be the man who holds Cher up and asks to lie on the ground in her designer gown—worth far more than the purse that he confiscates—or her father, who fails to notice that she is going out on a date in something that looks like underwear. If the role of the women is to be looked at, men, for the most part, are not looking in these films—both in terms of audience, and also, more surprisingly, within the films themselves.

Fashion and appearance in these films becomes a means of self-expression among women for other women. When Michele complains that she has no one to talk to, we sense that, in part, she has no one to talk to about her clothes. Clothing and appearance are major topics of conversation in these films. More than that they are the socially accepted topics of conversation, and the topics of conversation capable of creating strong emotional ties. In the case of *Romy and Michele*, fashion becomes their means of earning a living; it is equally true, if less directly evident, that it is Elle's knowledge of feminine culture, in particular hair care, that allows her not only to win her case in court in *Legally Blonde*, but also to gain access to the important political connection she needs to pass her bill preventing the testing of cosmetics on animals in *Legally Blonde 2*.

It would be a mistake to conclude, however, that feminine culture can provide the foundation for an ethical or moral system—because of the way that this culture obviously and inevitably circumscribes notions of sisterhood and agency within an ethos of individual fulfillment. In *Legally Blonde*, morality and altruism are the luxuries of the wealthy; Elle's support of animal rights as a sign of her ability to think beyond her own limited pleasures does not require any sacrifices on her part—her livelihood is never at issue. The happy resolution of Elle's dilemmas depends upon her initially privileged status. These films, then, suggest the complexities of feminine culture as well as the appeal of neo-feminism in terms of offering a more immediate solution to the problems of feminine embodiment than does feminism itself. Here, the neo-feminist heroine such as Elle offers an ideal that marries heterosexuality, sisterhood, altruism, fashion and accomplishment, but in a way that is made possible by the privilege of wealth. Elle's virtue is easily acquired demanding no sacrifices; her happy ending is complete, a fantasy in which conflicting desires can be reconciled.

A perspective that focuses on the individual and her dilemmas, while at the same time appeasing the criticisms of feminism, through invoking concepts like sisterhood, was compatible with the general climate of neo-liberalism that sought to limit notions of social responsibility by highlighting individual accomplishment. Elle as a "pink girl in a brown world," in the words of the film's production designer, Melissa Stewart, offered a fantasy resolution in which the neo-feminist subject triumphs in a world in which the logic of "and/and" holds true.[54] The practicalities that beset her are resolved through the privileges of wealth, which neo-liberalism promised was within reach of any well-intentioned "striver" who masks her elitism through her democratized "bricolage" style; however, in different ways, *Romy and Michele* (through the perpetual adolescence to which the young women are relegated) and *Legally Blonde* (because of the implausible privileges enjoyed by its heroine) suggest that this perspective, in spite of its promises, is fraught with irresolvable contradictions.

Chapter 5

Jennifer Lopez
Neo-Feminism and the Crossover Star

In *Romy and Michele's High School Reunion* (David Mirkin, 1997) and *Legally Blonde* (Robert Luketic, 2001), female friendship and the relations between work and femininity are both significant dimensions of the neo-feminist paradigm. *Maid in Manhattan* (Wayne Wang, 2002), in contradistinction, takes up the problem of race and immigrant assimilation as the obvious stumbling block in the neo-feminist success formula—a paradigm presupposing that hard work and goodwill inevitably result in wealth and self-fulfillment. The film seemingly offers a more democratic vision of the Cinderella story, with an emphasis on work and career. Despite its inclusion of a Nuyorican protagonist, *Maid in Manhattan* nevertheless offers a rigid set of norms to which the successful woman must conform.[1]

Exploring the initial premise of *Pretty Woman* (Garry Marshall, 1990) in the context of an inter-racial relationship, and the Cinderella fantasy at its origins, Wang's film recounts the story of an ambitious young mother working as a maid in a posh Manhattan hotel who aspires to one day enter hotel management (Jennifer Lopez as Marisa) and a rising politician from a patrician family (Ralph Fiennes as Chris) who overcome a number of obstacles to be happily reunited at the film's conclusion. Initially, unaware of her status, Chris falls for her, in part, as the result of her son's efforts as matchmaker—but also with the impression that she is, like he, a guest of the hotel. When the truth is revealed, she loses her job and her suitor, the young politician unwilling to accept that she had lied to him. Time and the efforts of her young son heal these wounds, and at the film's conclusion the couple are reunited, restored in amity. Intertwined in the tale of romance, recalling *Working Girl* (Mike Nichols, 1988), the film also recounts the story of Marisa's ambition to better herself, and her eventual success in rising to the rank of "manager" within hotel hierarchy—meaning that, in spite of her initial set-back, by the film's conclusion she enters into the ranks of the "new managerial class," to quote the words used in the film. Here, in contrast with *Pretty Woman*, Marisa is "saved" not by her suitor, but through her own efforts, perseverance and tenacity.

In fact, the script, originating with John Hughes and developed by Kevin Wade, was originally submitted to Julia Roberts with a view to casting her in the lead. While Roberts declined the role, she remained involved the project—tentatively titled *The Chambermaid*—through her production company, Shoelace Productions (later Red Om Films).[2] Initially, in an earlier draft of the script, the plot revolved around "a maid and a British prince who fall in love," their relationship overcoming the barriers of class in the time-honored manner of classical Hollywood films such as *It Happened One Night* (Frank Capra, 1934), or the later international co-production, *The Prince and the Showgirl* (Laurence Olivier, 1957).[3] The casting of a Puerto Rican, strongly "Latina" identified actress in the leading role of Marisa (largely through the good offices of Elaine Goldsmith-Thomas, co-producer on the film and former agent to both Lopez and Roberts) countered prevalent criticisms of feminine culture and its treatment of "race."[4] The film postulates, through its narrative, that the Cinderella template (and by extension the neo-feminist paradigm) can accommodate the variations in "race" and ethnicity that characterize a broad spectrum of the American population—in particular, a new generation of ambitious American-born Latinos.

Typical of second-generation immigrants, the members of this cohort consider themselves American and seek success as defined by the terms of the dominant Anglo-European culture. A significant portion of the Latino population, in particular the Tejano and Chicano populations of the Southwest, including Texas and California, are not children of recent immigrants, being, on the contrary, descendents of indigenous peoples and original settlers; however, these populations share with the more recently arrived Latino groups an ethos of self-improvement and a younger generation that has moved away from traditional culture and language, seeking to realize themselves within a recognizably American context. In 2005, the *New York Times* reported that 85 percent of the Latino population under the age of 18 in the United States were born in-country, of whom a significant portion were non-Spanish speakers of mixed national origin. In contrast, 54 percent of the Latino population over 18 was born outside the United States. Importantly, among young Latinos aged between 14 and 18, Lopez was the "favorite female celebrity."[5] The film, *Maid in Manhattan*, then, served to highlight the ambitions of a group of second-generation Americans, women in particular, who sought to emulate both Lopez herself and the character that she played, a young woman from the Bronx who desired, but had yet to achieve, the success that Lopez herself had already enjoyed. These aspirations, often described in terms of "choice feminism," or "commodity feminism," fall clearly within the discourse of neo-feminism in so far as they revolve around personal fulfillment and financial ambitions as exemplified in Lopez's own success as a star—with Lopez distinguishing herself from other icons, such as Helen Gurley Brown, or the television star Sarah Jessica Parker, through her self-proclaimed ethnicity.[6]

Initially, *Pretty Woman*, and the girly genre more broadly, were widely considered racist in the sense that the genre offered an image of the heroine as inevitably "white," a woman of European origins, often blonde. The feminist African-American scholar, D. Soyini Madison observed that, although "Vivian's race is not a subject of explicit significance within the film," nonetheless "it *is* fundamentally significant that only because she is a white woman, and a 'pretty' white woman, that the plot can unfold in the manner that it does."[7] *Maid in Manhattan*, by casting Jennifer Lopez rather than Julia Roberts or Hilary Swank (also mentioned in conjunction with the film), presented a counter-narrative in which the fact of "race" becomes an important element in the narrative, with the "raced" subject being offered her own version of the fairy story.[8] *Variety* commented that "[m]aking the maid a Latina is certainly realistic but never quite avoids the suggestion that upward mobility is best achieved though marriage into Anglo society."[9] While the loss of identity promoted by the film, in its presentation of what amounts to assimilation through marriage and cultural conformity, provoked criticism from academics and journalists, such criticism generally failed to consider how the star persona of Jennifer Lopez inflected the title role.[10] The neo-feminist paradigm that the film promotes derives as much from the media mythologies surrounding Lopez as it did from the plot itself.

The marriage-plot dimension of the film was not without importance in terms of providing a particular kind of fantasy for a predominantly female audience—a fantasy that permits the viewer, in the words of Ginia Bellafante, reviewing *Maid in Manhattan* for the *New York Times*, "to indulge in the cherished myth of class mobility and all its attendant promises of instant and effortless transformation."[11] The marriage plot propels the female protagonist to the achievement of her life-goals through marriage to a man, again in Bellafante's terms, a man who "will eventually emerge from the ether to recognize that you are a creature like no other. And you, already so uniquely pure of heart, will rise even further."[12] Bellafante hypothesizes that contemporary women, with their many conflicting demands, "can't help feeling like a chambermaids," hence the potency of this particular fantasy.[13]

In contrast, Lopez infused the film with her paparazzi-produced image as one of the successful "veritable media conglomerates," in the words of the *New York Times*, who was hardly a chambermaid and, if she had yet to encounter her Prince Charming, no longer needed "saving" from the "mess" of contemporary life. Lopez, in that period, was not simply as star; she was a franchise, in which her activities as a performer were part of a synergistic system in which she was associated with an array of products from CDs and DVDs to perfume, clothing and handbags. In short, she was "a one woman entertainment empire."[14] In July 2003, the *New York Times* reported Lopez as having earned as much as $60 million in the previous year from her acting, singing and fashion ventures.[15] Film scholars Alan Dodd and Martin Fradley underlined her ubiquity and profile: "Lopez's synergistic metamorphoses between dancer, singer, actress, fashion designer, perfumer, restaurateur and gossip column favorite cultivate a saturation omnipresence that is illustrative of ... the high accelerated commercial logic of contemporary 'celebrification.'"[16] As a Latina star, Lopez represented a new world order of femininity in which the ability to "look good" and work hard, and, thus, incarnate the ideals of the female "striver," became available to a broader demographic of women, on one hand, while maintaining stringent standards in terms of grooming and self-presentation, on the other.

Born in the Bronx in 1969, Lopez, only two years younger than Julia Roberts (b. 1967), had Spanish-speaking, mixed-"race" parents, David Lopez and Guadalupe Lopez, who were from Puerto Rico. Middle-class (her father was a computer technician and her mother a kindergarten teacher), Lopez, nonetheless, pursued a career in which her body rather than an education was her primary resource, much to her disappointment of her parents, whom Lopez "defied ... to fulfill her ambition."[17] She started as a dancer on television, as a "Fly Girl" in the Fox hit television series *In Living Color* (1990–94) following which she appeared in other series such as *South Central* (Fox, 1994), which led to her being identified with an American underclass. Subsequent films included *My Family/Mia Familia* (Gregory Nava, 1995), *Money Train* (Joseph Ruben, 1995), *Jack* (Francis Ford Coppola, 1996) and *Blood and Wine* (Bob Rafelson, 1996). Her performance in the title role of *Selena* (Gregory Nava, 1997), however, in which she portrayed the eponymous slain Tejana singer, thrust her into the limelight as a Latina star who represented a cohort comprising an amalgam of different groups—Latinos born in the United States, primarily English-speaking, whose parents derived from a number of different nationalities, including Mexicano, Cubano, Tejano, Chicano, Hondureno, Chileno, among others, and who were united in their ambitions to improve their economic and social position. In part, Lopez owed her success in the role to her uncanny resemblance to Selena (see Figure 5.1); nonetheless, this film proved to be a stepping stone to other featured roles in films such as *Anaconda* (Luis Llosa, 1997), *U Turn* (Oliver Stone, 1997), *Out of Sight* (Steven Soderbergh, 1998), *The Cell* (Tarsem Singh, 2000), *The Wedding Planner* (Adam Shankman, 2001), *Angel Eyes* (Luis Mandoki, 2001), *Enough* (Michael Apted, 2002), all of which preceded *Maid in Manhattan,* ensuring that Lopez came to the role of Marisa as an established star.

Though the sound track of the film featured original renditions by Selena, with Lopez lip-synching her performances, *Selena* also paved the way for

Figure 5.1 Jennifer Lopez as "Selena" (1997). Courtesy of Photofest.

Lopez's highly successful musical career as a performer.[18] Her albums released before 13 December 2002 (the date on which *Maid in Manhattan* opened) included *On the 6*, a reference to the New York subway line that links the Bronx with Manhattan, released in 1999, *J.Lo*, in 2001, *J to tha L-O!: The Remixes*, in 2002 and *This is Me ... Then* (2002), all of which were repeatedly cited obliquely in the film, in which, for example, the protagonist Marisa Ventura lives in the Bronx and takes "the 6" to work. In January 2001, before commencing shooting on the film—at that time still referred to as *The Chambermaid*—Lopez distinguished herself when her album *J.Lo* and her newly released film, *The Wedding Planner*, were number one on the Billboard Top 200 and at the box office, respectively. She was the first female performer to enjoy this status.[19]

The Wedding Planner and *Enough*, as well as *Maid in Manhattan* and subsequently *Gigli* (Martin Brest, 2003), starring Lopez and Ben Affleck, were distributed through Columbia/Sony, with "Epic Records, a label under Sony Music," holding Lopez's recording contract—prompting the *Hollywood Reporter* to claim that "[o]n the music side, Lopez has Sony ties as well."[20] The Sony connections suggest the complicated and extensive inter-media synergy that supported Lopez's quick rise to fame and fortune, and the creation of the Lopez star franchise, in which her persona emerged through a happy confluence of diverse activities. Lopez's success cannot be solely attributed to her talents—her acting and singing abilities—but also to the way in which she represented a certain ideal that appealed to a broad spectrum of women generally, and, in particular, to a specific ethnic group, the Latinas, who saw her as extending what I have been calling the neo-feminist paradigm to encompass diverse subjects for whom ethnic identity could be construed as an asset rather than an impediment, to be adopted, or not, as the situation demanded. Lopez explained in a frequently quoted statement: "I've always looked at my being Latina as something that kind of set me apart from the crowd and made me different and unique."[21] Baz Dreisinger, journalist and American Studies scholar, in a review of *Maid in Manhattan*, includes Lopez among "performers" who "prove that ethnicity is not such a stable entity," a point that she feels shapes the narrative of the film, which is, in her terms, "self-consciously about passing from Latin to WASP to Latin again—a theme that runs through Lopez's film career but also, I'd say, her real-life persona."[22]

The fact that Lopez's appearance was ambiguous, permitting her to play a range of roles that were frequently not Latino-inflected, was an important element in her persona; in contrast, her musical career tended to link her more consistently with her roots. As an actress, she incarnated variations on her "self," the consistency of which derived from her image—the fact that she was always recognizable as Jennifer Lopez, while remaining plausible in her many roles and in the range of identities that she assumed from Tejana in *Selena*, to American Indian in *U Turn*, to Italian-American in *The Wedding Planner*. In this sense, Lopez illustrated Richard Dyer's observation, in his now canonical work on Hollywood stars, that one of the functions of stars was seemingly to embody the cultural contradictions of their era; however, they did so through their "real existence" as a unique and specific individual, whose life was documented through the press—creating a narrative about that life that increasingly had a status independent of the lived experience of the star, but which, nonetheless, served to ground the star in the public's eye as a single and identifiable person.[23]

In Dyer's words, "[t]he disunity created by attaching opposing qualities to their images was nonetheless rendered a unity simply by virtue of the fact that each was only one person."[24] In Lopez's case, she mobilized a number of significant contradictions—here, most notably, the contradiction historically at the heart of the American body politic, in which a multitude of national and ethnic identities seek to conceive of themselves as "one nation indivisible with liberty and justice for all" —which she successfully brought together through her specificity as a distinctive individual, recognizable as such across her many different roles.[25] In particular, she represented an ideal of assimilation for young Latinos, one that paradoxically allowed the preservation of ethnic identity, when desirable, emphasized through the fluidity and diversity of Lopez's own performances (see Figure 5.2). Whether playing a Native American or Italian American, she was always Jennifer Lopez, her star identity never subsumed or "lost" in her roles.

Like many other stars associated with "chick flicks," such as Julia Roberts or Meg Ryan, Lopez was not noted for her virtuoso performances (as was and is, for example, the case for Meryl Streep), but rather for creating a specific persona across a number of genres (including interviews and photographs). Similarly, as a singer, she has not been noted for her technique or voice. *People*, attributing to Lopez "a savvy awareness of her own limitations," quoted producer Irv Gotti, who claimed that Lopez "can't make a record like Whitney or Mariah cause she ain't got a big voice." Her sound, according to Gotti, depends on "guys like me who can … enhance that voice."[26]

Lopez's most singular talent was to parlay what qualities she had into what fans accepted as an authentic representation of her "self," portraying a feminine ideal in which beauty and hard work are the key ingredients to achieving wealth and fame. Her limited talents contributed to, rather than detracted from, her persona because it enhanced, in Helen Gurley Brown's terms, her "mouseburger" status as an ordinary girl parlaying her resources through hard work and perseverance into a notable success story. Lopez effectively cultivated

Figure 5.2 Jennifer Lopez with Sharon Stone in 2002, an ideal of assimilation. Courtesy of Photofest.

an evolving persona that would be attractive to a media industry obsessed with celebrity, beginning with her first high-profile role in the bio-pic *Selena* in 1997, in which the media attention generated by Lopez was in excess of that produced by the film itself.[27] The film made a respectable $35 million at the domestic box office, comparing favorably to films like *Frida* (Julie Taymor, 2002) directed at a similar niche audience with a domestic gross of $26 million; however, it did not enjoy the broader success of a film like *The First Wives Club* (Hugh Wilson, 1996), based on the popular Olivia Goldsmith novel, released a year earlier, that targeted the broader women's audience, enjoying a domestic gross of $105 million.

Significant to the interest that Lopez generated in her role as Selena was the perception in Hollywood, and in service industries more generally, that the Latino audience was a potential market, which had not, as yet, been fully exploited. Banc One, for example, invested "more than $1 million on a series of marketing tie-ins" for the movie *Selena*, in an attempt to demonstrate the bank's "understanding" and "empathy" for "the Latino community."[28] In 1998, the *New York Times* reported: "Jennifer Lopez, the Puerto Rican actress, who played the title role in 'Selena,' now commands $5 million a film," locating Lopez's visibility and success within a larger phenomenon. In the same article, Marc Anthony, also Puerto Rican (and Lopez's third husband in 2004), was quoted as describing the increased interest in Latino culture and performers in the following terms: "The American market sees the potential of the new growth market and it's just trying to make money."[29] In a 1990 article, R. Serge Denisoff and George Plasketes quote producer Taylor Hackford as saying: "It is a market that Hollywood has ignored for its entire history."[30] The promotion of Jennifer Lopez indicates attempts to reach this market, but also the difficulties in creating material that would equally appeal to other markets to produce the kinds of box office revenues required by Conglomerate Hollywood.[31]

In fact, none of Lopez's films achieved a domestic box office gross of over $100 million, with *Maid in Manhattan*, at $94 million, her highest grossing film. In contrast, in the domestic market, *Pretty Woman* grossed $179 million, *The Devil Wears Prada* (David Frankel, 2006), $124 million, *Sex and the City: The Movie* (Michael Patrick King, 2008), $153 million. In the same year, Reese Witherspoon in *Sweet Home Alabama* (Andy Tennant, 2002) outperformed *Maid in Manhattan*, with a domestic gross of $127 million. Lopez's success, then, can only be understood in terms of the combined forces of her various enterprises, of which movie-making is only one, and which addressed a niche group, Latinos, whom other stars were not necessarily reaching.

During the period that witnessed Lopez's increasing prominence in the media as a celebrity, "Hispanic moviegoers" were reported to be "the fastest-growing ethnic group among film audiences … not only in terms of size but affluence."[32] As a bona fide representative of that group, who also emphasized her Latina identity, Lopez was able to command high salaries that went from $1 million for *Selena*, $9 million to $12 million for *Gigli* and then *Maid in Manhattan*, leading *People* to describe Lopez as "the highest paid Latina actress in movie history."[33] While stars like Cameron Diaz (b. 1972, and of Hispanic parentage) command salaries that are considerably higher than those awarded Lopez,[34] Diaz did not develop a specifically Latina profile, perhaps because, with her blonde, svelte and athletic physique, she conformed to a Hollywood type that did not single her out from other stars such as Michelle Pfeiffer and Meg Ryan, who tended to be coded as "white" and "Anglo" by audiences. Lopez, in contrast, was widely viewed as offering an alternative feminine ideal. According to women-on-the-street standards, Lopez at 5 feet 6 inches, weighing 120 or 125 pounds (her famous derrière estimated between 35 and 40 inches), did not entirely live up to her reputation as "short and curvy" (see Figure 5.3). In 2003, *American Demographics* reported: "The average woman is 5'4″ tall, weighs 145 lbs. with a dress size of 11–14, has a 36–37″ bust, is about 29″ around the waist and close to 40″ around the hips,"[35] pointing to the fact that Lopez was both taller and more slender than the norm. In Hollywood, however, she evoked a Latina body that challenged the conventional standards to which stars in this period adhered, distinguishing her from Jessica Alba (b. 1981) and Cameron Diaz (both of "Latino" extraction), but also from other stars of her generation.[36]

This departure from the Hollywood formula is deceptive since, unlike the activist actress Rosie Perez (b. 1964) also identified with her Puerto Rican roots, Lopez, both in her appearance, her relations with high-end fashion designers as well her attempts to develop her own fashion lines, emphasized the importance of consumer culture in the development and dissemination of her public persona and, thus, in keeping with the neo-feminist paradigm, can hardly be construed as contesting dominant social and economic structures.[37] In contradistinction, Salma Hayek, a Mexican national who became a U.S. citizen, offers an example of a Latina star who, albeit in a gentler manner than Perez, attempted to use her stardom to intervene in a certain kind of politics.[38] Notorious for her fervor about the benefits of breastfeeding, she also pioneered projects that challenged dominant Hollywood fare, such as *Frida* (Julie Taymor, 2002) which took as its subject the radical Mexican painter Frida Kahlo, who was and remains extremely popular with American feminists; however, Hayek, the daughter of an opera singer of Spanish descent, and a oil company executive of Lebanese origins, coming from a privileged background, with an imperfect command of English, never attracted the same fan base that Lopez shared with Selena herself, the striving American-born, English-speaking

Figure 5.3 Emphasizing Jennifer Lopez's posterior in *Maid in Manhattan* (2002). Courtesy of Photofest.

Latina. Hayek is not, unlike Lopez, a crossover star, that is a star who becomes "popular with a new audience," often by moving from one medium to another, or, perhaps more pertinently, among "non-white performers who succeed in becoming popular with white audiences."[39] In many ways, like the film *Frida*, and the painter herself with whom she identified, Salma Hayek served to represent a vision of Latinidad that resonated most strongly with "Anglo" audiences.[40] She was never able, at least within an American context, to mobilize the discourse of Latinidad that characterizes Lopez's star biography and, significantly, her activism, which contested feminine norms at least to some degree, resulted in a far more ambivalent relationship with the neo-feminist paradigm.

The media narrative surrounding Lopez throws into relief the continued importance of the cult of personality and celebrity to the dissemination and appeal of the neo-feminist paradigm, in which individual achievement and realization remain the primary goal. Channeling this philosophy through individual media celebrities enhanced and emphasized the focus on the individual rather than on other issues, notably social and political concerns. The neo-feminist paradigm promotes the idea that the primary pathway to self-actualization available to women is one that depends solely on individual achievement. In the 1990s, this was neatly articulated through a series of media exemplars that implicitly, and often explicitly, confirm that personality, rather than talent, skills or education, can ensure success. Lopez, like Brown and Sarah Jessica Parker, achieved prominence without specific education—for Lopez, in music, acting or dance. Her success belied the importance of training, deflecting attention away from what is conventionally considered the most effective path for advancement, especially in terms of increasing economic opportunity, for most individuals—that of higher education and advanced professional degrees. Narratives of achievement, such as that of Lopez, which center on celebrities, neither recognize nor contribute to the kinds of institutional reform (relating to employment and daycare, for example) that might benefit demographically significant groups of women, as opposed to a few isolated individuals. Such success stories, particularly revolving around media celebrities like Lopez, thus fueled the neo-feminist paradigm, implicitly suggesting that institutional and economic reform were without relevance, or of only minor importance, to the ambitious woman.

Also central to the neo-feminist paradigm defined by Helen Gurley Brown was "love," and "sex" as an extension of "love." For Brown, echoing Sigmund Freud's famous dictum, "work" and "love" were necessary to a woman's happiness, with work perhaps even more important than love without detracting from the latter's significance. In keeping with this vision of feminine accomplishment, Lopez's many and tumultuous love affairs, which accompanied her high-profile career, contributed to her star persona. Her highly publicized romances, in which she proved her optimism and her ability to renew and revive herself, provided the arena in which her character was tested, while providing fodder for the tabloids, whose interest in Lopez was crucial to her fame. The tendency among cultural critics was to see her unhappiness in love as a kind of retribution that "humanized" the star in the eyes of her fans, who might identify with her problems or even compare themselves favorably to Lopez in this regard. As scholars Dodd and Fradley have observed: "[a]bsolutely central to the Lopez star image are the catastrophic romantic liaisons that are the structurally necessary underside of her professional successes."[41]

Equally influential, if not more so, was the way in which Lopez, through her example, advocated a system of serial monogamy in which a woman is deemed to have the right to change her partner in her quest for her optimal mate, if that partner does not live up to her fundamental requirements. Lopez did not limit herself, in spite of her Catholic upbringing, to the expectations that confined women of her mother's generation to unhappy or unsatisfying marriages. Lopez's behavior indicated that a woman should persist in seeking out the relationship that she wants, and be prepared to change her partner should such an action seem advantageous. Lopez herself summarized her philosophy as one in which relationships, and by extension marriage, are never definitive, but part of an on-going process of self-realization: "I'm still figuring it out as I go along. ... I believe that in life you learn through experience. I'm old enough to know now that relationships take work. That it's not an easy thing."[42]

Like Sarah Jessica Parker or Julia Roberts, Lopez's lurid past, her unsuccessful marriages and liaisons, have not been portrayed as an impediment to a stable marriage, nor, significantly, to motherhood. With each unsuccessful relationship, Lopez renewed her faith in the fact that she, and by extension her fans, would find the right husband in order to have the family that she ultimately desired. She proclaimed in 1998, "I want everything. I want family. I want to do good work. I want love. I want to be comfortable."[43] Helen Gurley Brown had infamously condemned motherhood, at one point claiming that "[t]here is a conspiracy against women and I'd be the first to say so. ... But getting us to be beautiful ain't the problem! We are encouraged to be mothers, to be pregnant."[44] For the stars of neo-feminist cinema, such as Julia Roberts or Reese Witherspoon, motherhood has been an integral part of marriage and the neo-feminist paradigm (as a sign of its evolving status), with the "yummy mummy" competing with the single girl as a consumer-constructed feminine ideal. Lopez's very public romantic itinerary has highlighted feminine culture's debt to the neo-feminist paradigm initially articulated in the 1960s, as well as changes to that paradigm in the 1990s, which increasingly sought to include motherhood alongside romance and work as necessary to a woman's fulfillment.

At the time of *Maid in Manhattan*'s release, media interest in Lopez and her companion of the time, Ben Affleck, had reached a veritable frenzy, possibly because of a general feeling that, unlike her first two husbands or Sean

("P. Diddy") Combs, a media "bad boy," with whom she had also been linked, Affleck was her equal, an appropriately successful partner. Subsequent to the demise of her relationship with Affleck and the development of her seemingly calmer liaison and subsequent marriage to salsa star Marc Anthony in 2004, media interest in her waned; the birth of her twins in 2008, however, brought her *Bildungsroman* to a successful close, leaving Lopez as an example of a woman who has it all—according to the neo-feminist paradigm—which would not preclude her from seeking yet another partner in the event that Marc Anthony might prove inadequate.

One other man deserves mention for having played a crucial role in her career: entertainment mogul, Benny Medina, Lopez's manager (whom she met through Sean Combs), described in the *New York Times* as "the man who helped turn 'Jenny from the Block' into a household name."[45] Medina, who is listed as executive producer for *Maid in Manhattan*, masterminded many of her business ventures as well as her singing career, and was perhaps the most important force in terms of extending her franchise beyond acting into singing, and other ventures such as fashion, perfumes and product endorsements, such as Louis Vuitton, or even greeting cards.[46] The relationship, described as "a platonic marriage," lasted five years (1998–2003), coinciding with the period in which Lopez established herself as a cross-media star. In addition to enjoying her company (when traveling, "they stayed in adjoining hotel rooms"), Medina "received 10 percent of Ms. Lopez's earnings in film and television ... 14 percent of music publishing and recording and 10 percent of ancillary businesses." He also anticipated "50 percent of the producing revenues generated by ... Nuyorican Productions," Lopez's film production company, when their relationship was dissolved.[47] The fact that Lopez's break with Medina coincided with the advent of Lopez's relationship with Affleck seemingly confirmed that, in Affleck, Lopez had found a partner who exceeded Medina in meeting her needs, a man worthy of her exclusive attention who could furnish her with everything that she required and deserved. Medina commented:

> I've been there through boyfriends, husbands, new relationships. But now she has this new relationship, and it all changed. ... I have a tremendous amount of respect and love for her. We have gone through so many good times together and times of sadness, No. 1 movies and records—a fairy-tale life.[48]

The importance of *Maid in Manhattan* to this larger narrative is the way in which it punctuates Lopez's story, her journey towards her ultimate goal of establishing herself as a member of Hollywood's aristocracy with a suitable consort, a goal that continued to elude her, inspiring *Time* to remark, even in

2005, subsequent to her marriage to Marc Anthony, that "She may want to rule the world, but, like the lady says, at least in some way she's still Jenny from the block."[49] *Parade* observed:

> From the start, the thrust of Lopez's career strategy has been to hold on to her inner-city minority fan base while making inroads into mainstream America. Affleck is one of today's most powerful young movie stars, and J.Lo wanted to hitch her star to his Hollywood wagon.[50]

Though her generally increasingly "comfortable" (to use her word) financial standing was noted and applauded by the tabloids, especially during the years of her relationship with Medina, wealth was not sufficient in the absence of a suitable consort. Notably, her second marriage to dancer Cris Judd in 2001 inspired *MailOnline* to include Lopez among "the stars who stunned us by falling for the hired help," underlining Lopez's status as a member of the elite as well as her preference for the underclass. Liz Smith, the infamous columnist, also chastised Lopez for marrying down—in a move that reverses the role she would play in *Maid in Manhattan*, in which she aspires to "date" up. In both instances, the press expressed its consternation at the apparent inappropriateness of Lopez's choices, Liz Smith proclaiming "Two Mr. Wrongs for Lopez," on the occasion of her separation from Judd.[51] Ben Affleck, on the other hand, seemed more promising. Like Lopez he came from a middle-class background and, after a difficult period that included a stint in rehabilitation, he appeared to have reached that stage at which a star typically marries and has children. Not coincidentally, he, like Lopez, did in fact pursue that course of action, proceeding to marry Hollywood star, Jennifer Garner, in 2005, with whom he has had two children.[52]

Lopez and Affleck met in November 2001, on the set of *Gigli*, soon after Lopez's honeymoon with Judd. Affleck generated rumors in March 2002 by taking out an ad in the *Hollywood Reporter*, as did many others, when Lopez won the ShoWest 2002 Female Star of the Year award, highlighting Lopez's assets: "graciousness of spirit, beauty in courage, great empathy, astonishing talent, real poise and true grace," encouraging speculation in the tabloids about the nature of his relationship with Lopez.[53] The filming of *Maid in Manhattan* in the months that followed occurred during the high point of media interest in the couple, with Lopez's divorce to Judd finalized in January 2003, after the film's release.

Dana Kennedy reported in the *New York Times* that "Ms Lopez's handlers hope this romantic comedy ... will break her recent string of disappointing films and do for her what *Pretty Woman* did for Ms. Roberts." It would be more accurate to understand the film as offering the ultimate complement to Lopez's established star persona, in which the "striver" ethic that Lopez articulates in her media persona is given full representation through a film narrative. While *Maid in Manhattan* was Lopez's highest grossing film, unlike Roberts in *Pretty Woman*, or Witherspoon in *Legally Blonde*, Lopez's star persona was already well-developed when she accepted the role and the film; her persona and her sustained presence in the public's eye were crucial elements in the film's profile. In particular, the publicity surrounding the Jennifer Lopez/Ben Affleck relationship (2002–04) generated the context into which the audience's understanding of the film was, of necessity, inserted. The next chapter proposes to look more closely at the relations between this persona and the film itself, in particular with reference to the media interest surrounding the Lopez/Affleck relationship and its pertinence to the neo-feminist paradigm.

Chapter 6

Maid in Manhattan (2002)
A New Fairy Tale

As demonstrated in the previous chapter, *Maid in Manhattan* (Wayne Wang, 2002) distinguishes itself from girly films such as *Pretty Woman* (Garry Marshall, 1990) because of the way in which the film draws upon the persona of an already established star, Jennifer Lopez, who outside the film's narrative offers an exemplar of neo-feminist achievement that extends the ethos of the film beyond the cinematic experience. Lopez's involvement in the film highlights how the cult of celebrity contributes to, and supports, the neo-feminist paradigm by generating a discourse that encourages a philosophy of individual fulfillment while confirming the centrality of consumer culture in the viewer's life. Beyond the fact that Lopez as a star brought a specific set of characteristics and history to the role of Marisa, the film project occurred at a crucial moment in Lopez's own romantic development, leading to an especially resonant confluence between the film's theme and the star's life. During the period of the film's production and release, Lopez was involved in a relationship with Ben Affleck, one that appeared finally to offer her a possible resolution to the series of unhappy marriages and relationships that had heretofore marked her life as depicted in the tabloids. Affleck seemed to offer the fairy tale partnership that both Lopez and her fans seemed to anticipate as awaiting her in spite of two failed marriages.[1]

So prominent in the press was the relationship between Jennifer Lopez and Ben Affleck that they were dubbed "Bennifer," thus acquiring an identity as a media phenomenon. Notably, neither of Lopez's or Affleck's subsequent relationships have received the same degree of coverage, suggesting, perhaps, the importance of the inter-racial elements to the public's interest, but also the way in which the particular drama of that relationship elicited an interest that was in excess of the sum of its parts. The stars on their own did not have the same impact as they did as a couple whose tumultuous affairs were continuously in the public eye. For Affleck, the racial dimension of the relationship was crucial to the fascination that it exercised over the public. He remarked bitterly: "I'm white and she's Puerto Rican. That's what's underneath, although nobody says it because it's not politically correct."[2] Indeed, in 2003 "inter-racial" unions comprised only 7 percent of U.S. marriages, though "73 percent of Americans approved of such marriages."[3] In contrast, Lopez stressed, not their racial differences, but their similarities: "[w]e got along great ... Two kids who grew up in similar backgrounds, the same kind of neighbors, same kind of class—and we felt it right away."[4] The London *Observer* opined that "[i]t was no surprise ... that she would end up with someone like Affleck, who shared a similar upbringing, albeit in white, liberal Boston."[5]

This divergence of perspectives demonstrates how the couple served as a catalyst for the expression of contradictory desires and fantasies, suggesting the range of contradictions, in Dyer's terms,[6] evoked by Lopez's star persona. Affleck and Lopez represented an atavistic utopian ideal of melting pot culture, in which the worthy denizens of the middle-class, imbued with a Protestant work ethic, would achieve unimaginable success, wealth and prestige. As a couple, they embodied the American dream in which ordinary people might live extraordinary lives—in particular the lives of the extremely wealthy— while remaining untouched by corruption, with their work ethic, moral integrity and ethnic identity intact.

This same fantasy fuels the film *Maid in Manhattan*, which led Christopher Tookey to remark in *MailOnline* that the film "has an openness about ordinary people's desire for upward social mobility that is refreshingly honest."[7] Because the audience is aware of Lopez's notable successes, her own rise as a celebrity lends credibility to the fantasy, with Affleck serving as a kind of "prince consort," the "nice guy," by Hollywood standards, who can provide the companionship and lavish gifts that accompany this fantasy, while not necessarily challenging the prominence of Lopez as the primary focus of the fantasy as a fantasy for women. Indeed, as late as 2009, the French and Italian press were reporting that Affleck resented his position as a "prince consort" and the way in which Lopez controlled the life of the couple, while the American press indicated that Affleck felt that the relationship had had a negative impact on his "career."[8] In contrast, in 2005, Sandy M. Fernandez claimed in the *Washington Post* that Lopez created a persona that represented "an average Latina under the very best, luckiest conditions," her roles in films like *Maid in Manhattan* and the later *Monster-in-Law* (Robert Luketic, 2005) deriving their impact as much as from the character she plays in the film as from what Fernandez described as "her biography," which "reads like an immigrant archetype."[9]

Lopez is frequently portrayed as a hard worker, a dedicated professional, her accomplishments the result of determination and self-discipline rather than talent. The London *Observer* characterized her as "the product of her upbringing—a middle-class girl who puts a premium on hard work and improving her pension plan; conformist and close to her family,"[10] while *Variety* described her in 2002, on the occasion of her ShoWest 2002 Female Star of the Year award, as "one of showbiz's hardest working performers."[11] *Us Weekly* suggested that this trait served to naturalize the relationship between Affleck and Lopez, underlining their appropriateness as a couple: "She's so professional, and she knows what she wants. Ben's the same, and he was surprised to see there was somebody else with his same work ethic."[12] Unlike contemporary celebrities such as Nicole Richie or Paris Hilton, she neither drinks nor takes drugs—her major vice is perhaps shopping, which *People* characterized as Lopez's and Affleck's "common passion":

> In Philadelphia they laid out more than $1,000 on designer togs; in Coral Gables, Fla., they picked up an estimated $200,000 Aston Martin sports car; on a trip to Atlantic City back in August, Affleck dropped $50,000 on a Rolex for his beloved—and another for her mother, Guadalupe, 56.[13]

Pretty Woman's obsession with money returns here in the form of a preoccupation with the lifestyle and spending habits of the very wealthy that fuels both the "Bennifer" phenomenon and the narrative of *Maid in Manhattan*. While the film is structured by the love story, its visual interest lies in its depiction of upstairs/downstairs life in an unimaginably expensive New York hotel. Like the impromptu images shot by the paparazzi and coveted by the tabloids that feed the public's obsession with "Bennifer," the film offers insight into what the viewer might imagine to be the life of Jennifer Lopez herself. Lopez, then, can paradoxically occupy the position of the "maid," while her surroundings recall the enviable, in the eyes of her fans, excesses of the privileged, which she enjoys. As Marisa in *Maid in Manhattan*, she represents the "hired help" who attracts the attention of a member of the American political elite, while in her own life it is often she who has elevated the "help" in the case of her first two husbands, one a waiter and the other a backup dancer. Adding to this dynamic of alternating roles between underclass and upperclass, Lopez as a star is often portrayed in the popular press as a diva, not unlike the difficult clients on whom Marisa, as a maid, must wait, catering to their whims, moods and idiosyncrasies. *MailOnline* claimed that "Jennifer is said to have demanded that her coffee be stirred only clockwise. And during a recent appearance on *Top of the Pops*, she demanded ten dressing rooms decorated entirely in white."[14]

Yet another contradiction, then, at the heart of *Maid in Manhattan* revolves around the feminine ideal associated with the neo-feminist paradigm: on one hand, the ideal woman is modest, unassuming and hard working—still the "mouseburger" patronized by Helen Gurley Brown; on the other, she is a powerful demanding figure, who commands others—a captain of industry in which very often her body, as in the case of Lopez, is the initial resource upon which she must build her empire. The double ideal that Lopez represents as both diva and regular girl, as both her "self" as she has constructed her image in the media eye and as the protagonist of the film, Marisa, allows her to represent this contradiction without necessarily interrogating its norms. In this sense, she illustrates Richard Dyer's notion that "stars can be seen as ordinary people who live more expensively than the rest of us but are not essentially transformed by this."[15]

The prominence of "Bennifer" was encouraged by the growth of tabloid culture itself—in particular, the rivalry in that period between Time Inc.'s *People Magazine* and Wenner Media's *Us Weekly*, with *People* attempting to "blunt the impact of *Us Weekly*" as a relative newcomer. The bitter competition for images that depict "a famous person doing something unscripted" inflated the price of individual pictures. "[P]ictures that would have gone for $18,000 a year ago are now going for $200,000," reported Steve Coz, editorial director of American Media, with the *New York Times* claiming, "The most valuable images build the illusion of intimacy with stars by intruding into their everyday life."[16] In this atmosphere, the tumultuous love life of the very photogenic Lopez proved a fecund source for material sought by both the lower end publications such as *Star,* as well as *People* and *Us Weekly*. "The first photographed kiss between Ben Affleck and Jennifer Lopez ... reportedly went for just under $100,000."[17] While media attention may have had a negative effect on the relationship,[18] Lopez, in particular, mined the publicity generated by her amorous exploits, with both the press and Lopez herself eager to make the analogy between her situation and that of *Maid in Manhattan*'s fictional protagonist.

Us Weekly proclaimed that "Lopez's new fairy-tale life is just beginning. ... It's no secret that Lopez's offscreen Prince Charming is Affleck." The article's by-line: "Born in the Bronx: Made in Manhattan," makes explicit the implied analogy between the film project and Lopez's own life; another caption plays upon Lopez's own miraculous rise to success: "She may not wear a glass slipper in *Maid in Manhattan*, but J. Lo fits right in among classic cinematic fairy tales."[19] The *London Times* reported more succinctly on the occasion of the film's opening that *Maid in Manhattan* "echoes Lopez's rise from working-class girl in New York's Bronx to $50 million superstar."[20] Lopez herself, in a 2003 interview with *Esquire*, insisted, "But I am still Jennifer. I *did* grow up poor, and I did, you know, wear holey sneakers and hand-me-downs. I *did* sleep in the bed with my two sisters. And now it's different ... because I worked hard to get here."[21] Again and again, she parrots the sentiments expressed in her hit single, "Jenny from the Block," released the same year as *Maid in Manhattan*, in which she asserts her continued allegiance to her Latina, in particular Nuyorican, fan base and her own origins in the Bronx. In the single and the video, urging viewers to overlook her "rocks," she crooned: "I'm still, I'm still Jenny from the Block."

Lopez exploited the "Bennifer" phenomenon by including footage of herself and Affleck re-enacting scenes from their intimate life in her own music video that accompanied the single.[22] *People* commented: "For the 'Block' video, Lopez and Affleck recreated the Aug. 1 photos [the same photos for which *People* paid just under $100,000]—some front-seat smooching in her Bentley— that told the world their fling was the real thing."[23] Lopez explained the video as an ironic comment on the media's abusive intrusion into their private life, notably the infamously high-priced photographs.[24] Certainly, the video under- lined Lopez's conscious and obvious exploitation of her media image as part of her conglomerate, as an important element in the development of her star franchise as it would inflect *Maid in Manhattan*.

The analogy between *Pretty Woman* and *Maid in Manhattan* was frequently noted by reviewers, prompting Christopher Tookey from the *Daily Mail* to write: "*Maid in Manhattan* is a not very bright but refreshingly breezy romance in the upwardly mobile tradition of *Pretty Woman* and *Working Girl*."[25] Dana Kennedy commented in the *New York Times*, "While 'Maid in Manhattan' seems tailored for Ms Lopez's core fans, it may also appeal to those who will see authentic parallels between this story, which is more 'Working Girl' than 'Cinderella,' and Ms Lopez's own life."[26] The comparison with these two earlier films, *Working Girl* (Mike Nichols, 1988) and *Pretty Woman*, reveals significant changes as well as continuities, most of which move in the direction of enhancing the relations between the film and Lopez's own life story as it is represented in the press, but also pointing to developments in the neo-feminist paradigm itself.

Maid in Manhattan, like the two preceding films, offered a female protagonist at the center of her universe, who drives the story. Popular writers, Jo Berry and Angie Errigo, in their viewer's guide, *Chick Flicks: Movies Women Love*, recommend that the film "should be avoided by anyone with an aversion to J-Lo, as she is in every scene," highlighting Lopez's prominence in the film and the degree to which the film depends on her charisma and appearance as a star to attract its audience.[27] The centrality of romance to the film links it to *Working Girl* and *Pretty Woman*, rather than to later developments of the girly film—such as *Romy and Michele's High School Reunion* (David Mirkin, 1997), *Legally Blonde* (Robert Luketic, 2001) or *The Devil Wears Prada* (David Frankel, 2006)—in which romance (and the marriage plot) play a secondary role. Though Marisa is reunited with her paramour Chris, there is no suggestion of marriage. While the two are described as "going strong" at the film's conclusion, Marisa's newly and hard won success as a manager is equally if not more strongly emphasized, with the story of Marisa's ambitions to become a member of the managerial, as opposed to service, sector providing a significant counter-plot to the Chris/Marisa romance. Through this subplot, the film can be understood as bringing together themes from the neo-romantic comedy, the female friendship film, and a final sub-genre that might be called "women and work," the template for which is *Legally Blonde*, with *The Devil Wears Prada* offering a more recent articulation of the cycle in which men play a secondary role.

As is typical of the girly film, *Maid in Manhattan* offers a hybridized version of the classical romantic comedy, as though the genre itself were not adequate to the representation of the complexities of contemporary women's lives. The film thus ends not with the couple, but with an image of the new racially and ethnically diverse managerial class, comprised of Marisa and her fellow chambermaids, now emboldened to compete in the corporate world. Here the film both joins and departs from *Working Girl*, emphasizing Marisa's success but also her continued connection with other women. As *Working Girl* comes to a close, Tess finds herself alone in a self-contained office, one of hundreds in a corporate building, representing the isolation of the managerial class (see Figure 6.1). *Maid in Manhattan*, in contrast, with its upbeat tune and beaming working girls, seems self-consciously to recall the backstage musical of the 1930s, in which work and community combined to produce an ideal world in which each felt valued and included. While supporting the neo-feminist view of the rewards of work and career, this celebration of corporate culture has

Figure 6.1 Corporate anonymity at the conclusion of *Working Girl* (1988).

been roundly criticized by film scholars. Stephen Knadler described the film as a "jingoist pledge of allegiance to the hard working immigrant success story ... a cinematic allegory about ethnicity and assimilation in the United States for second-generation daughters." He explains that, in the film, "the all white management staff at the hotel is all too ready to embrace ... the Latina as the 'other white' in the nation's dream of integration."[28]

This "dream of integration" is reflected in discussion surrounding the election of Barack Obama, the son of an American woman of European origin and an African national, as President of the United States of America in November 2008, resonating with the ethos of self-improvement and ambition promoted by *Maid in Manhattan* with its promise of success to those determined to achieve it. American Studies scholar Gregory Smithers, commenting on Obama's memoir *Dreams from My Father*, points out that Obama couched "his personal story in a way that reflects the individualistic mythology of the 'American Dream,' the triumph, through hard-work and education, over humble origins to achieve social and economic independence." Smithers continues: "Obama's life story ... taps into the enduring image of immigrants coming to the United States and 'making it.'"[29] Steph (Marissa Matrone), a fellow chambermaid at the Beresford Hotel, explicitly evokes this same mythology on which Obama bases his successful political persona as she urges Marisa to enter the management training program, to the point of filling out her application, and encourages her by stating that "[t]hese are the golden years. We've got to prove our mothers wrong. Don't waste em"—a sentiment that speaks to the generational climate and element of female camaraderie that marks the film (see Figure 6.2).

The film's story more clearly echoes Helen Gurley Brown's Cosmo Girl ethos than does *Pretty Woman*—a man is important but a career even more so—because, as Brown commented in a 1988 television broadcast, Cosmo girls "wanted to achieve on their own."[30] The emphasis on career echoes the earlier less sentimental version of the single girl exemplified in Brown's own life. Marisa's desires to become part of a middle-management structure are modest in comparison to the "Supernova" status of Lopez herself and, as such, represent, not so much a fantasy of achievement, but the real possibility of advancement in which hard work and training play the crucial role. Marisa undergoes a rigorous education in hotel protocol under the supervision of the Beresford head butler, Lionel Bloch (Bob Hoskins), as a result of which she can come to embody the kind of European *savoir faire* that he represents. Lionel underlines for Marisa, and for the film viewer, that "class" is the prerogative of education and not birth, with perseverance being the primary ingredient. He tells her when she leaves the Beresford in disgrace that "[w]hat defines us is how well we rise after falling," echoing a time-honored Christian sentiment

Figure 6.2 Female camaraderie in *Maid in Manhattan* (2002). Courtesy of Photofest.

echoed in the biblical apothegm, "Septies enim in diem cadet justus, et resurget" (The just man falls seven times a day but rises again).[31]

Ultimately, Marisa is not educated in romance, but rather, like Elle in *Legally Blonde*, and unlike Vivian in *Pretty Woman*, her education revolves around her relationship with her self and her need to construct herself as an ethical subject—one who is capable of moral decisions, and willing to take responsibility for them. Elle chooses to be a lawyer and, in spite of the many reversals of fortune to which she is subjected, to use the "power of blondes" for good. Similarly, in *Maid in Manhattan*, a major turning point occurs when, subsequent to her failure at the Beresford, Marisa breaks with her mother, refusing to accept the compromise she proposes, which includes working as a cleaner, remaining determined to return to Manhattan in order to achieve success in the hotel business. She asserts to her mother with regards to Chris that "[i]t must really burn you that I think that I have the right to go with him." She ignores her mother's response, "you don't," by reiterating her resolve:

> I don't wanna clean houses. There's no where to go from there … I'll start over … And when I get the chance to be a manager … I'm gonna take that chance without any fear, without your voice in my head telling me that I can't.

Marisa's position is at odds with that of Lopez herself, who stated in 2003 that "[i]t constantly amazes me that somebody like me could be doing the stuff that I'm doing—I knew I could, because my mom always told me if you work hard, then you can achieve anything."[32]

This split between Marisa/Jennifer articulates the complicated relations between second-generation daughters and first-generation mothers—the conflict and the closeness as well as the importance of these relations within that cultural context. The second-generation daughter depends upon her mother (as does Marisa), but must surpass her to achieve the American dream. As in other girly films, in particular *Pretty Woman*, the father is absent—both Marisa's father and the father of Ty, her child. Family is matrilineal—as a source of strength and as a means of containment from which the protagonist must break free by means of a personal decision that must also respect the connection. Marisa is, then, careful to repeat that she does love her "Mom," but that this love will not prevent her from making her own decisions. Significantly, Marisa is a devoted mother herself. While Vivian as a prostitute in *Pretty Woman* is outside the family and the law until she is brought back into the fold, legitimated through Edward's choice of her, Marisa as a young and virtuous mother never leaves the family. Her legal status is never in jeopardy, her "borrowing" of hotel property a venal and minor infraction. Rather, she must make a certain decision about her future, a decision that was always available to her within the law and social convention, but that she had failed to recognize—that of acting on her own behalf, of becoming her own person.

Marisa's decision, the film suggests, leads to her eventual success, reiterating the philosophy of the do-over in the girly film, a second chance that this time will eventuate in the sought-after happy ending, an ending that focuses as much on the realization of her career dreams as on her romantic reunion with Chris. For this film, career may be more important than marriage. This emphasis on career and personal advancement is reiterated throughout the film. Earlier, when Lionel, who is aware of Marisa's flirtation with Chris, advises Marisa to choose between her ambition to become a manager and Chris, her fellow maids—Steph in particular—point out that the romantic fantasy endemic to the marriage plot is a myth, while the possibility of succeeding as a manager is not. Steph explains: "You are not in love with this man and he's not in love with you. You have no connections, affiliations or loyalties. You're from two different worlds." When Marisa reluctantly concurs, Leezette (Maddie Corman) attempts to comfort her: "Come on Maris'—you—you could be manager." Clarice (Sharon Wilkins) chimes in, "Think of it, girl, one of us out there." Leezette responds, "Ahh, in a blazer ... yeah." Yet, the film's conclusion, in which Marisa becomes a manager without giving up romance, undermines the film's pragmatism and reinstates the fantasy of later neo-feminism in which a woman can have it all. Nonetheless, this brief moment underlines that Marisa's night out with Chris (after which she has agreed to disappear, a modern day Cinderella) is only a fantasy. Nevertheless, this romantic fantasy commands such social power that reviewers and scholars can be forgiven for emphasizing this dimension of the film.

The film itself isolates and underlines the importance of a consumer-inflected romantic dream, represented through Marisa's Cinderella ball, a night as Chris's date at a benefit dinner held at the famous, and very chic, New York Metropolitan Museum. Steph, who orchestrates Marisa's first meeting with Chris by dressing her up in a guest's Dolce and Gabbana white coat and trousers (destined to be returned to the hotel store) (see Figure 6.3)—in which garb he understandably does not realize that she is a hotel maid—also makes possible, with the help of other hotel staff, Marisa's appearance at the fundraising dinner in order to re-enact the fantasy, to embody the dream that she herself has marked out as unrealizable. Here the film offers a hiatus, the "Happy Interlude" or "Bliss Montage" of the classical woman's film, in Jeanine Basinger's terms, in which the couple comes together for a night within the context of a consumer Green World provided by the hotel.[33] Marisa wears, on loan, a pink gown designed by Bob Mackie and a Harry Winston Wreath Diamond Necklace. Steph enjoins Marisa to enjoy her night because it is "like a dream … and for one night you're living it for all of us … Tonight, the maid is a lie. This—this is who you really are," pointing to the fact that Marisa is played by Jennifer Lopez, for whom red-carpet appearances, designer dresses and expensive jewelry are indeed her reality (see Figure 6.4).

Marisa's makeover, reprising a founding trope of the girly film, is not a transformation but an unveiling of Lopez as she is—neither a maid nor a single mother from the Bronx, but a red-carpet star. The film thus continually plays with Lopez's two identities, as Jenny-from-the-block and as "Supernova," another of her many nicknames, as a means of enacting the contradiction of her position. If *Pretty Woman* made Julia Roberts a star—and the film, indeed, in many ways recounts her transformation as a star, from being an ordinary girl at the film's beginning to a wealthy socialite at the film's conclusion—*Maid in Manhattan* tells a different story—that if a viewer saw Jennifer Lopez cleaning his or her bathroom, or walking down the street in a maid's uniform, he or she would fail to recognize her (see Figure 6.5). The film, pessimistically, suggests that the only way to emerge out of the invisibility to which Lopez's ethnicity initially relegated her is to become a star—contradicting the confidence expressed elsewhere in the film about Marisa's possibilities for advancement. The film, then, exhibits the "consistently inconsistent purpose and attitude" that Basinger claims characterizes the classical woman's film, a trait that extends to other Lopez vehicles.

Figure 6.3 Jennifer Lopez as "Marisa" in Dolce & Gabbana. Courtesy of Photofest.

Figure 6.4 Jennifer Lopez as "Marisa" in a Bob Mackie gown and "Harry Winston wreath." Courtesy of Photofest.

Figure 6.5 Jennifer Lopez as "Marisa" in her uniform. Courtesy of Photofest.

For example, in *Selena* (Gregory Nava, 1997), Lopez's character is humiliated in an expensive boutique, much as was Vivian in *Pretty Woman*; however, the saleswomen must change their attitude once they recognize that she is indeed Selena, a star—suggesting, again, how only exceptional stardom can move the Latina subject out of her initial subordinate position. Similarly, Marisa's downfall occurs because a hotel guest, Caroline (Natasha Richardson), recognized, not Marisa herself, but the Harry Winston necklace that she had borrowed for her Cinderella night. When Caroline sees Marisa slipping out of Chris's bedroom, it is again the necklace that attracts her attention, not Marisa herself. It is only by viewing Marisa on surveillance tape in her own Dolce and Gabbana coat that Caroline definitively identifies her—without ever recalling the name "Maria," with which she erroneously addressed her in their lengthy interchanges. While in the course of the film Caroline asks Marisa to purchase stockings for her and subsequently follows her fashion advice, she is unable to recognize her outside the context provided by her maid's uniform.

These moments offer a much more negative view of the melting pot ideology that the film promotes, underlining the invisibility of the groups, often illegal aliens, that support the service sector of American luxury industries such as hotel and clothing empires. In a certain sense, the film seems to suggest that a young Latina mother should aim only so high—middle-management should be her goal; to seek to live the dream is to risk the humiliation to which Marisa is subjected, brought about by the hubris that led her to "borrow" a Dolce and Gabbana coat and a Harry Winston necklace, to which, as her mother points out, she does not have "the right." Importantly, Chris himself, though he initially encounters Marisa cleaning his bathroom in his suite, does not "see" her until she dons her borrowed Dolce and Gabbana finery; for him too, at least initially, she is invisible in her maid's uniform. The film may lead us to understand that looking beyond the uniforms of his constituents constitutes a first step in his education; however, unlike Edward in *Pretty Woman*, the male role is so feeble and underdeveloped that is difficult to impute a deeper psychology to Fiennes's character. Indeed, the role of the Harry Winston necklace is at least as prominent and influential as that of Chris himself.

The highlighting of the necklace is no accident.[34] *Maid in Manhattan* is not a fashion film, signaled by the lack of a cutting-edge costumer and the relatively few fashionable garments—with the notable exception of Dolce and Gabbana, a designer often patronized by Lopez herself.[35] The pink ball gown that Marisa wears to the ball is by Bob Mackie, whose reputation is confined to the entertainment world, without extending into the universe of retail, of Dolce and Gabbana, for example. Nonetheless, the gown was widely copied, a favorite among young girls choosing a prom dress, testifying to the way in which the film created a climate favorable to consumer culture, and feminine consumer culture more particularly, in which the diamond necklace, the cause of Marisa's initial downfall, plays a significant role.[36]

In keeping with the fairy-tale dimension to Lopez's own life and her association with affluence and high-profile consumerism, the media in its discussion of *Maid in Manhattan* frequently highlighted the Harry Winston "6.1 [carat] rare pink diamond engagement ring" given to Lopez by Affleck (with a reported value of over $2 million), though she was still technically married to Chris Judd at the time.[37] The tabloids also highlighted the "Harry Winston bracelet of white and yellow diamonds" Affleck presented her earlier on the occasion of her birthday.[38] Elle, in *Legally Blonde*, lusts after a Harry Winston engagement ring, while Lauren Weisberger, the chick-lit author best known for *The Devil Wears Prada*, titles her third novel *Chasing Harry Winston*.[39] The ubiquity and status of the Winston name is the result of careful nurturing on the part of Harry, later his son, Ronald, and finally what is now known as the Harry Winston Group, often referred to as "the jeweler to the stars."

The tradition of lending diamonds to stars for red carpet events, in particular the Academy Awards, may have begun in 1943, but became a veritable policy in the 1980s as part of the firm's publicity efforts. Winston is reported to lend "each year ... a staggering $200 million worth of jewelry to celebrities."[40] Harry Winston is famously referenced in the 1953 film, *Gentlemen Prefer Blondes* (Howard Hawks), while Hollywood, generally, is attributed with promoting the diamond as a consumer item. Scholar Maura Spiegel comments that:

> if you wanted a piece of the glamour that you saw in the movies, you couldn't buy a miniature mink coat or a piece of a Rolls Royce, but you could buy a little tiny diamond or a ring with diamond chips in it and you had the real thing.[41]

Spiegel explained how the stars themselves cooperated with firms like De Beers and Harry Winston in promoting diamonds as a visible Hollywood symbol: "Stars welcomed publicity generated by their diamonds and the diamonds themselves served to confirm their glittering stardom, as well as their box office success."[42]

Lopez, both through the publicity surrounding her intimate life and through her role as Marisa, promoted the diamond industry in a tradition established in classical Hollywood, during which period this original "gem of mystery" associated with inherited power developed into "a common symbol" that denoted wealth,[43] with the result that "[b]eginning in the 1930s, jewelers began to place their diamonds in the movies, lending them to studios free of charge," with a view to increasing the visibility of their product.[44] Typically, then, Fred Joiallier provided Julia Roberts with "the ruby necklace set with diamonds," from his Rodeo Drive store, that she, as Vivian, wore to the opera. The necklace had a reported value of "$213,500" and included "14 carats of diamonds and 23.5 carats of heart-shaped rubies"[45] (see Figure 6.6). The Harry Winston Wreath appearing in *Maid in Manhattan* is part of an intensification of the phenomenon, with the almost hallucinatory repetition of the brand name during the late 1990s and early twenty-first century—evident in Lopez's own personal choices of gifts and engagement rings.

Not coincidentally, in 2000 the Harry Winston Group was looking to expand business by making stores "seem less forbidding" and by "offering jewelry priced as low as $4,000." The previous "entry point" had been "$6,000," while the average cost of a Harry Winston piece is "$100,000." The film also makes "unbranded jewelry," destined "for mass-market retailers like J.C. Penny Company, which are not allowed to disclose the origin of the items," constituting "about 20 percent of the company's business."[46] The success of Harry Winston Group's strategy can been seen in the fact that the wedding industry, and the sale of Harry Winston diamond engagement rings, have been reported as remaining relatively unaffected by the economic crises of 2008 and 2009.[47]

Harry Winston is an example of product placement within *Maid in Manhattan* that demonstrates how, through the repetition of a brand name (Harry Winston) associated with a particular product (jewelry, and by extension the diamond engagement ring), neo-feminist cinema supports the reproduction of the neo-feminist paradigm in which femininity is defined through the accumulation of a set of fashionable items. An important dimension of neo-feminist cinema, then, is the circulation of talismanic consumer culture objects within a variety of interlocking discourses and media environments, in which the narratives that the media produce about the stars of a particular film are as significant as the plots of the films themselves. It is probably appropriate to conclude a discussion of *Maid in Manhattan* with the Harry Winston Wreath because it highlights how despite the film's emphasis on a feminine work ethic of self-discipline and independence and on family, and female friendship, and even its ethnic star and protagonist, it cannot escape its fundamental role as the purveyor of feminine consumer culture and the articulation of feminine desire and ambitions in terms of the acquisition of consumer items in a price range appropriate to the subject's income. The film encourages female viewers, who constituted 60 percent of the film's audience, to aspire to a diamond, perhaps a Harry Winston diamond, or failing that, a J.C. Penny equivalent, as the mark of her success.[48] The film's function as a "shop window" for its viewers reaches frenzied proportions that will continue to intensify in subsequent girly films, in which the emphasis on consumer culture is so self-evident that they are often referred to as "fashion

Figure 6.6 Vivian's necklace. Courtesy of Photofest.

films"—films such as *The Devil Wears Prada* and *Sex and the City: The Movie* (Michael Patrick King, 2008).[49] Finally, then, neo-feminist cinema is a proponent of a system of feminine culture and a feminine ideal in which differences in "race" can be accommodated through the acquisition of appropriate consumer culture items, which then become the arbitrators of status in a system of privilege that depends solely upon a subject's individual economic achievement. The next chapter will investigate the development of the event film for women, and the fashion film more specifically, as particularly dense expressions of the neo-feminist paradigm and the intensifications of its ties with consumer culture.

Chapter 7

Hit Movies for "Femmes"

Chick Flicks and Chick Lit

Maid in Manhattan (Wayne Wang, 2002) offered a means by which to explore the ways in which the narrative model and box office success of *Pretty Woman* (Garry Marshall, 1990) could be rewritten to incorporate a "raced" and "ethnic" subject. The film, with a worldwide box office gross of $154,906,693 and a budget of $55 million, was a success within its genre, though hardly equaling the earlier *Pretty Woman*, which had a worldwide box office gross of $463,406,268 and a budget of $14 million. In contrast, a film like *Something New* (Sanaa Hamri, 2006) that deals with inter-racial relationships, in spite of largely positive reviews, as well as two charismatic if less well-known stars, Sanaa Lathan and Simon Baker, had a dismal worldwide gross of $11,468,568, pointing not only to the importance of Lopez's already established fan base to *Maid in Manhattan*'s success, but also to the relative difficulties of managing race within the context of popular cinema. For example, *I Think I Love My Wife* (Chris Rock, 2007), a remake of the French 1970s classic *Chloë in the Afternoon* (Eric Rohmer, 1972) featuring a largely African-American cast, earned only $13,196,245 worldwide at the box office in spite of the fact that Chris Rock, the star and director of the film, enjoyed an international reputation as a television personality.

Both *Something New* and *I Think I Love My Wife* have in common female characters who exemplify the neo-feminist paradigm, indicating the pervasiveness of its influence, while underlining the dominance—at the box office in any case—of the "white" ideal. Like the aging woman, the woman of color must be exceptional, perhaps even a star, to enjoy the full fruits of neo-feminism and serve as the subject for a successful girly film.[1] Nonetheless, it is important to recognize that the paucity of older heroines and of ethnically and racially diverse heroines cannot be attributed to the neo-feminist paradigm itself, as films like *Maid in Manhattan* or *Something's Gotta Give* (Nancy Meyers, 2003) demonstrate. Rather, it is in part a function of what Thomas Schatz calls "Conglomerate Hollywood," dominated by "a half-dozen global media superpowers."[2]

A consequence of the development of Conglomerate Hollywood in the 1980s was the subsequent "rapid development of three distinct film industry sectors dominated by three different classes of producers—the traditional major studios, the conglomerate-owned indie divisions and the genuine independents—which generate three very different classes of movie product."[3] Most girly films fall into the second category, though these categories themselves are not as distinct as they might initially appear. *Maid in Manhattan* was produced by Revolution Studios, technically an "independent," described by Joe Roth, its co-founder, as "a little boutique making little movies trying to make a profit";[4] Revolution Studios films are, however, distributed by Sony/Columbia, one of "the so-called Big Six media conglomerates," and, as such, should hardly be considered "independent."[5] The media conglomerate industry structure is "hit-driven," meaning that it depends upon large scale blockbusters, known as "tentpoles" ("the top two or three runaway hits that generate most of the studios revenues and thus prop up the entire studio operation"[6]), often franchises, such as *Dark Knight* (Christopher Nolan, 2008), which earned over one billion worldwide at the box office; however, Conglomerate Hollywood also produces counterprogramming, films that would appeal to that segment of the audience typically not attracted to the male-oriented "tentpole" films, such as *Sex and the City: The Movie* (Michael Patrick King, 2008), which, though ranked number 11 in terms of domestic box office return in 2008, earned only $152,647,258, compared with *Dark Knight*'s $533,345,358 at number one. The ideal film—such as *Titanic* (James Cameron, 1997), with its $1,842,879,955 box office gross worldwide, attracts all four audience quadrants: males under 25, males over 25, females under 25, females over 25—is a movie that "plays across all sectors: young, old, male, female, US and international";[7] however, *Pretty Woman*, with its unprecedented (for a romantic comedy) foreign box office success provided a formula that would predominate among a specific type of counterprogramming films that address the female audience, or "female-demo films," in the words of *Variety*. Such films primarily target only two quadrants, females under 25 and females over 25, with their development and content being designed to allay any fear that only one of these quadrants will respond to any given film.[8]

The conglomerates, as their influence and power consolidated over the 1990s, as well as the tag-along independent studios like Revolution, sought to develop strategies that would enable their films to reach an audience whose tastes could easily be predicted, one that could be relied upon to take up a certain film, which often meant a film that had an already established fan base, whether through its star, its genre or its relations to previously successful material circulated through other media forms. In 2003, the co-head of United Talent Agency Book Department asserted, explaining why "Hollywood is drawn to the more commercial, femme pop-boilers": "The bottom line is easier to envision with a female crowd. That demographic is known."[9] Accordingly, the media conglomerates, ever risk adverse, increasingly sought from the 1990s to mobilize that known demographic with its important disposable income, still by and large white—to the disadvantage of groups less well-represented demographically in terms of numbers or disposable income. Crossover films that can reach the broader known audience through an already established crossover media phenomenon—perhaps a novel, music or, more commonly, a star with a following within a specific group but whose popularity crosses over into more mainstream audiences—might provide occasional instances of diversity, as was the case with *Waiting to Exhale* (Forest Whitaker, 1995) with a worldwide box office gross of $81,452,156, or, more recently, *Dreamgirls* (Bill Condon, 2006) at $154,937,680 worldwide, as well as the significantly less successful *Joy Luck Club* (1993) and *Maid in Manhattan* (as discussed in the previous chapter), both directed by Wayne Wang, all of which did less well in their categories than their "whiter" counterparts.

The desire to minimize risk—notably for the girly film—encourages the adaptation of popular novels for women in the hope that the film will appeal to an already established group, and perhaps increase sales of the original novel at the same time. *Legally Blonde* (Robert Luketic, 2001), for example, was based on a novel of the same name, self-published by Amanda Brown in 2001, and republished in 2003 (the book was optioned before it was published). The movie itself, *Legally Blonde*, spawned two movie sequels (one in 2009 that went straight to DVD), a *Legally Blonde* Barbie doll, a Broadway musical and the "Legally Elle Woods" book series for young adults by Natalie Sandiford—illustrating the cross-media scope of the successful girly film.[10]

Often novels solicited for adaptation with a view to targeting a female demographic fall into the category of what is popularly called "chick lit," and are clear expressions of the neo-feminist paradigm, though to varying degrees.[11] A groundbreaking example of this kind of synergy is *Bridget Jones's Diary* (Sharon Maguire, 2001), based on the 1996 novel by Helen Fielding, also credited with inaugurating "chick lit" as a specific literary genre. Though the tradition of popular fiction for women has a long history, going as far back as the eighteenth century, "chick lit" represented a significant development in the area at the end of the twentieth century.[12] Owing a great deal to the "bonk busters" of the 1980s as well as the popular format romance of the 1970s and 1980s, "chick lit" distinguishes itself from previous popular fiction because of the way that it testifies to the power of the "female demo" within the world of publishing. Like the woman's film of classical Hollywood as defined by Jeanine Basinger, the novels draw upon an number of generic conventions, but have in common a female heroine or group of heroines that are at the center of their universe, in which their experiences and problems are their and the novel's primary preoccupations.

Kathy Lette's *How to Kill Your Husband (And Other Handy Household Hints)*, for example, revolves around the problems of three married women in their early forties, while also incorporating a detective/thriller strand to the narrative, with one of the friends accused of murdering her husband.[13] While two will end their marriages, the third, the organizing sensibility of the novel, will resolve her difficulties with her husband, providing the happy ending characteristic of "chick lit." Though the novel is in many ways a parody, illustrating the hybrid nature of "chick lit" in general, the heroine's problems as a working woman (she is a primary school teacher and her husband is a vet) are treated with a greater degree of seriousness than those of her wealthier friends. Friendship, marriage and children take center stage, with the murder providing an amusing subplot; consumer culture and fashion, though mentioned in passing, are not significant motivating themes.

In contrast, *Handbags and Gladrags* by Maggie Alderson, though including the theme of friendship, focuses more clearly on the romantic problems of a single heroine who works in the fashion industry as a "fashion editor" at a fictitious fashion magazine, *Chic*. The novel, again a first-person narrative,[14] inserts the names of well-known designer labels and fashion figures at every opportunity, reveling in lengthy descriptions of the heroine's workout strategies, of the correct way to wash a "TSE cashmere cardigan," and other routines in a young fashion editor's life, while remaining much more reticent about the details of the heroine's sexual exploits: "I don't want to go on about the sex in detail, because it would just sound yuck and it was so, well, beautiful really."[15] *How to Kill Your Husband* was more forthright, with the heroine's sexual problems garnering significant attention.

As "chick lit," both novels have in common—unlike other genres directed at women readers, such as format romances—an ironic, self-deprecating tone, that scholars like Whelehan see as distinctive to the form, claiming that "self-deprecating humor has taken over as the dominant register."[16] In spite of variations in style and topic within "chick lit," exemplified by the two novels above, there is a general sense that the popularity of *Bridget Jones's Diary* and the subsequent sequels and movie adaptation served to confirm the commercial viability of material directed at women. Within the realm of fiction publications this conviction has inspired a renaissance of novel writing for and by women. For most popular culture scholars, Bridget as the heroine of the novels and films constitutes, rightly or wrongly, the defining figure of the new "chick-lit" generation.

Bridget, characterized by constant self-deprecation, represents what is commonly referred to as the Singleton in British culture (as opposed to the enthusiastic and optimistic Cosmo Girl). She is motivated solely by her own self-interest, and in many ways actively rejects feminism. Considered a contemporary version of a Jane Austen marriage plot, the novel in the form of a diary and the film recount the various perambulation of Bridget's unimpressive career and, perhaps more importantly, her disastrous romantic attachments, concluding with her rescue by a suitable man. Indeed, Imelda Whelehan in her study of best sellers for women sees the heroine of British "chick lit," represented by Bridget Jones, as expressing the sentiments of a younger generation of women who view "femininity as something essential to them under threat by feminism."[17]

While the film earned \$280 million worldwide, its domestic gross was only \$71,543,427. The sequel, *Bridget Jones: The Edge of Reason* (Beeban Kidron, 2004), exhibits a similar split—\$40 million domestic, \$262,520,724 worldwide—suggesting the way in which the films and the novels, though circulating extensively within an international market, represent a British rather than an American articulation of the neo-feminist paradigm. As a point of comparison, *Pretty Woman* earned \$178,406,268 domestically, more than twice as much as the first Bridget film, and over four times as much as the second, with a worldwide box office gross of \$463,406,268, over \$180 million more than the first Bridget film and \$200 million more than the second, largely because of its superior domestic performance. Notwithstanding, the Bridget films were successes in their category, and serve to refine the formula that would increasingly drive the women's film—if not in terms of the characteristics of the heroine herself, at the very least in terms of the industry context that the films created.

In particular, the Bridget films illustrate the move towards "the female event film," in which the release of the film, independent of its qualities as cinema, garners significant media attention because it is an adaptation of an already popular novel, part of a series, based on a historically successful television series, the vehicle for a charismatic star, the re-enactment of a controversial political event, etc. In 2008, screendaily.com explained:

> Just having a good movie isn't enough, of course—a project needs to have that huge "want-to-see" factor to drive up mega box-office. That can be spurred by established brand awareness from past films, books or graphic novels; a must-see news angle; an A-list cast; or when the stars align, all of the above.[18]

President of Paramount Pictures International, Andrew Cripps, elaborated: "You've got to have some form of pre-established awareness to get huge box-office success."[19] The event film model, largely associated with tentpoles, also provided a production pattern—though on a smaller scale—that becomes typical of films for women in which the media conglomerates play a crucial role.

Bridget Jones's Diary, as the adaptation of an already popular model and the vehicle for an established star, Renée Zellweger, demonstrated the potency of this model. *Bridget Jones's Diary* was produced by the European companies Canal+ and Working Title, but distributed by Miramax (owned by Disney), and Universal (owned by General Electric)—members of the "Big Six." In terms of content, however, *Bridget Jones's Diary* distinguishes itself from the dominant American girly film in two ways. The first difference is that its heroine, Bridget, is not a "striver"—or rather, as much as she might wish to be a striver, she is incompetent, lacks judgment and is a compulsive liar, traits that she shares with other chick-lit heroines, such as the British Becky Bloomwood of the extremely successful Shopaholic series created by Sophie Kinsella, also the basis for a film, *Confessions of a Shopaholic* (P.J. Hogan, 2009). If the term "striver" is often used today to describe the ambitious and effective young woman, Becky and Bridget are "stumblers," comic figures whose mishaps elicit the reader's and viewer's sympathy rather than admiration. Whelehan explains that "the chick lit heroine is sometimes too anxious to make simple decisions and seems instead to celebrate instances in which she fails, as well as resignedly suggesting that character flaws are a part of one's unchangeable personal make-up."[20]

Though Bridget may in some ways recall Romy and Michele, the latter redeemed themselves through their undeniable competence in the arts of fashion, their admirable physique and sense of style, the generosity of heart that motivates their friendship and, finally, their capacity to choose joyfully the noble position of woman alone rather than accept the compromises of marriage as defined by the film. In contrast, Renée Zellweger, who plays Bridget in both films, was widely portrayed as having to put on weight and "dress down" in order to incarnate the inadequate Bridget, who was as homely as a film star is allowed to be outside independent films such as *Monster* (Patty Jenkins, 2003), in which Charlize Theron was also famously required to "fatten up" in order to play the serial killer, Aileen Wuornos (see Figures 7.1 and 7.2).[21] In addition to her failure to conform to the ideals of grooming and body-type incarnated by the Cosmo Girl, Bridget exhibits an unbelievable level of general incompetence, another trait that she shares with Wuornos as depicted by Theron. But unlike Aileen Wuornos, Bridget Jones is ultimately rewarded for her ineptitude and general lack of capacity; she is "saved" by a supremely accomplished and patient man, whose devotion cannot be explained in rational terms, and who embodies the romantic mythology of the perfect husband—a fantasy soundly criticized by Helen Gurley Brown.

Comparing Theron's portrayal of Aileen Wuornos with Renée Zellweger's Bridget may seem incongruous; however, I wish to underline the utterly

Figure 7.1 Renée Zellweger in *Bridget Jones's Diary* (2001). Courtesy of Photofest.

Figure 7.2 Charlize Theron (right) in *Monster* (2003). Courtesy of Photofest.

fantastic nature of the film's (and the novel's) resolution, and the degree to which Bridget represents a persona that challenges the conventional heroine of the girly film, to the extent that she has more in common with the unhappy Wuornos, a tragic "stumbler," than with the typical neo-feminist protagonist, from Vivian to Marisa. In contrast with Romy and Michele, who ultimately choose work and self-sufficiency over marriage, Bridget and Becky, who is also saved by an inexplicably devoted man, exemplify, in the words of film and literature scholar Suzanne Ferriss, "contemporary women's renewed desire to be rescued by men from the complications of life as an independent woman."[22] Neither Bridget nor Becky subscribe to an ethos in which self-fulfillment is found through work; rather, they seek immediate and direct self-gratification as the most important motivation for their actions, their selfishness softened by genial good nature and a servile desire to please.

The second difference from the American girly film is that the Bridget books and films (here, Fielding's series distinguishes itself from Kinsella's) do not emphasize the consumer culture dimension of the neo-feminist paradigm to the same degree. Though Bridget aspires to the standards of grooming and dress dictated by Helen Gurley Brown—for Whelehan, she is "governed by the schizophrenic edicts of glossy magazines and trend watchers"[23]—she has neither the discipline nor the financial assets to reproduce these consumer culture ideals—in other words, to undertake the intensive work required to transform a "mouseburger" into a "glamour puss," in Helen Gurley Brown's terms.[24] Similarly, if in the third volume, *Shopaholic Ties the Knot*,[25] consumer culture ultimately provides Kinsella's Becky with gainful employment as a personal shopper in the high-end department store, Barneys (also featured in *Maid in Manhattan*, as well as the television series, *Sex and the City*), it is also the source of her worst humiliations, largely involving her tendency to overspend and lie as though she were caught in an uncontrollable addiction. Here, consumer culture does not provide a safe haven but is fraught with dangers and difficulties as well as pleasure.

Within the neo-feminist paradigm, though shopping and consumer culture are a source of gratification as well as providing the instruments with which to perform the labor of self-development, they are rarely dangerous. If personnel in the form of shop attendants are not always as attentive as might be desirable (as was the case most notably in *Pretty Woman*), and may even be hostile, the neo-feminist heroine will inevitably triumph, proving her competence as a woman of means and discerning taste, as well as her ethical superiority revealed in her ability to overcome social prejudice. The successful girly heroine within Hollywood, then, mobilizes the lineaments of the American dream within the context of feminine consumer culture and thus distinguishes herself from the failed and flawed heroines that populate many "chick lit" novels, in particular those associated with British Singleton culture.

A number of feminist scholars see a connection between the British Singleton prototype and American television characters such as Ally McBeal (Calista Flockhart) on *Ally McBeal* (Fox, 1997–2002). While McBeal, a single working woman who battles bad relationships and her ticking biological clock, does exhibit the kind of anxiety that Whelehan attributes to the chick-lit heroine, she is also a capable and effective professional, in many ways excelling in her role as a lawyer, in spite of her "anxieties."[26] In general, there is a tendency to view the heroines of *Bridget Jones's Diary*, *Ally McBeal* and *Sex and the City* (in its various media incarnations) as being, in Whelehan's words, "the most eminent singleton triumvirate,"[27] without paying sufficient attention to the distinctiveness with which each articulates the predicament of the contemporary single woman, and to the heterogeneity of chick lit itself beyond the three figures of Bridget, Ally and Carrie. Similarly, feminist media scholar Diane Negra states that "[a]lthough Bridget Jones was the most high-profile and perhaps the pioneering figure of the new pathetic single woman, the specter of singlehood abounds in print, film and broadcast media," suggesting a return to a pre-Helen Gurley Brown version of female singleness.[28] In contradistinction, the Hollywood girly film offers, as a rule, a very different image of the contemporary single woman, one that owes more to the continuing tradition of the Cosmo Girl than to that inaugurated by Helen Fielding, in which whatever anxieties she may feel are expressed through brash achievement and a perfectly toned and garbed body.[29]

While the girly heroine may face set backs and disappointments, these are also the means of the education that she undergoes, which will ultimately enable her to persevere in the face of adversity. Wendy Healy, one of the three heroines of *Lipstick Jungle* by Candace Bushnell (who as the author of the original *Sex and the City* is also credited, alongside Fielding, with inaugurating "chick lit" as a popular trend) states at the novel's conclusion that "it's so easy to solve your problems when you're a successful woman and you have your own money."[30] Wendy's education emphasizes self-reliance, with all three heroines of the novel, including the inveterate single girl, Victory Ford, portraying a very different vision of the "chick lit" protagonist than does *Bridget Jones's Diary*. In particular, Wendy, a successful film producer, represents the new working mother who realizes that "I can do this. I *do* do this. ... This *is* me. I have my career, and I have my kids. And I want them both. I need them both ... I just decided that I wasn't going to feel guilty."[31]

The complexities of "chick lit," which incorporates the "Singleton," the "Yummy Mummy" and the "Older Bird," while manifesting clear national inflections, suggest that it is difficult to pinpoint a single prototype that would represent the ideals of the genre; the genre's cohesion derives, rather, from the fact that the books are both written and read by a group that is assumed to be uniformly female, constituting the "female demo." In contrast, the heroine of the successful girly film offers a more coherent set of attributes that serve to assist her in achieving a feminine version of the American dream that, arguably, may have a broader appeal than the British Singleton, at least within the United States. The Hollywood girly film, then, departs from the pattern set by chick lit through the Bridget books that in many ways might be seen as a reaction against the neo-feminist paradigm as well as feminism itself. Whelehan recalls:

> Helen Gurley Brown had promised success through utter self-discipline; and as if in reaction to the unattractiveness of this, chick litters respond by celebrating a clutch of women who consistently fail to achieve the aims they set themselves and lack any kind of discipline at all.[32]

In contrast, girly films celebrate the neo-feminist paradigm articulated by Brown, while smoothing over some of her harsher edicts, such as the need for self-denial or the dangers of waiting for a prince charming. For Brown, marriage, like glamor and employment, can only be achieved through strategic investment and dedication. Girly heroines are able to achieve their goals through perseverance and discipline—a discipline that involves the body, grooming and clothing as well as the more traditional areas of education and training.[33] As Whelehan explains, Helen Gurley Brown offered "a regime rather than a lifestyle, requiring dedication and endless self-sacrifice because discipline in matters of diet, exercise, social stratagems, and even interior design and style, are all equally important" to the success of the Cosmo Girl.[34]

Indie Films for the Female Demo: *My Big Fat Greek Wedding* (Joel Zwick, 2002) and *Mamma Mia!* (Phyllida Lloyd, 2008)

Not all films directed at woman are girly films, strictly speaking, nor do they all emerge out of the practices encouraged by Conglomerate Hollywood. It is difficult, nevertheless, to find examples of successful "female-demo" cinema that do not bear the marks of the neo-feminist paradigm or the strategies of the "Big Six." Films that seem to deviate from the norm, such as *My Big Fat Greek Wedding* and *Mamma Mia!*, both produced by Tom Hanks's Playtone Pictures, in fact have more in common with productions like *Maid in Manhattan* than might first meet the eye. *My Big Fat Greek Wedding*, "the most successful independent film of all time," according to the *Wall Street Journal*,[35] does in many ways invoke the neo-feminist paradigm by offering a homely heroine who improves her job skills, and, moving from waitress to travel agent, undergoes a mild makeover that serves not so much to change her into the skinny fashion adept advocated by Brown, as to transform her into an ordinary American girl, erasing her immigrant Greek status; in so doing, she is able to find a husband and a rewarding life that includes work, love and family, thereby achieving the American dream that lies at the heart of *Maid in Manhattan*, but without the intense emphasis on consumer culture that Lopez brought to this film.

Nonetheless, the press was quick to point out the conventional nature of the film's story. In the *Village Voice*, Leslie Camhi commented that, with regard to the film's concluding couple, "it's hard to see their marriage as a victory for feminist ideals of self-realization."[36] David Denby in *The New Yorker* complained, "*Wedding* is not all that different from a sitcom." Mike Goodridge remarked in *Screen International* that the film "is a crowd-pleasing romantic comedy which has more in common with *Pretty Woman* than *Sex, Lies, and Videotape*."[37] Colin Brown, editor-in-chief of the same publication, opined that "this is not a true independent film at all but a small-budget film masquerading as an old-fashion film that plays to the general populace"[38] (see Figure 7.3).

While the star, Nia Vardalos, developed the screenplay on the basis of a one-woman theatrical performance, Hollywood insiders, the mega-star Tom Hanks and his wife Rita Wilson, initiated the film project. Wilson, who is of Greek origin, saw Vardalos perform and recommended her to her husband. Without the tenacity and vision of Vardalos, there would have been no film; however, the profile and experience that Hanks brought as a producer and a star were also essential.[39] In this sense, in terms of its production process, the film, through Hanks, was already part of Conglomerate Hollywood, which relies heavily on stars such as Hanks to put together profitable "packages" such as *My Big Fat Greek Wedding*.

Considered the most successful independent film to date, *My Big Fat Greek Wedding* achieved a domestic box office gross of $241,438,208 (number three in 2003 among domestic grosses) and $368,744,044 worldwide, significantly more than both Bridget films; however, *Screen International*, commenting on the film's achievement, noted that "it's a 'freak hand' that results in success,"[40] and that the film's "box office performance defies logic and tradition."[41] Assessments of this nature underline the anomaly represented by the film, which cost $5 million, with a marketing budget of reportedly "around 30 million."[42] Tom King in the *Wall Street Journal* "credits the movie's unusual staying power to an old-fashioned 30-city road show in which the star, Nia Vardalos, and John Corbett … hit places like San Antonio and St. Louis to talk up the film to local radio talks shows and papers."[43] The film's slow-release distribution strategy—in opposition to the saturation release employed routinely for

Figure 7.3 Nia Vardalos in *My Big Fat Greek Wedding* (2002), "an old fashioned film."
Courtesy of Photofest.

tentpole films—which relied heavily on word-of-mouth, was engineered by Bob Berney of IFC (the film failed to find a "Big Six" distributor). Berney is also credited with the successful US releases of other independent films such as *Whale Rider* (Niki Caro, 2003) and *Y Tu Mamá También* (Alfonso Cuarón, 2002). A marketing consultant, Paula Silver devised a "grassroots campaign" that targeted Greek-American communities.[44] Thus, if the nature of the film's story and its production were not entirely at odds with Conglomerate Hollywood, its distribution and marketing strategies placed it within the independent category.

Mamma Mia!, based on an already widely profitable stage musical, which recounts the story of an aging single mother and her daughter, concluding with a double wedding, was another singular "counterprogramming success story,"[45] the result of the passionate commitment necessary to the creation of a "hit movie" that does not follow Hollywood tentpole norms on the part of three women: Phyllida Lloyd (director), Catherine Johnson (writer) and Judy Craymor (producer); however, it also illustrates the trend in twenty-first-century independent production described by media historian, Thomas Schatz, in which "indies" are increasingly

> more "commercial" as they're more closely aligned with and effectively controlled by (at least in terms of financing and distribution) the majors. So-called indie films now require stars, name directors, and a clear genre hook—which means they look more and more like mainstream studio films.[46]

Variety described the film as "the most successful movie musical in history," "the #1 film of all time in the UK," accompanied by "Universal music's biggest selling album of 2008."[47]

Critics were less glowing. Some accepted the film as light fare; others were less generous. "*Mamma Mia!* is a (Shirley) valentine to 50-something-we're-not-done-yet broads," proclaimed Ella Taylor in *LA Weekly*.[48] Andy Klein, in *LA City Beat*, remarked, "But once again we have a movie that seems so designed for a certain demographic that it excludes everyone else (by which I mean: me)."[49] The *LA Times* was quick to exploit this demographic by offering instructions on how to reproduce the "design ideas" behind *Mamma Mia!* through judicious purchasing of products carried by national conglomerates like Crate & Barrel and Pottery Barn, underlining the consumer culture base of even the most innocuous films.[50]

Mamma Mia!, though technically a UK film, was also produced by Tom Hanks, again with the support of his wife and partner, Rita Wilson, but distributed by Universal, one of the Big Six. This double success from Hanks (both *My Big Fat Greek Wedding* and *Mamma Mia!*) highlights, yet again, the ways in which Conglomerate Hollywood uses industry figures such as Tom Hanks to provide counterprogramming to studio-produced tentpoles. Based on a long running musical that debuted 10 years earlier in London's West End, in addition to featuring stars such as Meryl Streep, Pierce Brosnan and Amanda Seyfried, the film drew on an existing fan base (the stage version was seen by over 30 million people), both in terms of the musical itself and the songs of the 1970s Swedish pop group ABBA.[51] It grossed $144,130,063 at the domestic box office and $609,711,574 worldwide, outperforming in the international arena all girly films discussed to date, while significantly under-performing at the domestic box office in comparison with *Pretty Woman*, *Sex and the City: The Movie* and *What Women Want* (Nancy Meyers, 2000). The film's performance points again to a split between the international and American audiences in terms of taste, with American preferences often setting the Hollywood production agenda, in spite of the increasing financial impor-tance of the international market.

Mamma Mia!, a weakly plotted film, takes place on a Greek island and revolves around a young woman's wedding, an occasion that spurs her to find the father she has never known and in so doing reunite her mother, the film's central protagonist, with that same man. The film concludes in a Shakespear-ean manner with all couples suitably paired, incorporating many attributes of the girly film: the happy ending depends on viewers' belief in "the do-over" and "the second chance," with protagonist Donna Sheridan (Meryl Streep) married to the father of her now adult daughter after a 20-year hiatus; chastity is discarded as an outmoded virtue without impeding the film's celebration of marriage and conventional heterosexual relationships; female friendship plays a significant role for both mother and daughter. Like the girly film more gen-erally, the film presents independent, energetic and resourceful heroines, in this case two—one who has raised a daughter on her own, and manages to triumph against all odds to achieve her happy ending, and another capable of engineering a suitable wedding for both herself and her mother, and in so doing providing herself with both a husband and a father.

Within the film, however, consumer culture is not underlined as necessary to a woman's success; indeed Meryl Streep's Donna, clad in overalls with lank blonde hair flopping around her shoulders, recalling an aging California hippie escaped from the Haight, seems to promote a very different image of ideal femininity, one that does not prevent her union with Sam Carmichael (Pierce Brosnan) at the film's conclusion (see Figure 7.4). If the film serves to bring the wayward independent woman back in line, safely married, it also offers, more optimistically, a vision of a woman who has it all—independence, daughter and finally husband—without the kinds of compromises advocated by

Figure 7.4 Meryl Streep in *Mamma Mia!* (2008). Courtesy of Photofest.

Helen Gurley Brown. In this sense, the film departs, as did *My Big Fat Greek Wedding*, from the neo-feminist paradigm, though it seems unable to escape its influence.

I have spent some time discussing these two films, *My Big Fat Greek Wedding* and *Mamma Mia!* because, as highly successful films that address a largely female audience, they appear to offer alternatives to the girly film; however, as I have shown, a closer examination of both films demonstrates that, while not girly films, the films' premises and narratives have strong connections to the neo-feminist paradigm and, as such, do not constitute significant counter-examples. Both films also illustrate the ways in which Conglomerate Hollywood encourages independent films that will occupy a particular slot and will bring in a return that attempts to reach the standard set by *Pretty Woman* through targeting a "known demographic," often by relying on conventional stories and on already established fan bases.

In her 2000 study of what she calls "feminist Hollywood," Christina Lane concludes that 1990s independent cinema provided counterprogramming to the media conglomerates, and as such created opportunities for women directors making films for women. She claimed that even after the studios became increasingly implicated in counterprogramming production by purchasing independent studios such as Miramax (now owned by Disney), "heightened studio involvement stood as evidence that films bucking conventional formulas and including aesthetically jarring visuals, even films that contain politically leftist themes, were commercially viable."[52] Yet, *The Piano* (1993), the top box office film of highly acclaimed woman director Jane Campion, grossed only $40,157,856 domestically, almost $140 million less than *Pretty Woman*, which demonstrates the superior financial viability of conventional over unconventional narrative in providing counterprogramming, from a studio's commercially driven perspective. This discrepancy in performance between a highly acclaimed film by a woman auteur director, widely held to be a box office success in its category, and *Pretty Woman* points to why Conglomerate Hollywood increasingly emphasizes the girly formula, and by extension the neo-feminist paradigm, when producing films directed at the female audience.

In the same vein, this brief analysis demonstrates that targeting the "female-demo," using *Pretty Woman* as a narrative model, will privilege films that highlight an established and glamorous star, preferably with a high-fashion profile, that have established fan bases and obvious consumer-culture tie-ins, and that generally create a context that is favorable to consumer practices ranging from a potential buy-through market for DVD release to product placement; however, the range of films available to the female audience is further reduced by the conglomerates' acknowledged reluctance to deviate from its blockbuster standards. In spite of the kinds of successes represented by the films discussed above, the "Big Six" under the current Hollywood production system remain disinclined to produce what is referred to as "femme fare," because of the concern that films directed at the female audience will reach only one quadrant. In a 2008 article, *Variety* quoted Alan Horn, then president and chief operating officer for Warner Brothers, one of the Big Six, as asserting that "every studio wants to do the same thing—get as many quadrants as possible." *Variety* explained, "The knock on chick flicks is that they might not cross over to men, who have been known to avoid female-centered titles."[53] The consensus is that females will typically follow males to the movie theaters. America's pre-eminent actress, Meryl Streep explained. "When you're in high school you go to the movies that the boy wants to see and that hasn't changed. When they say, 'oh, but the women pick,' women pick because they pick what he wants to see. They're not stupid."[54]

The fact that "from 2002 to 2007, Hollywood's top ten releases averaged an astounding 25.6 percent share domestically and a 25.5 percent market share worldwide" explains why the producers of women's films will continue to struggle;[55] even the most successful women's films of 2008, including, for example, the unusually profitable (by femme fare standards) *Sex and the City: The Movie* and *Mamma Mia!*, were not in the top 10 domestically and thus garnered a significantly lesser share of the market than the higher budget but much higher grossing films targeted at males under 25 and over 25, including family films like *Kung Fu Panda* (Mark Osborne and John Stevenson, 2008) at number six, and *Dr. Seuss' Horton Hears a Who!* (Jimmy Hayward and Steven Marino, 2008) at number 10. Thomas Schatz, a media historian, judges that:

> The conglomerate-controlled industry is all about tentpoles for young males … and in trying to control the indie sector, about which the major studios are fundamentally clueless, they've [the major studios] been systematically stifling any semblance of independent filmmaking—including "specialty films" for specific segments that are "outside" their purview (including the fairly large segments of "girls" and "women"). There has been no systematic cultivation of these segments, but the occasional hit has certainly caught the studios' attention.[56]

The feeling that films for women, and women in general, are disadvantaged in Hollywood is supported by statements such as the notorious October 2007 proclamation by then president of production for Warner Brothers, Jeff Robinov, that "[w]e are no longer doing movies with women in the lead," posted by Hollywood insider, Nikki Finke, on her widely read blog, *Deadline Hollywood Daily*.[57] Whether true or not (Finke is known for her honesty, if not her tact), the controversy generated by the posting indicates that treatment of women, women stars and women's films remains an issue in Hollywood.[58]

It is within this context that I wish to consider two extremely successful films directed at women: *The Devil Wears Prada* (David Frankel, 2006), and *Sex and the City: The Movie*, both of which illustrate the difficulties confronting films for the female demo and the ways in which these difficulties encourage the production of films that offer a variant on the neo-feminist paradigm, in particular the fashion film, of which both are an example.

Chapter 8

The Devil Wears Prada (2006)
The Fashion Film

In the previous chapters I argue that *Pretty Woman* (Garry Marshall, 1990), while mobilizing a sentimentalized version of the neo-feminist paradigm, offered a narrative format that would prove influential in the subsequent decades in which a striver heroine, as well as romance, female friendship and consumer culture, are important elements. As Marshall remarked in 2000, reflecting on the film's release, "Back then the general opinion was that no romantic comedy could make it internationally because they only wanted action."[1] *Pretty Woman* proved the economic viability of the woman's film within an international arena; however, as the previous chapter argued, the subsequent success of films like *Bridget Jones's Diary* (Sharon Maguire, 2001) suggested the desirability of producing films with a "want-to-see factor" or "some form of pre-established awareness"[2]—films that I have called the female-oriented event film. *The Devil Wears Prada* (David Frankel, 2006) illustrates this trend: based on a successful novel, it also exploits the tendency exhibited in films like *Romy and Michele's High School Reunion* (David Mirkin, 1997) and *Legally Blonde* (Robert Luketic, 2001) to highlight contemporary fashion as "another character in the movie,"[3] giving rise to the term "the fashion film," or "fashion flicks."[4]

While the connection between film and fashion is of long standing, dating back to classical Hollywood studios, the tendency was, with a few notable exceptions, to eschew haute couture in order to devise more approachable versions of French designs that would be attractive to the American audience, produced by their own personnel.[5] Shifts in the post-World War II fashion industry resulted in the reformulation of haute couture houses such as Christian Dior as advertising vehicles for ready-to-wear, mass-manufactured lines, which became the core business of fashion. As a result, the fashion industries were eager to advertise their creations to the masses, increasingly their primary clients.[6] In the post-World War II years, high fashion designers, happy for the exposure, often collaborated with the costumer for a film, who tended, increasingly, not to produce original designs, but to borrow and assemble "outfits." Examples included the studio designer Edith Head and the French couturier Hubert de Givenchy, who together created the costumes for the original *Sabrina* (Billy Wilder, 1954), as well as films like *The Great Gatsby* (Jack Clayton, 1974), whose costume designer, Theoni V. Aldredge, introduced the fashion designer Ralph Lauren to the wider world when he contributed the wardrobe for Robert Redford (who played the lead). By the 1980s, according to costume designer Deborah Nadoolman Landis, product placement was an important dimension of clothing in films, with costuming devolving into a combination of "designing," "renting" and "shopping," in part because of diminishing budgets.[7] Landis, however, puts much of the responsibility for the increased use of recognizable labels in film on the designers themselves: "There are definitely pressures to exploit the medium. ... Fashion designers would love every star to be sporting their clothes all the time."[8]

A fashion film takes the logic of product placement one step further. The film's function as a shop window is not secondary to its story. Rather, it is "the sort of film that could easily be watched minus the soundtrack, to better appreciate the clothing," explained one fan.[9] The fashion film should thus be distinguished from films about the fashion industry such as *Roberta* (William A. Seiter, 1935), or the more recent *Prêt-à-Porter* (Robert Altman, 1994), or documentaries such as *Unzipped* (Douglas Keeve, 1995); though fashion films are often about the fashion industry, such as *Funny Face* (Stanley Donen, 1957) or *Slaves of New York* (James Ivory, 1989), it is the interest elicited by the clothing displayed in the movie (rather than the inclusion of material about the fashion industry and its creators) that defines this genre. While earlier films might be designated as such a posteriori by fans, the twenty-first-century fashion film self-consciously plays upon the attraction that fashion and style, as an element in the larger media industries, may hold for its potential audience as part of the film's conception and promotion.

While costume serves to highlight character, fashion refers neither to character nor to clothing per se, but to a set of objects defined by specific discourses generated from an array of sources. These include fashion shows, coverage of fashion shows in newspapers and on the internet, television reportage and programming, and, most importantly (arguably), by fashion magazines such as *Vogue* (1892–) and *Harper's Bazaar* (1867–), or by what are known as women's service magazines such as *Good Housekeeping* (1885–), including the more recently established *O, The Oprah Magazine* (2000–), which sponsor affiliated internet sites. Fashion must be understood not only in contrast with clothing as an expression of character, but also with beautiful and opulent costumes that do not necessarily reference the fashion industry— as, for example, in historical costume dramas such as *The Duchess* (Saul Dibb, 2008), which won the 2009 Academy Award for Costume Design.

The HBO television series, *Sex and the City* (1998–2004), was a significant influence in the development of the contemporary fashion film. As film scholars Stella Bruzzi and Pamela Church Gibson commented in 2004,

> The process of extravagant costume display has developed its own independent existence with the series and, bolstered by various extra-diegetic factors, has acquired a separate momentum. Parker [Sarah Jessica Parker who plays Carrie Bradshaw, the series' lead] has become a fashion icon in her own right.[10]

Bruzzi and Gibson elaborate: "The spectacular use of fashion … is … at the heart of the series' mission and appeal—fashion as an element independent of character and action rather than subservient to it."[11] By "spectacular," Bruzzi means, as she explains in another influential volume, clothing that takes on an identity of its own, that may even arrest the narrative, drawing the viewer's attention to the world outside the story, or outside what Bruzzi and Gibson term the diegetic universe of the film. Bruzzi underlines that "fashion" at the cinema "allows for clothes to be the objects of the spectatorial gaze and to be admired or acknowledged in spite of the general trajectory of the film."[12] This tendency is at odds with traditional perspectives on costume design that claimed that "[c]ostumes are not mere garments. They are the visual tools used to release the soul of a character—a way to lift a character off the page and into the three dimensional world."[13] The fashion film explicitly incorporates a dimension of clothing that is not about character, but about fashion as part of the attractions that it offers its viewers, situating the discourse about clothing that it mobilizes in terms of the larger fashion industry and culture.

Sex and the City was not the first television show to highlight contemporary high fashion, and fashion more generally. In the 1980s, "current flamboyant fashion" began routinely to appear on American television as part of a given program's appeal,[14] in particular through fictional material such as *Miami Vice* (NBC, 1984–89) or *Dynasty* (ABC, 1981–89), and also through shows that reported on contemporary fashion, such as *Style with Elsa Klensch* (CNN, 1980–2001), *Fashion Television* (CTV Toronto, 1985–) and MTV's *House of Style* (MTV, 1989–2000). *Miami Vice*, in particular, displayed the clothing of high-end designers such as Giorgio Armani, Hugo Boss, Vittorio Ricci, Gianni Versace and Perry Ellis, while popularizing Ray-Ban Wayfarer sunglasses, circulating the idea (then novel for Americans) that men could be interested in fashion. As one of the show's costume designers, Bambi Breakstone, claimed, "The concept of the show is to be on top of all the latest fashion trends in Europe."[15] High fashion designers for women were, however, more skeptical about television. Fashion on television for women, such as that featured on *Dynasty,* also a significant sartorial influence in the 1980s, tended to be less concerned with European trends, with the exception of coverage offered by programs like *Style with Elsa Klensch*, which was, in fact, often critical of more adventurous designs. Klensch herself promoted a more conservative approach to personal style.[16]

A decade later, *Sex and the City* delivered high fashion to a wider public, extending the logic of *Miami Vice*, addressing and expanding the already style-conscious female demographic, bringing European designs such as those of Manolo Blahnik, Jimmy Choo, Roberto Cavalli and Prada to the attention of the American public: high fashion as well as product placement and various magazine tie-ins became crucial factors in the program's popularity internationally. In the process, the show made the costume designer and stylist, Patricia Field, a media celebrity in her own right. A number of extended studies of *Sex and the City* (the television program) have described the import and impact of the program on the female viewer and its relations to feminine culture.[17] Christina Binkley stated in the *Wall Street Journal*:

> As anyone who lived through it can testify, the TV show "Sex and the City" was wildly influential over the past decade. It not only introduced a generation of women to high-fashion brands like Blumarine and Chloé and pushed the concept of mixing pricey brands with flea-market finds; it also fostered pride in feminine friendships and pursuits.[18]

Here, I wish to emphasize, in the context of neo-feminist cinema, that the show provided the groundwork that made the twenty-first-century fashion film possible by cultivating a viewer sensibility receptive to and interested in films that featured designer clothing. The same designer clothing could be incorporated into magazine and newspaper features and spreads, cultivating awareness of the film well before its release.

Typically, the *New York Post* featured a three-page spread detailing "the movie's million dollar wardrobe," on Wednesday 21 June 2006, nine days before *The Devil Wears Prada*'s release on 30 June.[19] Similarly, Sarah Jessica Parker appeared on the cover of *Vogue*'s June 2008 issue, which also included an interview with Parker conducted by "pink lit" novelist, Plum Sykes, further photographs by Annie Leibovitz, who shot the cover photo, as well as a letter from the editor, Anna Wintour, noting that Parker first appeared on the cover of *Vogue* in 2002. The issue would have appeared on newsstands a few weeks before the 30 May opening of *Sex and the City: The Movie*, which itself included a number of important scenes involving *Vogue*, illustrating the happy collaboration between the two media in developing a context for the fashion film that would in turn support the fashion industry.

In cultivating an environment that would be hospitable to the fashion film, *Sex and City*, however, was not operating in a vacuum; rather, the program was symptomatic of the 1980s and 1990s, which saw fashion and style become a significant preoccupation of the culture at large. Contemporaneous developments in media and celebrity culture stimulated an investment in fashion among viewers in terms of its links to the lifestyles of the rich and famous, particularly media celebrities. This trend was given visibility through the proliferation of programming like *Entertainment Tonight* (1981–), a syndicated series originally produced by Paramount Television, and in the development of the Comcast Entertainment Group, which operates the E! Entertainment Network (launched in 1987 as Movietime, renamed in 1990), E! Online, and the Style Network (American launch in 1999)—all of which offered broadcast material that supported the development of a viewing culture that would be receptive to the fashion/celebrity dimension of *Sex and the City*, the television series, as well as the later fashion films.

The mounting success of *Sex and the City*, and the increasing attention it received in terms of setting styles and trends among viewers, also assisted Field, initially a New York stylist and retailer, in developing a network of relations within the fashion and magazine industry that would enable her in her subsequent projects to draw upon the wares of the fashion industry, while developing a mutually beneficial (for films and for designers) public awareness about the clothing that a film's characters might wear. For example, while the *New York Post* reported that for the filming of *The Devil Wears Prada* "Field had a costume budget of a mere $100,000," Field claimed, "We must have used at least $1 million worth of clothing." She explained: "we never could have done it without my friends in the fashion industry helping us along. It would have been impossible. The level of fur coats, and designer bags—oh my God."[20] (See Figure 8.1.)

Not coincidentally, Patricia Field was the costume designer for both *The Devil Wears Prada* and *Sex and the City: The Movie*. Her participation contributed to the pre-fabricated "hype" or "buzz" surrounding both films. Though Field had worked on films previously, most notably on *Miami Rhapsody* (David Frankel, 1995), in the course of which she met Sarah Jessica Parker, it was her role on *The Devil Wears Prada* that established her reputation within cinema, a reputation that would continue to build with *Sex and the City: The Movie* and subsequent films like *Confessions of a Shopaholic* (P.J. Hogan, 2009).

If films like *Pretty Woman*, *Romy and Michele's High School Reunion* and *Legally Blonde* to increasing degrees highlighted the role of fashion, as opposed

Figure 8.1 Meryl Streep and Patricia Field on the set of *The Devil Wears Prada* (2006). Courtesy of Photofest.

to costume that serves to reveal character, the twenty-first-century fashion film exploited its ties with the fashion world in order to create the "buzz" and media attention that encouraged a profitable opening weekend, considered crucial to a film's success. Though independent films like *My Big Fat Greek Wedding* (Joel Zwick, 2002) might build an audience over time, Conglomerate Hollywood increasingly depended on a splashy and popular opening weekend in order to ensure continued bookings as part of its saturation campaign. Films that did not do well within the first week of their release had little chance of building an audience over time, hence the Conglomerate's dependence on films that were already receiving attention even before they opened.

The work of stylists like Field, who needed to cooperate closely with both the fashion industry, the fashion publication industry and with the stars who wore the clothing and posed for magazines, was facilitated by developments in magazine celebrity culture in the 1990s, such as the inauguration of *InStyle Magazine* in 1994, by Time Inc.[21] The magazine was symptomatic of new directions in the relationship between fashion and celebrity, and quickly challenged established fashion magazines like *Vogue*.[22] *InStyle* was designed to focus on "the lives and homes of celebrities";[23] however, it developed distinctive editorials, directing readers to put together outfits from an array of sources, ranging from the modestly priced to haute couture. *Publishers Weekly* described *InStyle* as "a premier fashion magazine, with the idea of bringing the fabulous to the many."[24]

The magazine offered advice that breached the distance between celebrity style and the practices of the readers themselves, avoiding the conceptual and artistic aspirations of fashion magazines, as well as fashion models, using either media celebrities, in particular film and television stars, or the clothing itself in, at the time, innovative, but now widely copied, layouts. For example, *InStyle* popularized a layout that instructed readers on how to achieve a high fashion look through the purchase of more modestly priced items from what are commonly referred to as "High Street" fashions, such as those offered by Zara, the chain, owned by the Spanish company Inditex Group, with stores around the world that specialize in modestly priced, relatively speaking, "knock offs" of high fashion items.[25]

The focus on fashion that was both affordable and yet also linked to high fashion was complemented by the magazine's focus on the celebrity—not surprising, given that the magazine's creator, Ann Moore, is also credited with "*People's* huge buildup." (*People* is also owned by Time Inc.[26]) The focus on celebrity also became a pronounced trait of the high fashion magazine, in particular *Vogue* under Anna Wintour (1988–), a strategy that she inaugurated in her bid to compete with the recently established American version of *Elle*. Early in her tenure as editor-in-chief, Wintour explained her policy: "People want to read about fashion and controversy and gossip. ... If *Vogue* can't give it to them, who can?" The ground-breaking cover of her first issue, featuring a "jewelled Christian Lacroix T-shirt" and a "$50 dollar pair of blue jeans" was meant to illustrate that, in Wintour's words, "a woman can make an outfit her own by how she puts it together."[27] She elaborated: "I wanted the covers to show gorgeous real girls looking the way they looked out on the street."[28] The *New York Times* asserted that this "may well be the first time blue jeans have appeared on a *Vogue* cover—without a belt and with the model's tummy showing, no less."[29] This more democratic approach to design that highlighted styles readily copied by young women on a budget through a process of mixing and matching different pieces expanded the terms of the fashionable beyond the wealthy, high society matrons that were *Vogue's* traditional readers. In so doing, Si Newhouse, head of Condé Nast, which owned *Vogue*, and Wintour hoped to expand the magazine's circulation and to compete with *Elle,* who already attracted a younger readership.

As well as favoring a more youthful look that foreshadowed the approach of stylists like Patricia Field, Wintour also often placed celebrities on the magazine's covers, including Madonna, Sandra Bullock, Claire Danes, Sarah Jessica

Parker (as noted earlier), the Spice Girls, Renée Zellweger, Oprah Winfrey, Hillary Clinton and Michelle Obama.[30] The combined thrust of her policies created an environment that facilitated links and synergies with television programming and films directed at women audiences and the larger fashion scene, particularly in view of the highly influential position that she held as editor-in-chief of arguably the most important fashion magazine in the world at the time. Many celebrities were quick to exploit the link between fashion and celebrity by creating their own clothing lines, such as film star Sienna Miller's Twenty8Twelve,[31] Sarah Jessica Parker's Bitten or Justin Timberlake's William Rast, with varying degrees of success.[32]

The intensification of celebrity culture, and the alacrity with which the media and consumer culture more generally sought to mine it, inspired journalist Maureen Orth to dub the phenomenon "the celebrity-industrial complex." She asks: "Why are millions who have never watched *Sex and the City* so well acquainted with the clothes, shoes, and baby-in-the stroller outings of Sarah Jessica Parker?" She explains:

> Celebrity culture, which now extends beyond the arts and sports into politics and business, has become such a huge area of interest with so much monetary and cultural impact that it demands as much investigative reporting as the White House or Wall Street.[33]

The fashion film is a symptom of these same forces, uniting as it does the public's interest in style and in celebrities, an interest that extends beyond the small group of elite consumers, historically the participants in the world of high fashion.

Importantly, the clothing lines initiated by media celebrities were not necessarily directed at the high-end consumer; rather, the field of the fashionable was expanded in an effort to create the broadest possible market. Patricia Field herself developed a collection for Marks & Spencer, the British retailer, known for stores offering practical and affordable clothing, household items and even food. The collection was promoted on the basis that it served an international cohort of women: "For the first time ever, women all over the world will have a chance to own for themselves one, or more, of the sexy, glamorous and individual styles of Patricia Field."[34] A concern with fashion was presented as a primary dimension of the new democratic feminine popular culture.

The fashion film and the kind of publicity that it generated was thus part of a larger extremely profitable economic and cultural movement that had placed fashion and style in the forefront of the public's imagination. Conglomerate Hollywood sought to exploit this development, privileging material that cultivated an interest in fashion, a trend that supported the tenets of neo-feminism, for which appearance and glamor were important concerns. With regards to *The Devil Wears Prada*, fashion, however, was only one factor in producing the kind of interest necessary to a film's success, suggesting the way in which the successful female event film must operate simultaneously on a number of levels. The film was based on the successful chick lit or "pink lit" novel by the same name, largely assumed to be drawn from Lauren Weisberger's (the author's) experiences working for American *Vogue*'s editor-in-chief Anna Wintour. In spite of the fact that Wintour was depicted in a highly unflattering light, she did little to impede the book's popularity. On the contrary, she seemed to encourage the visibility that the book afforded her, even agreeing to a documentary, *The September Issue* (R.J. Cutler, 2009), which, though softening her image to a degree, also confirmed a number of the traits described by Weisberger in her novel. Wintour's strategy was successful. As her biographer, Jerry Oppenheimer commented: "What the book did do, besides giving Weisberger her fifteen minutes, was to place Anna squarely in the mainstream celebrity pantheon."[35]

Given the existing interest in fashion, the popularity of the novel, as well as the high profile of Wintour herself on whom the novel was assumed to be based, it is not surprising that Fox 2000, a subsidiary of the media conglomerate News Corporation, "paid a reported $600,000 for ... *The Devil Wears Prada*."[36] Producer Wendy Finerman, whose credits include *Forrest Gump* (Robert Zemeckis, 1994), became interested in the project when it was still only a 100-page book proposal, even though at the time, "'soft' female movies had become a tough sell in Hollywood." Kirsten Smith, screenwriter for *Legally Blonde*, claimed that "[e]ven romantic comedies are centering on male characters and their issues."[37]

Fox 2000 president, Elizabeth Gabler, was fundamental to the film's development, in particular, the choice to avoid the temptation to adapt the book into a typical "broad romantic comedy, where the plucky heroine not only lands the guy in the end, but gets back at her wicked, evil boss, too," a kind of updated *Working Girl* (Mike Nichols, 1988).[38] Gabler, however, "has long been identified with adult films and romantic comedies," achieving "[e]very year ... a breakout or two."[39] *Variety* noted that Gabler's string of successful films inevitably "fall outside the tentpole sensibility of the major studios, and the genre taste of most specialty divisions."[40] Noted media analyst, Anne Thompson, remarked that Gabler's "success argues for a reexamination of the big-studio model. Taking more time to make fewer movies at a lower budget makes high-quality control more possible."[41] Thompson's comment underlines the difficulties encountered by films that address a female audience with regard to even the most obvious projects, such as *The Devil Wears Prada*. Based on a best-selling novel that provided an established fan base, and which had a built-in celebrity interest factor that had already garnered media attention, the project required the support of a producer and studio head considered mavericks by their peers, because of their successful track record with films outside the Conglomerate norms. Box office potential remains the primary concern, with the growing economic clout of the female demographic the single most important consideration.

If *The Devil Wears Prada* is an example of the "adult-oriented pictures" for which Gabler is known, it signals the constraints to which any project for "diversity of creative advocacy" (the ostensible purpose of creating Fox 2000 in 1998) is subjected in Conglomerate Hollywood.[42] Through its focus on the figure of Miranda Priestly, played by Meryl Streep, the film departs from the typical romantic comedy, the vehicle for girly stars such as Kate Hudson or Jennifer Garner, by offering an important place to an older woman in a plot that does not center on romance; however, in other ways the film rehearses a number of significant "girly" film themes—notably, the makeover, the striver ethos, the importance of appearance, the do-over, the double ending, the lack of interest in chastity, and other traditional feminine virtues, as well as the emphasis on consumer culture and its importance to the feminine subject. Rather than presenting the plot in a purely comedic mode, the film alternates between satire and melodrama, producing a generically hybrid narrative typical of many "girly" films, notably *Pretty Woman*, itself. As such, the film could hardly be considered a "break out" film in terms of the types of material that Hollywood had been routinely producing for women since *Pretty Woman*.

While the plot of *The Devil Wears Prada* uses elements associated previously with successful girly films, in particular *Legally Blonde* and *Working Girl*, in terms of its focus on a young woman and her career, it nonetheless highlights relations between women, but without recalling the female friendship film. Indeed, the film proposes another kind of relationship between women, one that is outside family and friendship, and that devolves within a purely professional arena. While *Working Girl* depended upon a conflict between two women, one blonde (Melanie Griffith) and the other brunette (Sigourney Weaver) of relatively equal capacities, and similar ages, it had only one protagonist, Griffith as Tess McGill, encouraging the viewer to follow the trials and tribulations of a young woman's drive for success. In fact, Melanie Griffith, born in 1957, was only eight years younger than Sigourney Weaver, born in 1949, though the characters they play are the same age in the film itself. In contrast, *The Devil Wears Prada* had the potential to provide two protagonists, a potential that was more fully realized in the film than the novel. Gabler commented: "It had dual protagonists, one relatable to older women, one younger women. There hadn't been a working girl kind of movie in some time. It had the added guilty pleasure of the fresh perspective on the glitzy New York fashion world."[43]

Gabler's comment above clearly lays out the attributes that she felt would ensure the film's success and that attracted her to the project: it had the potential of attracting a broad audience of women, females under 25 and females over 25, a dimension that was heightened by casting, with Meryl Streep (b. 1949) in the title role 33 years older than Hathaway (b. 1982) as the younger woman; it relied on a proven formula; it exploited current celebrity culture because of its topic as a *roman-à-clef* about an already visible public figure in the world of fashion, itself a topic of increasing media attention. Gabler's comment also highlights the importance of location to "girly" films, such as *Maid in Manhattan* (Wayne Wang, 2002), *How to Lose a Guy in 10 Days* (Donald Petrie, 2003), *13 Going on 30* (Gary Winick, 2004), *Raising Helen* (Garry Marshall, 2004), *Bride Wars* (Gary Winick, 2009) and *Confessions of a Shopaholic*, which are increasingly set in New York, in particular Manhattan—a trend encouraged not only by the "glitz" of the New York fashion scene, but also by film-television tax incentives sponsored by the New York State Legislature and the city of New York.[44]

As the fashion center of the United States, and arguably the world, with the declining influence of Paris, Manhattan as a setting affords multiple opportunities to highlight designer wares, strengthening the links between the girly film as a genre and the fashion industry. Sarah Jessica Parker, commenting on HBO's *Sex and the City*, went so far as to assert that New York was "the greatest character ever written," inspiring Ron Simon, curator at the Paley Center for Media, to describe Manhattan as "the mecca for single living," citing the fact that "unmarried New Yorkers head 48 percent of households in the city."[45] Jane Arthurs, media scholar, in a widely read article, described how the program, in turn, "contributed to New York's reputation as city 'brand' in the global system of capitalism as a source of new fashion ideas."[46] In focusing on the New York setting, Gabler pointed, yet again, to the desirability of creating a consumer friendly environment, one that would also, coincidentally, encourage a neo-feminist perspective for films directed at a female audience.

In spite of these constraints, *The Devil Wears Prada* signals a noteworthy development in the girly film, one that yet again ties it to the neo-feminist paradigm, which emphasizes achievement in the workplace: *The Devil Wears Prada* takes as its topic the already successful and powerful woman, Miranda Priestly (Meryl Streep), viewed through the eyes of a young woman, Andy (Anne Hathaway), embarking on her life's journey. The introduction of the powerful woman may recall characters from Hollywood's past, such as Lora Meredith (Lana Turner) in *Imitation of Life* (Douglas Sirk, 1959), Amanda

Farrow (Joan Crawford) in *The Best of Everything* (Jean Negulesco, 1959), the much earlier Alison Drake (Ruth Chatterton) in *Female* (Michael Curtiz, 1933), or even Diana Christensen (Faye Dunaway) in *Network* (Sidney Lumet, 1976). Miranda Priestly distinguishes herself from these earlier boss ladies because of the way in which the film highlights her relations with other women; though romance has a small role in the film, it is almost incidental to its drama.

Working Girl's Tess (Melanie Griffith) with her "head for business and bod for sin" prevailed through perseverance and intelligence but, even more importantly, a canny seduction of her supervisor's boyfriend; in contrast, *The Devil Wears Prada* views "the desire for sex ... as relatively unimportant." Desire revolves around "power and ... very beautiful things," in the words of film critic David Denby.[47] The focus on career and fashion within a story that hinges on relations between women promised to deliver a "two quadrant film," by spanning the generations, contributing to the view that the project would prove successful at the box office. The producers and screenwriter, Aline Brosh McKenna, made significant changes in adapting the novel to the screen, changes that highlight "girly" elements and enhance the film's potential appeal, transforming the initial story about a young woman's suffering under her tyrannical boss into a "coming-of-age tale about a smart Cinderella named Andy who undergoes a total makeover," and in the process comes to understand her ambitious nature, but also the directions in which her ambitions lie—which are not in the area of fashion.[48]

The film, in typical girly manner, stresses both a work ethic that is almost Protestant in its fervor, and also the need to be true to one's self. The conclusion is happy; Andy does, as a direct result of her experiences at *Runway*, where she ultimately wins Miranda's approval, find employment as a journalist at a newspaper with a social conscience—the very position that had eluded her a year earlier. She does not suffer in vain, and emerges with a sense of identity and purpose, one that highlights career (in keeping with the neo-feminist paradigm) rather than romance. Though, in spite of her sexual infidelity, she repairs her relationship, agreeing to a commuter partnership, the real satisfaction in the ending derives from Andy's success in the workplace, and perhaps from the fact that though no fashion victim, she is no longer the awkward frumpy recent college graduate of the film's beginning, but a trendy, stylish career woman.

The novel itself recounted the tribulations of a young Ivy League graduate (in the film, Andy attended the more plebian Northwestern University as a journalism student) who aspired to write serious fiction (lacking the social conscience that motivates the film's heroine). She accepts employment as the assistant of Miranda Priestly, the editor-in-chief of the fictional *Runway*

Magazine, a demanding and abusive boss, in order to eventually find a less stressful occupation, writing articles for other magazines through the connections that she had gained by working for Priestly. The story offers no strong perspective on the heroine's education, except perhaps to encourage young women to be ruthless, manipulative and opportunistic. The novel, as reviewers underlined, lacked subtlety, or even a clear focus, other than the complete disdain and hatred with which Andy regarded her employer. Janet Maslin, a *New York Times* reviewer, claimed that Weisberger's "sour, sarcastic, self-involved heroine is too much of a pill to be endearing."[49]

Given that Weisberger did in fact work for *Vogue*, much of the pre-publication discussion of the volume centered on the celebrity gossip potential of the work. Weisberger's efforts had the additional virtue of offering a thinly veiled portrait of an already well-known figure, that of Anna Wintour, who had only a few years before been hounded by the tabloids over a much publicized extra-marital affair and divorce.[50] Though reviews were largely negative, by June 2008 the book had over four million copies in print worldwide, creating the media interest in the film that Gabler had anticipated.[51]

McKenna (the screenwriter) made substantial revisions to the novel as she prepared the script that served to humanize "the boss" and place her squarely at the film's center. Kate Betts in the *New York Times* bemoans the fact that Lauren Weisberger "seems to have understood nothing about the isolation and pressure of the job her boss was doing, or what it might cost a person like Miranda Priestly to become Miranda Priestly." She calls for a more complex and nuanced understanding of the character, whom, having worked for Anna Wintour herself, she clearly admires:

> Surely there are much larger social forces at work in fashion, as in all subcultures, and the Mirandas of the world, as much as they seem like casualties of their own psychology, are also reflections of us—our ideas of style, our hunger for glamour, our age-old need for a consummate antagonist in a chic red suit.[52]

McKenna's script seeks to remedy this failing, with the film serving as a vehicle for Meryl Streep's interpretation of Priestly. According to reviewer A.O. Scott, "the movie, while noting that she can be sadistic, inconsiderate and manipulative, is unmistakably on Miranda's side."[53] David Edelstein, in *New York Magazine*, dismisses the film—"If there's any drama here, it's slender—maybe a size 2."[54] He, however, is full of praise for Streep: "A heavenward tilt of the head and the tiniest sigh of impatience and *The Devil Wears Prada* becomes, so briefly, a Restoration comedy."[55] David Denby concurred: "In all, this has to be the most devastating boss-lady performance in the history of cinema."[56]

Meryl Streep as Miranda Priestly incarnates a schizophrenic vision of the woman in power, overshadowing the girlish Hathaway as Andy, whose transformation contributes to Hathaway's reputation as "Hollywood's makeover queen," inaugurated with *The Princess Diaries* (Garry Marshall, 2001).[57] Streep, in contrast, through a carefully orchestrated performance, offers a multilayered portrait of the successful female executive (see Figure 8.2). Though hardly the stereotypical figure drawn by Lauren Weisberger, Priestly remains a cold, ruthless and predatory creature. She differs, however, from the earlier version of the female boss as portrayed by Sigourney Weaver in *Working Girl*, played for broad comedic effect, because Streep brings to bear the weight of her age and experience as an actress on the role. Film scholar Karen Hollinger describes Streep's reputation as "the finest actress of her generation,"[58] while Cher depicted her as "an acting machine in the same sense that a shark is a killing machine."[59] The role of Miranda Priestly provided Streep with an opportunity to demonstrate the technical capacities of that "machine," in a context that highlighted her glamor as well as her skills as a thespian.

Much of the film's coherence, then, resided in the way that it showcased Streep's virtuosity and subtlety as a performer who, unlike the typical girly star, stressed, in Hollinger's terms, "characterization," the ability to lose herself in a role.[60] Streep is not, then, a diva but an artist. As Belinda Luscombe proclaimed in *Time*, "Meryl Streep is not a star. A legend, but not a star."[61] The director, Frankel, was full of praise for Streep's performance. "She's able to play the drama with a hint of comedy. ... You always feel that there's something else on her mind, some depth, some sadness, some manipulation, some cruelty, some genius."[62] He further commented about Priestly, confirming her centrality, "That was the character that appealed to me, that you could paint a portrait of the contemporary media world with the character of Miranda."[63] Ultimately, Frankel considered Priestly as a representative of excellence. "If there are boundaries of humanity that get crossed in aspiring to excellence, is that not possibly a sacrifice that's worthwhile? ... It's a question ... the movie does stir that idea."[64] He added, a comment that might be equally applied to Streep: "I'm in awe of anybody who's excellent. That is the crux of the movie for me."[65]

Importantly, however, neither Miranda nor Streep are girls. Streep's Miranda exhibits few of the more girlish features associated with Anna Wintour (in terms of appearance, Wintour is slight, wears fitted clothing with short hemlines and slides her saucer-like eyes apologetically towards the camera), or with the Miranda of the novel (who, for example, wears a signature white scarf and tiny white Chanel tennis shorts). Streep's Miranda is not girlish in her behavior or her hairstyle and wardrobe. Because, since the age of 40, "Streep has mostly played people taking charge of their own destiny, if not actual ballbusters,"[66]

Figure 8.2 Meryl Streep as "Miranda Priestly." Courtesy of Photofest.

Streep's own persona pushed the character towards a more womanly, as opposed to girlish, interpretation of the role—a tendency enhanced by the wardrobe and hair style choices made by Streep herself. Streep explained: "Most of the models for the character were on the male end of the species."[67] Field added, "I just wanted to present a powerful woman running a magazine. I wanted it to be an original character."[68] Streep's apparel was described as "understated and high-end chic ensembles for the film, conveying the moneyed and privileged world of couture chroniclers,"[69] leading Ruth La Ferla in the *New York Times* to describe Miranda as "too bland and bankerlike and ugh!—far too pretty."[70] Indeed Field revealed:

> The studio thought that she looked like a lady who lunches. I had to explain to them that Meryl liked them, and we were taking these over-done jackets and putting them with a pinstripe skirt and a white shirt, and that is the look of this powerful woman in fashion. It's not a lady-that-lunches look.[71]

The "frosty white wig" that she wore for the role was Streep's idea, devised with her "longtime makeup artist and hairstylist, J. Roy Helland,"[72] suggesting the manner in which Streep maneuvered the initial focus on "fashion," dictated by the film's genre, back to a more traditional notion of costume as intrinsic to the creation of character, which did not prevent Field from dressing her in high-profile designers. Streep had around 40 changes of costume, including a black Valentino gown, praised by reviewer David Denby, which indicates how, notwithstanding Streep's efforts, fashion remained in the forefront of viewer's preoccupations (see Figure 8.3).[73]

Streep's persona as an accomplished actress, together with the modifications that the screenwriter Aline Brosh McKenna brought to the role of Priestly, moved the film's articulation of femininity away from the most prevalent form of neo-feminism, which values the cultivation of a girlish appearance; however, the character's emphasis on a very individualized program of ambitious self-advancement remained very close to more general neo-feminist ideals. McKenna described the character:

> Obviously, her priorities are a little different from most people's, but basically, Miranda's a working mother. She's trying to do the best she can, and she's trying to keep her personal life afloat, and this is the only way that she knows to live—completely devoted to her work.[74]

The fundamental thrust of the film, however, lay in appealing to the viewer's voyeuristic interest in a world of almost unbelievable affluence. As A.O. Scott

Figure 8.3 Meryl Streep in a Valentino dress and bolero, Fred Leighton earrings. Courtesy of Photofest.

commented in the *New York Times*, "the vicarious thrill is ... conspicuous consumption: all those lovingly photographed outfits and accessories, those warehouses' worth of Chanel and Jimmy Choo, those skinny women decked out (by the tirelessly inventive Patricia Field) in expensive finery." For Scott the film, like the fashion magazines it references, provides "the most sumptuous goods imaginable—or fantasy images of them, in any case—to the eager eyes of the masses."[75]

In general, the reviewers were critical of the way that the film depicted the fashion scene and fashionable clothing, with Booth Moore claiming in the *Los Angeles Times* that "*The Devil Wears Prada* is a film about insiders that has been costumed for outsiders." This perspective, shared by Ruth La Ferla of the *New York Times*, indicates how distinctions are maintained among the fashionable in the era of mass consumption, generated by fashion writers and editors, such as Wintour herself, or, more obviously, her close colleague at *Vogue*, Grace Coddington. Yet this same discourse, filtered through the likes of Patricia Field and the proliferation of licensing practices by haute couture designers such as Valentino, also encourages the development of a wider demographic that might be responsive to the fashion industry more broadly defined, fueled by a notion of style that is ever receding and out of reach. Sidney Toledano, president and chief executive of Christian Dior, explained in 2004:

> If Haute Couture activity exists only for the client, it doesn't work. However through the fashion show, it appeals to the public and it greatly affects ready-to-wear, perfume, etc. It's more than publicity. I feel that Haute Couture product is more important as a concept than as a product itself.[76]

The fashion in films such as *The Devil Wears Prada* fulfills the same purpose as the fashion show, but within an even broader more popular context and with the fuller range of affect that cinema provides as an individual and social experience—as an event that is both lived through and talked about. The efficacy of the strategy internationally is highlighted by the box office success of *The Devil Wears Prada*, with a worldwide gross of just under $327 million, despite the fact that two-thirds of the opening weekend audience was female and "over half was aged 25 and over." *Variety* reported, "The $35 million pic raked in $40 million in its first five days." Frankel, the director, asserted: "The Holy Grail of this movie was to create an event movie for women."[77] The film's success at the box office, and the attendant media frenzy surrounding the film, suggest that it met its goal; however, more importantly for the development of the fashion film, and films for women more generally, the achievements of

The Devil Wears Prada served to pave the way for the even more strongly event-oriented movie directed at the female demo, *Sex and the City: The Movie*. In this sense, *The Devil Wears Prada* was an important step in promoting a production profile for women's films that would increasingly resemble that of the franchises typically directed at young males, in which the existence of an already favorably disposed group of fans was an important element in gaining the financial support necessary to producing and distributing a film.

Chapter 9

Sex and the City: The Movie (2008)
The Female Event Film

The success of *The Devil Wears Prada* (David Frankel, 2006) was crucial to the decision made to move forward with a movie sequel to the extremely successful television program, *Sex and the City*. The cinematic version, *Sex and the City: The Movie* (Michael Patrick King, 2008), performed even better at the box office than *The Devil Wears Prada*, with the former grossing $415 million worldwide, preceded and accompanied by a media extravaganza that was unprecedented for a film directed at a female audience. Warner Brothers' Dan Fellman described the event: "It's a cultural phenomenon; it's an absolutely incredible opening."[1] Josh Feldman observed in the *Los Angeles Times*, "Because of its loyal following, ... 'Sex and the City' is more like a 'fan boy' movie for women, with eager customers already turning opening night into an event."[2]

From an institutional perspective, however, the film's reception largely served to confirm the pattern of the fashion film by presenting a movie that overtly announced its topic as "labels," as in clothes and accessories made by high-end designers, relying upon a pre-established fan base to promote awareness of the film before it opened. Appropriately in the title song "Labels or Love," pop star Fergie, recruited in a bid to expand further the movie's audience, provocatively states: "Love is like a runway but which one do I love more." Judging from the multiple postings about the song, which began even before the film's domestic release, and included reactions such as that of "Ainnet 4rom NYC!," the strategy was successful:

> Thiz is the Best song ever fergie has done in her career and I luv her musik, so stop hating! And the Sex n the City Movie was da Best Movie out..... "I be lo0kin 4 labels I aint lo0kin 4 luv. My Pharse 4life! [*sic*][3]

Fergie herself commented:

> I grew up watching *Sex and the City* and I know a lot of my girlfriends did as well. ... We felt like these characters were our friends, so to be part of this project has been amazing. ... I would die to do a video with the girls.[4]

The opening song, "Labels or Love," written for the film, demonstrates how its marketing corresponds to the larger trends of Conglomerate Hollywood, and how the neo-feminist paradigm that unites consumer culture and romance, circulated through a number of media, continues to inform contemporary cinema for women.[5] The mobilization of the internet through Fergie's fan base also illustrates the cross-media nature of the female event film as a characteristic of Conglomerate Hollywood. *The Devil Wears Prada* featured songs from U2, Madonna and Alanis Morissette—artists no doubt selected to appeal to a female demographic—augmented with cosmopolitan contemporary electronic dance music that enhanced the film's status as offering a view of the New York scene;[6] however, its sound track did not significantly contribute to the advance attention that the film received.

The use of the Fergie song to promote *Sex and the City: The Movie* suggests not only the increasing refinement of the female event film as the product of marketing in which the quality and nature of the actual movie is of secondary importance, but also the way in which films directed at a female audience continue to imitate *Pretty Woman* (Garry Marshall, 1990), which had exploited the marketing potential of its sound track in keeping with marketing strategies of the period, as a model for targeting its potential demographic. Though the internet has subsequently provided a new avenue for circulating music to fans, the use of music to stimulate interest in a movie was already a facet of the *Pretty Woman* campaign, which drew upon the trend, begun in the 1970s and well-established in the 1980s, of exploiting "potential for cross-promotion ... between the film and recording industries," with "movies and records ... commonly marketed to sell one another."[7]

The *Pretty Woman* sound track was produced through a joint venture with the record label EMI. Natalie Cole, an EMI artist, wrote a song for the film, "Wild Women Do," which "plays over a shopping montage that lasts a minute and a half" within the film, but which was released in February 1990 in advance of the film (the film was released on 23 March 1990).[8] A video accompanied the single, which included "Cole in a black-and-white photo shoot as well as several models, also in black and white, 'playing' musical instruments. Interspersed, in color, is a Cliffs Notes version of *Pretty Woman*, showing quick snippets of nearly the entire movie."[9] The aggressive, rebellious tone of the song and its "female power" message, as well as its circulation on MTV, would have contributed to creating awareness of the film before it opened, as well as appealing to a younger fan base with feminist sympathies, if not aspirations; however, in other ways, the song works against the pro-social message promulgated by *Pretty Woman* as a Disney film. In fact, during this period Cole was developing a more pop-oriented style. In many ways, then, the association between the song and the movie seemed contingent, motivated by a strategy designed to highlight EMI artists, which, in the case of Cole, was extremely effective. In contrast, suggesting an increasing synergy at work in the film's very conception, Fergie's "Labels or Love" underlines one of the major attractions of *Sex and the City: The Movie*: its function as a showcase for clothing and accessories produced by high fashion designers—an aspect of the film featured by magazines ranging from *Vogue* to *Hello!* for several months before the film's release. *Variety* reported that there were "63 pages in the May 23 edition of *Entertainment Weekly* alone."[10]

Significant attention was paid to setting up what are known as "promotional partners" for the film. The president of marketing at New Line, the studio producing the film explained: "So we want to align only with those brands that make sense, the match up with the 'Sex and the City' brand, ... and extend our footprint, not duplicate it."[11] "Promotional partners" are a key factor in the film's capacity to produce pre-movie awareness:

> The partner brands are included in the film in ways that range from mentions in lines of dialogue to numerous appearances on screen. In exchange, the owners of the brands will help publicize the movie with commercials, posters, sweepstakes, viewing parties, events in stores, contests, ticket giveaways and even products with labels inspired by "Sex and the City."[12]

In the case of *Sex and the City*, the film was confronted with an array of silent, unofficial partners—in particular, contemporary designers,[13] such as Manolo Blahnik and Jimmy Choo, whose shoes were featured throughout the "94 episodes of the TV series,"[14] in order to, in the words of HBO producer, John Melfi, "establish the reality of the world the characters lived in."[15] (See Figure 9.1.) While these designers were keen to augment the film's costume budget by lending clothing, this "world" defined by high fashion also provided an environment attractive to other, official, promotional partners. Though the emphasis on selling albums or singles was no longer a primary motivation in 2008, the year of *Sex and the City*'s release, the cooperation between media industries in publicizing a product, whether it be a singer, a designer or film, while leaving an imprint on the content of a film, was crucial to creating the critical mass of pre-movie interest that might produce the kind of opening weekend that would ensure the success of the film.

Among films targeting the female audience, the fashion film offered a number of different means of generating pre-opening attention, in particular the general interest among the targeted demographic in style itself.[16] The fashion film also encouraged repeat viewings so that audiences could better appreciate the details of the various outfits that they glimpsed only fleetingly

Figure 9.1 Manolo Blahnik shoes in *Sex and the City: The Movie* (2008).

in an initial viewing, thus possibly prolonging the film's success in theaters, subsequently, on cable, broadcast television, VOD and DVD. While the emphasis on fashion at the expense of love in the title song underlined the importance of cross-media marketing to the pre-opening interest generated by the film, the narrative of the film itself highlights romance as a crucial ingredient in a woman's life, whether in the form of a permanent relationship or a series of relationships. Nonetheless, the film's visuals, which included over 300 "outfits" worn by the four female leads, "the girls," underlined the importance of fashion to a feminine sense of self as defined within the movie, invoking a very clear reiteration of the neo-feminist paradigm, in which self-fulfillment in terms of both "labels" and "love" provides the primary goal for a woman's life. Katie Barker in *Newsweek* characterized "the girls" as ultimately having "won it all: true love, self-worth and fabulous shoes."[17]

Notwithstanding the seemingly obvious commercial potential of *Sex and the City: The Movie*, Michael Patrick King, the film's writer, director and producer (with Sarah Jessica Parker and Darren Starr), reported that initially the project was stalled because "there was nothing to point at that it would be a money-making venture." This perception, King adds, changed with the success of *The Devil Wears Prada*, and suddenly there was a renewed interest in the project, which had fallen to the wayside after initial discussions immediately following the series' discontinuation. In King's words, "It became, 'Maybe we missed the buck on making the bucks'—literally."[18] The *Los Angeles Times* explained: "Hollywood worships so-called four-quadrant films: movies that draw males and females both young and old." He added that "[i]t's easier to find $2-a-gallon gas than a straight man" disposed to attend a screening of *Sex and the City: The Movie*,[19] though the film hopes, "like the TV show, to attract an unofficial half quadrant in the form of gay males."[20] Notwithstanding, the film's production was haunted by the fear that the film might appeal only to "a single audience slice"[21]—females over 25—in spite of the fact that the series, released on DVD and broadcast in syndication, most notably in the United States on TBS (also owned by Time Warner), had not only maintained its fan base, but also reached new audiences.[22]

Women under 25, teenage girls in particular, were a growing segment of the series' fan base, developed largely through the broadcasting of the series in syndication, often involving a highly "sanitized" version of the original program; however, the film's R-rating raised concerns because many of these new fans "aren't old enough to get into an R-rated movie."[23] *Variety* concurred: "Younger teen femmes, who tend to drive repeat business on chick flicks, won't be able to add to New Line's take."[24] Two days later, *Variety* noted that "the pic is rated R, making it tougher for teen girls to see, and it may not play as well in smaller markets," which are typically more cautious about R-rated films.[25] From a studio's perspective, the problems stemming from an R-rating extended to the marketing of the film, particularly in the wake of a Federal Trade Commission report in 2000 that "accused Hollywood studios of inappropriately marketing adult content to children."[26] This report led Warner Brothers to undertake "not to show ads for R-rated movies during any programming where about 35% of the audience was under 17 years old," a resolve that did not prevent the marketing of the film to some adolescents.[27] Indeed, it was reported that ads for *Sex and the City: The Movie* ran during television programming such as *Gossip Girl* (2007–current) on CW (also part of the Time Warner family), "which had an under-18 audience of about 23%" in the spring of 2008.[28]

Shelley Zalis, CEO of a consumer research firm, OTX, claimed that "Sixteen is the new 20. ... Sixteen-year-olds want to see films with more adult subject matter."[29] Michael King averred:

> The reality is that most of the marketing is very grown-up, but that's OK—it's supposed to be aspirational. ... I'm not expecting that 16-year-olds would have a Louis Vuitton bag [featured in the film, author's note]. It's all supposed to be a little out of everyone's reach.

The defunct ym.com and teenvogue.com, websites targeted towards adolescents, featured entries on Sarah Jessica Parker, the film's lead, and her clothing line, Bitten (the low prices of which were popular with adolescents), as well as on the film itself, illustrating the way in which neo-feminism as a form of femininity defined through consumer culture reaches out through media franchises to new generations of women. Unlike the older character of Miranda Priestly, who marked an exception to the girly mode of neo-feminist cinema, the characters in *Sex and the City: The Movie* emphasize a girlishness that extends from 15 to 55 as a mode of being and an identity—despite the fact that "[t]he film's stars are ancient by Hollywood's unfortunate standards— Parker and Davis are 43, Nixon is 42 and Cattrall is 51," inspiring the sobriquet "Menopause in the City," during the initial development stage.[30]

David Edelstein commented in the *New York Magazine* that "these women are in their fifth decade, and age is a more insistent subtext. The time for do-overs is almost up."[31] The film, nonetheless, contrives to offer each character a "do-over," as one of the defining traits of the girly film: "Carrie" (Sarah Jessica Parker) severs her ties with "Big" (Chris Noth), her long-time beau, only to renew them once again at the film's conclusion; "Miranda" (Cynthia Nixon) reunites with her husband "Steve" (David Eigenberg), yet again; "Samantha" (Kim Cattrall) decides, yet again, that life within a couple is not for her; "Charlotte" (Kristin Davis), after adopting, discovers that she can again conceive in order to enjoy the rewards of motherhood a second time with a biological child. The film promotes the fantasy, through these endless do-overs, that girlishness as the sign of perpetual adolescence, with its promise of change and development and its rejection of stasis and fixity as the fate of the mature woman, offers a desirable and attainable identity, biological age notwithstanding, to the predominantly over-25 female audience.[32] Slim, toned, elaborately garbed and expensively shod, the four friends of *Sex and the City* are routinely referred to as "the girls" in the press,[33] their "girlishness" signaled through their endless belief in the "do-over" (see Figure 9.2). Their devotion to each other, and to themselves, in particular through the common ground of fashion that they share as friends, also extends the premise of the television program to the film, with the film supplying the further experiences of the four "girls," following on from the final episode of the series, as they—women now over 40—negotiate the perils of life in New York City and beyond.

In contrast with the movie, the earlier television series actively engaged with the much repeated fallacy—a misquotation that haunts both chick lit and chick flicks (originally propagated by *Newsweek* in a 1986 cover story "The Marriage Crunch")—that "[s]ingle women over thirty-five are more likely to be killed by a terrorist than get married."[34] The program's finale, however, provided all four friends, if not with husbands (two were married), with permanent heterosexual relationships. Thus, another consideration was whether or not the interest excited by the series, particularly after the mixed success of

Figure 9.2 "The Girls" (2008). Courtesy of Photofest.

other shows based on a similar premise about female friends confronting the vagaries of urban life together, such as *Lipstick Jungle* (NBC, 2008–09) and *Cashmere Mafia* (ABC, 2008–), would sustain a major film. Typically, legendary columnist Liz Smith asked in 2004, when discussion of a film version first emerged, "Does anyone really think a feature film of the famous HBO series, which was a half-hour each week, with quick cuts and quicker dialogue, could be expanded into a full-length movie?"[35]

These perceived constraints on the film's box office potential undoubtedly fed into Warner Brothers' decision to turn the project down, though "HBO's profit participation deal" was also reported to be an issue, in spite of the fact that both Warner Brothers and HBO are part of the Time Warner conglomerate. The film was eventually picked up by New Line, another subsidiary of Time Warner that subsequently "folded into its larger corporate sibling," Warner Brothers itself,[36] prompting many, such as King, to dub *Sex and the City: The Movie* "the swan song of New Line," which had earlier produced hits like *The Lord of the Rings* trilogy.[37] New Line was initially wary of shooting in New York because of costs. John Melfi, HBO producer, explained: "New York is about 30% more expensive than shooting elsewhere, but with the tax credit, it's become quite affordable. The tax credit calmed them down." Erik Holmberg, New Line co-president, concurred that the "rebates" provided by the city were crucial in enabling the New York location.[38]

In general, the city was receptive to the film because of the way that the series had enhanced New York as a tourist attraction. Katherine Oliver, commissioner of the Mayor's Office of Film, Theatre and Broadcasting, stated: "If we can do our part to marry entertainment and tourism, and bring more people here to visit our great city, that's added value in terms of economic impact on New York." By and large, "New York City ... bent over backwards for the film."[39] Similarly, the fashion industry, beyond the designers themselves,[40] was supportive of the project because of the power that the series had demonstrated in transforming "many of fashion's most upscale brands into household names." Fern Mallis, senior vice president of IGM fashion, judged: "The series was critical in teaching a television audience about fashion." IGM fashion is "the company that produces Mercedes-Benz Fashion Week in New York," arguably one of the most influential fashion events of each year.[41] Not coincidentally, the movie included scenes at the "Bryant Park-based Fashion Week," and "Mercedes-Benz erected and then deconstructed its branded tents for the shoot—saving the film hundreds of thousands of dollars."[42]

The shooting of the film became an event in and of itself, attracting tourists to New York as well as a flurry of media interest in the progress of the film, with the informants leaking small items about the plot on a routine basis. For example, *TV Guide* reported in its 11 May 2008 issue that "an on-set spy says a new wedding scene was shot in the Brooklyn courthouse," after having raised doubts about a "wedding scene at Saint Patrick's cathedral," in its 15 October 2007 issue. This kind of media attention fueled speculations about whether Carrie and Big in fact finally marry, one of the major points of potential audience curiosity concerning the film's plot on an international level, with London's *Hello!* asking, "Is *Sex and the City*'s most famous singleton really going to tie the knot?"[43] The *Los Angeles Times* in November 2007, more than six months before the film's release, commented: "The photos are everywhere because the devoted cult of *Sex and the City* can hardly contain its excitement," explaining that "with a gazillion on-location photos already posted on the Internet, it's hardly a national secret what Sarah Jessica Parker and the gals will be wearing"[44]—a comment emphasizing how fashion was regarded as equally, if not more, as important as plot.

The production of the film itself generated similar interest. *Hollywood Reporter* observed, that, while the film opened on 30 May 2008, "hundreds of thousands have been watching it piecemeal since September, when the first of 57 on-location days began shooting in New York."[45] The director, Michael Patrick King, reported: "I would see a scene on 'Access Hollywood' before I saw the dailies." *The Daily News* published the film's production locations and fans would turn up each day with video and digital cameras, posting their footage on Flickr and YouTube, "while the tabloid newsmagazines shows were sharing their own footage."[46] The production team exploited the media interest by shooting multiple scenes and endings in order to raise further questions in the public's mind. A fan, who traveled from Virginia to watch, commented: "It's cool to be here, knowing this is going to be in the movie. ... Unless this is one of those things they do to throw us off."[47]

If the publicity around the on-location shooting in New York served to feed the "enormous audience awareness" that was a major factor in the film's success, Sarah Jessica Parker as the film's lead (she was also a producer) was another crucial factor. As testimony to her power to attract an audience, the domestic weekend opening "ranked as the strongest ever for a movie carried by a female lead (at least if ticket-price inflation is not taken into account)."[48] Parker was also instrumental brokering the arrangements that allowed the film to feature "fashion and its key players" as one of its primary attractions. John Melfi, HBO producer, admitted: "We definitely piggybacked onto Sarah's relationships. ... There was just so much good will there."[49] Through her role as Carrie on the television series, Parker had developed a highly successful celebrity persona that was intimately tied to the fashion world, receiving the kind of treatment from the media usually reserved for film stars;[50] however, given that "[i]n show business, the big money is made in movies,"[51] Parker's decision to move from television into film (she is largely credited with the decision to conclude the series), underlines that, above all, she is a "disciplined business woman" who has understood how to capitalize on her relatively meager talents as an actress and a face and physique that are far from the norms dictated by the beauty industries.[52] Kim Cattrall, commenting on why she and the "girls" were continuing with a movie after ending the series "on such a high note," also revealed that "if we were going to go back into it, money was definitely a factor."[53]

Parker's less than perfect features contributed to her high profile and popularity with audiences. Plum Sykes, describing her in her cover article for *Vogue*, observed: "She's perfect-imperfect. ... She's not a model, but she's model beautiful—people can imagine themselves as her."[54] Sykes's words point to one of the fundamental characteristics of Parker's persona in which one of her primary roles was to showcase fashion, both high fashion and street wear, offering herself up to the gaze of her women fans as precisely a kind of "model" who wore clothing to which they could aspire. Similarly, Liz Smith characterized her in the following terms:

> Sarah Jessica Parker, fashion icon! The size zero "Sex and the City" star has the bod and the attitude wanted by most trendy designers—the better to advertise their wares. Just having Parker carry Christian Dior's scarf print bag ensured a sellout.[55]

At the same time, her exceptional ordinariness as "not a model" lent legitimacy to her portrayal of the fashionable woman whose style might be copied by the wider public. Like Jennifer Lopez, Sarah Jessica Parker's persona seemed to embrace both the ordinary and the extraordinary as a facet of her charisma while at the same time appealing to a much broader group of women than did Lopez, extending across race and national lines,[56] with Julia Baird claiming in *Newsweek* that the series "has been broadcast in 200 countries."[57]

Through "Carrie," a character to whom her persona was irrevocably wedded, Parker represented a democratization of style, echoing Anna Wintour's inaugural *Vogue* cover:[58] "It wasn't about how much the pieces cost, it was about how you wore them. More than fashion, the show was about personal style," stated journalist Booth Moore.[59] For example, Parker described a typical "Carrie" outfit that she wore for an interview with *People*: "The pants are Yves Saint Laurent. Someone gave them to me. I got the blouse at a flea market in Paris. And the shoes are Marc Jacobs shoes that I got on sale."[60] Discussions of the film expressed nostalgia for the "cheap chic" look of the series, claiming that the girls have "turned into rich bitches, clothed and cared for by men!"[61] Such views did not, however, impede the international circulation of Parker as a contemporary icon of style.

In the years leading up to *Sex and the City: The Movie*, in spite of a-rags-to-riches story, a series of unhappy relationships that included Robert Downey, Jr., and John F. Kennedy, Jr., marriage to Matthew Broderick and a child,[62] Parker's personal life had inspired far less interest than her image—in contrast with most female stars, such as Lopez.[63] The coverage of Parker ran counter to the dominant trend described by film scholar Christine Geraghty in which "[w]omen are particularly likely to be seen as celebrities whose working life is of less interest and worth than their personal life."[64] It was not, however, Parker's work as an actress (as was the case for Meryl Streep)[65] that attracted media attention—rather, it was her role as an American fashion icon, her appearance in endorsements for her own projects, such as perfumes, in advertising campaigns such as that of the lower-end clothing conglomerate Gap, or the seemingly unremunerated numerous red carpet appearances in high-end designer dresses (see Figure 9.3). SJP (Parker's nickname), through her widely circulated public image in this period, her constant reiteration as literally a "clothes horse," appeared to advocate that the self created by a woman through grooming, exercise, clothing and accessories was her "real" work and the site of her identity. Though in the months leading up to the film's début in 2008 the tabloids dissected her domestic life, in particular, her role as wife and mother, this coverage paled in comparison with the reproduction of the endless images—from Gap ads to those for her own Coty perfume "Lovely"—of the style icon, beautifully dressed and coiffed with an ever evolving sophistication.

Figure 9.3 Sarah Jessica Parker in a red carpet appearance (2003). Courtesy of Photofest.

In an influential essay on contemporary stardom, Christine Geraghty has emphasized its "dual nature" in contemporary culture, articulated through the opposition "working life" and "private life."[66] The itinerary of SJP suggests a third category: that of fashion icon—a persona in Parker's case that sits neither comfortably within her private life as wife and mother, nor in her working life as an actress, most notably as Carrie Bradshaw in the television series. While "Carrie," who was as much the creation of Patricia Field as of Parker herself,[67] bears a distinct relationship to SJP as fashion icon, the two are not identical, with the fashion icon, for example, receiving in 2002 the title as "best-accessorized woman in America by the Accessories Council" and the 2004 "Style Icon" award from the Council of Fashion Designers of America.[68] While Sarah Jessica Parker's stardom is a complex issue, one that reflects the intricacies of what Maureen Orth calls the "celebrity industrial complex" (a topic that perhaps deserves a book-length study of its own),[69] it is her role as a purveyor of fashion that is most significant to an understanding of the female event film and the concomitant success of *Sex and the City* in this category. Fashion in the era of the celebrity industrial complex is ideally embodied through the persona of a particular star that can be translated into a series of photographic images, destined to be circulated through the press, including the internet, thus contributing to an awareness of the film before its release.

Sex and the City: The Movie had a distinct advantage over *The Devil Wears Prada* in that no specifically fashion conscious star was associated with the latter film, the place of which was taken by Patricia Field, the costumer, as a media celebrity in her own right. *The Devil Wears Prada* compensated by featuring actual fashion celebrities; for example, supermodel Giselle Bündschen appeared as "Serena," a *Runway* employee, and legendary designer Valentino as himself. *Sex and the City: The Movie* followed suit, including, for example, Patrick DeMarchelier, the fashion photographer, Plum Sykes, the fashion writer, and André Leon Talley, *Vogue's* editor-at-large, who "styles" "Carrie" at a fashion shoot held at *Vogue*, as part of the film's plot. These celebrities, however, rather than adding to a general credibility of the film as a reflection of the fashion scene, functioned specifically to highlight "Carrie"/SJP's legitimacy as a fashion icon. André Leon Talley's comments on this scene are typical: "The movie got (editor) Anna Wintour's blessing. It's all very *Vogue* and of course, Carrie Bradshaw is the ideal *Vogue* woman."[70] Though other stars may fulfill the role of fashion icon to varying degrees, as was the case for Jennifer Lopez,[71] the intensity of interest that surrounds "Carrie"/SJP's fashion choices, and the degree to which she has been able to exploit that interest to keep herself in the public eye, sets her apart from her contemporaries and was an important factor in the creation of media interest in the film before it opened.

While Sarah Jessica Parker stands out as one of the drivers of the project, both as a producer and as the focal point of the film and its surrounding publicity, her identity as part of the group, as a member of "the fab four,"[72] produced a specific kind of collective celebrity in which the four gained their significance through their association. Though Parker did have a separate identity, particularly within the fashion media world (though one that was informed by her role as "Carrie") and to a degree as a film actress, the other three actresses were much more clearly identified with their roles in the series, their celebrity being tied to their status as a member of the group. The possibilities for arousing fans' interest through fashion layouts was multiplied and focused in the film itself through the group (rather than the star). The three other women, in their roles as "Miranda," "Charlotte" and "Samantha," elicited attention rarely awarded the star personas of the actresses themselves—again, at least in part, because of the celebrity enjoyed by Field, who continued to dress them for the film and its attendant publicity (see Figure 9.4). In fact, *People* reported on 16 June 2008, a little more than two weeks after the film's 30 May release date, that the best-selling "key look" from the film was "Miranda's $150 Maggy London frock," which was "flying off the shelves: Though currently sold out, the label is manufacturing 2,000 more of the dresses, which will be available in July."[73] This focus on the group of four, then, marked an extension of Parker's status as a fashion icon, while also expanding the sartorial idioms that the film invoked.

In addition to expanding the fashion base of the film, the group added a necessary dimension to the film that humanized and sentimentalized the experience of the film for its fans by foregrounding female friendship. In fact, the film's tagline might have appropriately read "labels" and "friends," with friendship playing a much more significant role than heterosexual "love." The focus on fashion and female friendship were elements that clearly placed the film in the category of "chick flick," a term often avoided in Hollywood because of the stigma attached to "single quadrant" films for women.[74] Some media experts, such as Lisa Rosen, writing for the *Los Angeles Times*, questioned the pessimism expressed about the film's possibilities as part of this stigma:

Much has been made in the press (including this newspaper) about the films' narrow appeal. After all, what about those magical four quadrants that presage a hit? Can a movie said to appeal only to women over 30 open big? That term "only" rankles some people. After all, the box office bonanza *The Devil Wears Prada* should have put the lie to that thinking two years ago.[75]

Figure 9.4 Patricia Field on the set of *Sex and the City: The Movie* (2008). Courtesy of Photofest.

Rosen is not alone is expressing her dismay at the implicitly misogynistic thinking of the entertainment press. Warner Brothers' Dan Fellman commented: "With movies that appeal to boys and men, you never hear the conversation, 'I hope we get the women.' We have a movie that skews heavily female and while we would love to get as many men as possible, we can do extremely well without them."[76] In fact, the film proved the naysayers wrong, by taking top place domestically over *Indiana Jones and the Kingdom of the Crystal Skull* (Steven Spielberg, 2008), which had already been out for some time, with "the best opening ever for an R-rated comedy," grossing an estimated "$55.7 million." *Variety* commented, "[t]he film's unexpected boffo performance mystified Hollywood and shattered the decades-old thinking that females—particularly older ones—can't fuel the sort of big opening often enjoyed by male-driven event films."[77]

Reviews of the film, like those for many "girly" box office successes, were mixed and largely negative. Exceptionally, Ginia Bellafante, writing for the *New York Times*, described *Sex and the City: The Movie* as investigating "the means by which love and identity can be reclaimed, the great theme of the so-called comedies of remarriage in the 1930s." Bellafante maintained that with the series' conclusion "its four heroines had been taken from their frothy protracted adolescence and submerged into the adult world of anguish and aggrievement," a trend that continued in the movie, which offered "Mr. King's effort to illuminate the complications of happiness and the complexities of friendship" as the characters move forward into an inevitable, if delayed, maturity.[78] In the course of the film, Carrie and Big, or John James Preston, Carrie's long-time on-and-off lover, finally marry, after a false start, such that, in a time-honored manner, the film includes a break-up (a crisis point at which the two lovers lose each other) but concludes with a reunion—the reunion of Carrie and John, but also Miranda and Steve, and Samantha with herself as the most important person in her life. Charlotte has the child that she has anticipated for many years and finally the four women seem to have settled into their lives—not to the degree, however, that would preclude a further sequel.

The thematic of maturity and family notwithstanding, the film was frequently attacked because of its opulent and gratuitous display of consumer goods. Eric Wilson observed in the *New York Times*, "Carrie Bradshaw represents the ultimate endorsement of a luxury system that is built on the aspiration to look rich or famous. Buying $1,000 handbags brings fulfillment. Buying knockoffs brings emotional impotence."[79] Anthony Lane described the film as resembling "a TV show on steroids," while the characters' "gallops of conspicuous consumption seem oddly joyless, as displacement activities tend to be."[80] It was rare, however, for reviewers not to sneak in a kind word. Carina

Chocano asserted that "what feels most remarkable about the movie is its unapologetic embrace of middle-aged women,"[81] although Ella Taylor in the *Village Voice* dismissed the movie as "virtually plotless, not to mention pointless."[82] Vivienne Westwood, iconoclastic designer, whose wedding dress is featured in the film proclaimed: "I thought *Sex and the City* was supposed to be about cutting-edge fashion and there was nothing remotely memorable or interesting about what I saw. I went to the premiere and left after ten minutes."[83] Here, Westwood echoed criticisms of *The Devil Wears Prada*, suggesting that high fashion that is edgy, innovative, artistic and interesting does not crossover to the big screen.

Westwood's perspective is in marked contrast to that of the series' devoted fans, of which there were many, who cited female friendship and the clothing as the film's more moving dimensions. Jessica Henry told Lisa Rosen of the *Los Angeles Times*, reflecting back on her first viewing of the film the previous night at a sold-out midnight screening: "I cried and laughed. I'm going to see it again on Sunday with two other girlfriends. We loved it. I had mascara running down my face by the end of the movie."[84] *New York Magazine* also emphasized the emotional reception that the film received by fans ("And when they cried they cried tears of fashion"), claiming to have overheard two girls at the film's New York premiere: "Girl 1: Did you cry? Girl 2: So much. First, it was tears of joy, then it was tears of fashion." The theme of tears was already routinely associated with the series. For example, a tour guide, a woman of 28, introduces her clients to "Carrie Bradshaw's house" with these words of caution: "I know it might be overwhelming. ... I might see a few tears walking down there. It's a magical place. But try to stay calm, and quiet."[85] The emotionalism with which the audience viewed the series and greeted the film, embracing both the dimension of female friendship and the clothes that the characters wear, suggests the powerful sway that this version of neo-feminism holds over certain women too young to have been exposed to feminism itself as a political movement. Female empowerment for this generation limits itself to individual aspiration; the goal of a more utopian social organization that might foster self-fulfillment is outside meaningful feminine experience as they have encountered it.

These young women, unmarried and with an income whose primary purpose is their sustenance and gratification, represent an important market for the selling of consumer non-durables. Not insignificantly, "the girls" of *Sex and the City* appear to have no biological family: they exist for themselves and each other as a reflection of themselves. Ginia Bellafante remarked about the film: "One aspect of the women's depiction that remains fixed is the sense that they have emerged from nowhere, with no lives to speak of before they were old enough for snakeskin and small dresses with tinier straps."[86] In some ways, the needs of these new urban orphan girls are modest: they have neither mortgages nor cars; they are not providing for their children's education; at least as yet, medical care is not one of their major concerns. While their tastes fall outside products geared for the home or family, they represent ideal consumers of other kinds of goods, in particular luxury goods—objects with no purpose except the enhancement and gratification of their owners. In an oft-cited article, *The Economist* explained in 2001 a crucial dimension of the growing category of single young females (SYF) and their companions who animate "the rich world's city life" in New York and London, extending to Tokyo, Stockholm, Paris and Santiago: "They are the main consumers and producers of the creative economy that revolves around advertising, publishing, entertainment and media. More than any other social group, they have time, money and a passion for spending on whatever is fashionable, frivolous and fun." Coining the phrase "the Bridget Jones economy," *The Economist* explains: "Because young singles have so much disposable money and because they set so many trends, they are a market that many companies long to sell to."[87]

Kay Hymowitz extends the notion of the Bridget Jones economy to include *Sex and the City*: "The *Sex and the City* culture has spread far with women from Beijing to Warsaw now asserting their independence and economic power." She continued: "The globalization of the SYF reflects a series of demographic and economic shifts that are pointing much of the world—with important exceptions, including Africa and most of the Middle East—towards a New Girl Order." The characteristics of SYF as part of the New Girl Order evoke the principles of what I have been calling neo-feminism. While perhaps not as goal-oriented as Helen Gurley Brown's Cosmo Girl, the SYF has a strong work ethic and subscribes to a program of self-improvement. The *Economist* reports that SYFs are "especially likely to jog, play tennis and take exercises classes," noting, however, that the most significant distinction between the SYF and "her married sisters is the amount of time and money she spends on simply having fun."[88] Vicky, a SYF from Beijing, China, claims as her motto, "work hard, play harder," not only recalling the characters on *Sex and the City* in their younger incarnations (Samantha, in particular), but also suggesting the ways in which the SYF represents the culmination of the rise of the Modern Girl in the 1920s and 1930s as an international phenomenon.[89]

The success of *Sex and the City: The Movie* illustrates how the New Girl Order provides the kind of audience that Conglomerate Hollywood would find desirable because this audience would be responsive to and supportive of the media synergies necessary to "opening big"; however, this group, nonetheless, remains a second-class audience from a conglomerate perspective—the target of counterprogramming, rather than of "tentpoles," or major productions. While in 2008, *Sex and the City* garnered a very respectable international box office take of $415 million, it pales in comparison to the $1,001 million earned by *The Dark Knight* (Christopher Nolan, 2008) in the same year. Thus, the girly film, in spite of its relative success at the box office, highlights the reality that women audiences are less significant than ones that include men, both under and over 25.

Female stars occupy a similar position, with only Julia Roberts routinely appearing among the top 10 stars in terms of box office earnings. When asked to comment on the unusual success of *Sex and the City: The Movie*, Sarah Jessica Parker exclaimed: "I am so excited about the possibilities for movies about women."[90] More than a year later, Ann Hornaday in the *Washington Post*, was far less optimistic. She asked, "With female characters, why does Hollywood fear that the stronger they are, the harder they fail?" She continued, "Strong women, for now anyway, are out." Hornaday reported that Nia Vardalos, of *My Big Fat Greek Wedding* (Joel Zwick, 2002) fame, was asked to transform her heroine into a hero because "women don't go to movies." Recent successes, such as *Sex and the City*, were dismissed as "flukes."[91] Samuel C. Craig explains that the studios' reluctance to produce the relatively "smaller films" that appeal to women is because these "typically have much more limited, if any, opportunities for ancillary revenues." He adds, however: "There are also the less tangible issues of egos and bragging rights," highlighting that the nature and personality of the male executives who continue to dominate the industry is also a factor.[92]

Producer Lynda Obst notes that the need for "'unaided awareness,' which is where you get this addiction to toys and comics and old titles," also leads studios to focus on male-oriented material. As a consequence, Obst explained, "it's easier for male executives to get jobs now." According to Obst, "[g]irls don't grow up reading comic books or playing video games, or with Transformer or G.I. Joe toys," all of which have provided the basis for the kinds of franchises that studios prefer. Obst continued: "So the material that they're looking for isn't necessarily as familiar to female executives who read books, which is becoming practically a liability. That's the real problem. That's how it becomes systemic."[93]

Another less obvious implication of Obst's observations is that when films are produced that address a female audience, they must meet similar criteria to those exhibited by the male-oriented franchises, limiting the kinds of films that will be made. Female-oriented films must target a demographic that is likely to consume the kinds of goods that create desirable media synergies and that will ensure that a film "opens big." In order to appeal to the New Girl Order as a potentially desirable demographic, the film's topic has to be such that it will also be likely to benefit from "unaided awareness," through a highly visible star, previous exposure in another medium such as television or novels, and various consumer oriented tie-ins that will enable the project to gain the support of other industries, including location in cities such New York that will garner media attention and significant financial advantages. Finally, these films must replicate successful formulas in order to minimize risk. Among the limited band of films that interest Conglomerate Hollywood many reproduce the neo-feminist paradigm because of the way that it supports feminine consumer culture and the larger tenets of celebrity culture with its focus on individual achievement. Thus, an important reason for the continued popularity of the neo-feminist paradigm is the way in which it is compatible with the goals of Conglomerate Hollywood and the media industries more generally, from the fashion magazine to television networks.

Ultimately, nothing breeds success in Hollywood like success itself, condemning women audiences to a limited range of films that are based on previously successful marketing and narrative formulas and that often support the neo-feminist paradigm. While films produced by women directors for women might initially hold at least the promise of an alternative, in fact these productions tend also to reproduce a version of the neo-feminist paradigm. There are a very few women directors who have the experience and credibility based on past achievements to promote a project that derives from an original script; however, the constraints of Conglomerate Hollywood seldom permit significant deviation from proven formulas—even in the case of these privileged directors. Furthermore these directors, such as Nancy Meyers and Nora Ephron, are themselves products and proponents of neo-feminism. As a result, though films such as *Sleepless in Seattle* (Nora Ephron, 1993) may exhibit traits that are at odds with neo-feminism, such as the relative lack of importance accorded fashion in this film, by and large these productions also serve to confirm the importance of the neo-feminist paradigm for contemporary audiences. The next chapter proposes to investigate the role of neo-feminism in a film by auteur director Nancy Meyers, *Something's Gotta Give* (2003), as means of further exploring the pervasiveness and limitations of this perspective.

Chapter 10

Something's Gotta Give (2003)
Nancy Meyers, Neo-Feminist Auteur

Nancy Meyers as a contemporary writer, producer and director occupies a privileged position in Hollywood. Michael Allen in his introductory work *Contemporary US Cinema*, published in 2003, noted that "[t]he American film industry, even in these liberated days, is overwhelmingly controlled and operated by men." He described Meyers as one of the few exceptions, "a particularly interesting mainstream woman director ... who has scripted many of the more significant women-centered films of the last 20 years."[1] Allen characterized her work as "gentle comedy" explaining that "[t]he gentleness of the comedy, however, does not necessarily mean that these films do not offer pertinent observations about women in contemporary America."[2] While Meyers has been involved with a series of box office successes as a writer and producer, such as *Private Benjamin* (Howard Zieff, 1980) and *Baby Boom* (Charles Shyer, 1987) and as writer and director for films such as *Parent Trap* (1998), or writer, director and producer for films such as *The Holiday* (2006), her work, unlike that of directors such as Katherine Bigelow and Jane Campion, has been largely neglected by feminist scholars.[3] *What Women Want* (2000), which she produced and directed (and for which she also served as an unacknowledged co-writer[4]), in 2009 remains the top-grossing romantic comedy directed by a woman.[5] Though appreciated by the public, the film was for the most part ignored or condemned by critics and scholars, as is the case for neo-feminist cinema more generally. In this chapter, I will argue that Meyers brings a distinctly neo-feminist perspective to her comedies that not only becomes one of the marks of her style, but also facilitates the marketing of her films within Conglomerate Hollywood. A notable dimension of this neo-feminist perspective is her view of heterosexual men, who are portrayed as significantly disadvantaged, even to the point of suffering a disability, over women in the game of love, and her interest in the older, often very successful, woman, who typically stars in her films.

A comparison with other contemporary comedies directed at women audiences suggests that within the woman's film, in particular within hybridized comedies as the new privileged form of the woman's film, two disabilities emerge as significant impediments to romance: masculinity and advancing age.[6] Heroes who find themselves the protagonist in a "girly film" (such as *What Women Want*) discover that their gender works against a satisfying conclusion, while the "biological clock" constitutes a primary disability that many a heroine must overcome. If the single girl provides the model for the new romantic heroine, how does this ideal work for a character who seems past the age of marriage, whose potential partners suffer from debilitating forms of masculinity that have hardened with advancing years? The film *Something's Gotta Give*, based on Meyers' own experience as a single woman in her late fifties, which she transformed into a star vehicle for Diane Keaton, engages with this question.[7]

As a vehicle for Diane Keaton, *Something's Gotta Give* depended heavily upon her long-established star persona. Within a cinematic arena, the career of Diane Keaton demonstrates the various permutations of femininity and its conclusive girlishness in the twenty-first century. Her role as Annie Hall in the eponymous film (Woody Allen, 1977) inaugurated a mode of dress that reconciles femininity and feminism, and which offers itself as an alternative to the "tarty" plunging necklines promoted by *Cosmopolitan Magazine*. Throughout her career, which is exceptional in terms of its longevity, she incarnates a number of different "style" options while maintaining a persona that suggests independence of thought and continuity. Like other significant female stars, such as Jane Fonda, who managed careers that continued through several decades, Diane Keaton's star persona might be described as embodying "serial authenticity," in which the ability to undergo transformation while remaining recognizably herself is a significant trait.[8] The whimsical "men's styling" of *Annie Hall* in the 1970s gave way to the aggressive career look of her characters in the 1980s, culminating in her role as a magazine editor in *Hanging Up* (2000), which she herself directed. Her character "Georgia" recalls Grace Mirabella, a former editor-in-chief at *Vogue* (1971–88), who, like Georgia in *Hanging Up*, started her own magazine, *Mirabella* (1989–2000). Amy Taubin, writing in *The Village Voice*, goes so far as to say that "Keaton's character ... is such a blatant caricature of Grace Mirabella that she might have grounds to sue."[9] As Georgia/Grace, Keaton offers a double neo-feminist icon by representing both herself and a high-powered career woman clearly based on an actual public figure—a far cry from her original Annie Hall incarnation, whose fey charm countered the potential threat of her career successes.

Relative to other stars of her generation, such as Jill Clayburgh (b. 1944), Goldie Hawn (b. 1945), Candice Bergen (b. 1946) or Marisa Berenson (b. 1947), Diane Keaton (b. 1946) offers a catalogue of possibilities to her viewers, moving from youth to middle age, that counter the more overt consumer-culture images circulated in magazines like *Cosmopolitan*, or the more recent spate of celebrity magazines such as *Hello!* Her hair, a soft golden brown, flowing and unstructured, between chin and shoulder length (a seemingly natural look), a soft feminine figure (neither buxom nor muscular), quirky clothing that covered rather than revealed, eccentric jewelry—together create a distinctive and influential style that matures over time. From the flighty, hesitant neophyte of *Annie Hall* she evolved into a career woman, sometime mother and wife—but always autonomous. Her determination, softened by her girlish and slightly loopy charm, offset the decisiveness that characterizes her later roles, as in her incarnation of a CEO-type who suddenly finds herself responsible for a child in *Baby Boom* (Charles Shyer, 1987), on which Meyers served as a writer and producer. Yet, Carina Chocano notes about Keaton that "what we want most is to keep seeing her as she's made us believe she really is—free-spirited and rebellious, and not just somebody's mom."[10]

Keaton's 2003 role as Erica in *Something's Gotta Give*, directed by Nancy Meyers, for which Keaton won a Golden Globe, an NBR Award and a Golden Satellite Award, marked a departure from the stylistic choices associated with her previous mature roles, which always retained something of the whimsy associated with her off-screen persona, mitigating the potential abrasiveness of her more forceful incarnations. Erica, the character played by Keaton in *Something's Gotta Give*, avoids the kooky wardrobe associated with Keaton's star persona (in particular, the menswear look that Keaton pioneered in *Annie Hall*) conveying a more conventional, more mainstream sensibility. Erica's palette is light. Beige and white predominate in opposition to the dark suits that Keaton wore in her previous "mature" roles, except when these neutral colors give way to black for emotional emphasis at certain points in the film. Keaton as Erica not only avoids the colorful palate associated with youth, but also the severity of the suits associated with her career roles, as well as the eccentricity of dress she exhibits in such roles as Daphne Wilder in *Because I Said So* (Michael Lehmann, 2007), or Natalie Swerdlow in *Surrender Dorothy* (Charles McDougall, 2006) in which she (as in *Something's Gotta Give*) plays a "girly" mother.

As Erica, her silhouette is sharply defined: she appears significantly thinner and fitter than in previous films such as *Town and Country* (Peter Chelsom, 2001). There is something nostalgic about her "look." Her "date" dress, in which she catches of the eye of both Jack Nicholson (b. 1937) as Harry Sanborn and Keanu Reeves (b. 1964) as Julian Mercer, recalls the classic LBD (little black dress) popularized by Chanel in the first half of the twentieth century. It is sleeveless with clean lines, a gently flared skirt that stops just

Figure 10.1 Diane Keaton in *Something's Gotta Give* (2003). Courtesy of Photofest.

above the knees, a neckline that plunges discretely to reveal subtle curves. Keaton is reported to have said, "Nancy kept forcing me to wear all these open clothes, which I can't stand. I would have liked it more buttoned up."[11] (See Figure 10.1.) Her look is spare—no bold accessories except for large hoop earrings, a chunky ring and a lariat choker—from time to time and never all at once. Her hair is styled and streaked—a coiffure appropriate to a younger woman, while equally suited to the mature matron. Liz Smith of the *Los Angeles Times* remarked: "If only Keaton would wear in real life the divine, simple clothes she sports in the movie, she'd probably become fashion's comeback kid."[12]

This shift in style highlights the role that Keaton played for the writer, director and producer of the film, veteran Hollywood player Nancy Meyers, for whom Keaton functions as an alter ego—such that Meyers' stylistic choices temporarily displace Keaton's own persona, without, paradoxically, under-mining our sense of Keaton as Keaton. "'Clearly, Erica is more Nancy than me,' says Ms. Keaton of her character, Erica Barry, a divorced playwright and self-described 'high-strung, over-amped, controlling, know-it-all neurotic who is incredibly cute and lovable,'" reported the *New York Times*. The *Times* further commented, referring to Meyers: "She looks strikingly like a petite version of Ms Keaton, down to her streaked, affluent-mom hairstyle and cream turtleneck."[13] (See Figure 10.2.) Similarly, *Variety* claims:

Figure 10.2 Nancy Meyers (2003). Courtesy of Photofest.

> The female protagonist played with disarming and flighty charm by Diane Keaton in writer-director-producer Nancy Meyers' latest film *Something's Gotta Give* is, in many ways, a reflection of Meyers herself. It's a device she used before in her previous films *Private Benjamin* and *Baby Boom*.[14]

Meyers actually wrote the role of Erica for Keaton, consulting with Keaton and Jack Nicholson (Keaton's co-star) in the course of producing the script and tailoring the characters to suit these particular actors, while using her own experience as her source.[15]

Of Jack, Meyers says: "I had his picture by my computer."[16] Nicholson brought a similarly powerful star persona to his role that exercised a significant influence over the development of the script; however, this persona highlights how neo-feminism assumes that men are disadvantaged within the feminine realm, and thus must be managed and manipulated, according to the Cosmo tradition, or need to be educated, as was the case for Edward in *Pretty Woman*, by the neo-feminist heroine. Nicholson, who has the reputation of being "a shrewd curator of his own legend,"[17] nonetheless leaves open the possibility that he might be at some point redeemed by a woman, in particular a woman like Diane Keaton. Thus, he confides to *Playboy*: "I happen to think Keaton is fantastic—one of the most idiosyncratic, interesting people I know. But I have a kind of open affection for Diane anyway, ever since I was with her in *Reds*."[18]

The *Observer Review* summarizes his reputation: "He's sneering, lecherous and misogynistic—and Hollywood loves him for it," qualities that Meyers was able to mobilize in creating a foil to Keaton's charms.[19] The *Los Angeles Times* reported that "Mr. Nicholson freely admits he prefers to date women between 25 and 38, though he does see older women."[20] Widely circulated statements of this nature lent credibility to Nicholson's portrayal of the male lead in *Something's Gotta Give*, a serial womanizer who breaks the heroine's heart.

Nicholson's persona assisted the film in its representation of masculinity as something that must be tamed or even surmounted if the neo-feminist heroine is to reach her goals, while giving Meyers full reign to express her own amorous disappointments onscreen. By creating a male lead whose major task was to provide a backdrop upon which the heroine's dilemmas might be played out, Meyers was, through Keaton, able to emphasize the autobiographical dimension of the film. Thus, Meyers claims: "It's a real story I'm telling about what it's like to be her age and single ... To have been married for a long time and to be without that, and the shell she shrinks inside of."[21] Meyers could tell this story entirely from her own perspective since the male lead was, even before the movie began, through association with the star persona of Nicholson, an example of masculine self-absorption and insensitivity, and hence unworthy of the viewer's sympathy. Feminist scholar Molly Haskell is quoted as claiming: "In all of his movies, he legitimizes sexism. That's part of the package. There's something obnoxious going on there, and people have called attention to it, but somehow he's so hip ... he's managed to keep his anti-Hollywood credentials while remaining the ultimate Hollywood playboy."[22] Meyers exploited these qualities to engage the viewer's interest in the sentimental plight of the heroine.

Meyers' work with her former husband produced "glossy sentimental comedies that paid lip service to feminism but celebrated old fashioned bourgeois values at the core," according to Nancy Griffin.[23] *Something's Gotta Give* is no exception. The film recounts the story of Erica (Diane Keaton) and Harry (Jack Nicholson). Harry meets Erica during the course of what he hopes to be a "fun-filled" weekend with her daughter; however, before the fun can begin, he has a heart attack. Erica is reluctantly left to care for him, during which period, the mother comes to occupy the daughter's place and the couple falls in love. Once Harry returns to the city, their romantic idyll comes to an end as Harry reverts to his philandering ways. Erica takes her revenge: she dates a young doctor Julian (played by Keanu Reeves) and writes a hit Broadway play, in which Harry appears as Henry, a satirical figure who dies at the end of the second act.

Harry has less success in sublimating the feelings generated by his failed loved affair. Subject to acute anxiety attacks, he attempts to change his ways, briefly retreating to a tropical island, which fails to soothe his distressed spirit. He ultimately finds solace by seeking forgiveness from every woman he has ever hurt. At the conclusion of what proves to be a long and arduous process, Harry finds himself in Paris, asking Erica's forgiveness, at which point Erica relents, leaving her impossibly handsome and sensitive doctor for the contrite, if still coarse and egotistical, Harry. The film concludes with a happy scene, the olds and the youngsters reconciled and properly paired with age-appropriate partners—the new granddaughter the apple of Harry's eye!

The principal plot runs parallel to a subplot that focuses on Erica's relations with her daughter, Marin (played by Amanda Peet), and her daughter's father and her ex-husband, Dave (Paul Michael Glaser). Marin, who is on the road to becoming a female version of Harry, is arrested in her path by Erica's stirring defense of love, emphasized through her lack of bitterness over her failed marriage and failed romance with Harry. Her mother's tears, in which happiness and loss combine to define in her words "the time of my life"—that is, the time of a woman's life—give Marin the moral courage to marry a suitable young man (unlike her father who marries a much younger woman) and have a child—the granddaughter that delights Harry. In this crucial scene, Erica tells Marin that "[y]ou can't hide from love for the rest of your life. ... I let someone in and I had the time of my life." Marin responds: "I've never had the time of my life." Erica retorts: "I know, Babe. ... What are you waiting for?" Marin, of all the women who dated Harry (albeit in her case the relationship was never consummated), expresses no bitterness towards him when he seeks her out as part of his journey of penance.

Both mother and daughter, then, are able to move forward on the path of personal fulfillment, with both being singled out by their exceptional beauty, style and professional success. Importantly, in terms of their identity as successful women, mother and daughter adeptly manipulate the codes of feminine performance—Erica from her casually sleek vacation wear to her seductive black dress, Marin from a bikini-clad Lolita to a killer auctioneer—a transformation emphasized in the film by the fact that this takes place onscreen: Marin strips and dresses in her office while talking to her mother just before a crucial bidding war.

Keaton, through her various roles and transformation as an actress, as well as through her role as Erica, emphasizes the importance of the consumer-constructed persona for a successful professional woman, while distancing this persona (who represents taste and refinement) from the cruder and crasser versions propagated by television shows such as the British *What Not to Wear* (BBC One and Two, 2001–07) for middle-class audiences. The character of Marin, along with her capacity to transform herself from beach bunny to auctioneer and finally to mother, while conforming to the mandate of bourgeois good taste, suggests the power of this particular legacy. Women who do not participate in the play and performance of feminine culture are marginalized, such as Zoe (Frances McDormand), Erica's sister, who teaches Women's Studies at Columbia. While the film portrays her affectionately, it also positions her as being outside the culture of self-fulfillment represented by Erica. Zoe is childless, without a partner—a lovable eccentric among the high-powered movers and shakers who provide the film's focus.

Through this emphasis on the importance of appearance and the woman's capacity to control her appearance, *Something's Gotta Give* transforms the makeover trope emphasized in films such as *Pretty Woman* (Garry Marshall, 1990) and *Romy and Michele's High School Reunion* (David Mirkin, 1997) into a continuous regime of renovation and self-improvement, which extends into home-decorating and language acquisition.[24] A sign, then, of Erica's worthiness as "A Woman to Love," in Harry's terms, is her studious apprenticeship in French and then Italian as well as her dedication to redoing first her beach house, and then her New York apartment (never shown onscreen).

Scott Foundas in *Variety* identifies the film's "endless fascination with the peccadilloes of New York's obscenely wealthy" as one of its defining characteristics, seeing this as a reflection of the ways in which the film's cultivation of the self extends beyond the body into its surroundings, that of the "white-linen New York beach community scene."[25] Décor was the object of lavish attention, and the beach house (in fact a Hollywood set) "rated an *Architectural Digest* spread."[26] Another reviewer comments: "Set and costumes look like someone hit the shopping mall and bought Pottery Barn and J. Crew out of much of their inventory," again emphasizing the film's dependence upon an aesthetic defined by the visual vernacular of tasteful (and expensive) consumerism.[27] Typically, the March 2006 issue of *Architectural Digest* included a feature called "Discoveries by Designers: Editors Present Designers' Sources" that highlights a particular shop, complete with address and phone number upon whose resources Meyers called to "furnish Diane Keaton's Hamptons home in *Something's Gotta Give*."[28] With a total of three articles appearing in *Architectural Digest* on the film's set, the press coverage of the set design serves to emphasize the role of popular cinema, and this film in particular, as a literal shop window, as in the case of the fashion film, here, redeployed to include home wares.[29]

Meyers' understanding of character extends this now well-documented consumer culture dimension of the cinema. Cinema is not merely a shop window; the goods that it displays are crucial to its art. Surroundings, for Meyers, create character. She claims: "I tend to write movies that take place in bedrooms, kitchens and living rooms rather than on grand landscapes. It's fun for me to continue to define the characters through the places they choose to live."[30] Even more pointedly, she remarks: "But if you've spent a chunk of your life writing a character and someone puts them in the wrong clothes or in a bed with sheets you know she would never own, it's as if someone's written dialogue."[31] Literally, then, in a Meyers' film, the self of the character is defined through its manifestations in its environment—a filmic technique that works to support the developments of consumer culture. This expansion of the self to its surroundings mimics the evolution of makeover culture extending through the various parts of the body to the body's environment as the required arenas of cultivation, manifest in the proliferation of makeover programming on television, covering the body, clothing, cooking, gardening, home improvement, etc.[32] Consumer culture norms, then, can be applied to every aspect of the individual's material existence as an expanded self in need of constant renovation and improvement. The focus of this cultivation is an autonomous self that seeks its own fulfillment as its primary goal, ultimately challenging the notion of a natural order associated with the traditional romance.[33]

While the film nominally upholds a conventional reading of gender and of the family within this consumer culture environment, it also systematically undermines codes of gender difference. The film concludes, in typical Shakespearean fashion, with a set of couples that appear to conform to a "natural" order; however, the manner in which the film reaches its conclusion raises questions about that "order"—in particular, the film offers an interrogation of the relations between age and gender. Age as a "disability" that literally embraces all men and women paradoxically reinvigorates a romantic model that at the film's beginning is presented as beyond all repair. Initially, it might seem that age creates a level playing field; however, even age cannot erase the difficulties that contemporary hyper-sexualized masculinity, as licensed by the sexual revolution, represents for the romantic comedy. While the film may not necessarily be optimistic in all its conclusions, it provides an exercise or experiment in precisely what the genre can and cannot do.

Something's Gotta Give unites two significant thematics in contemporary romantic comedy that are characteristic of a category I shall call the "neo-romantic comedies," identified by Frank Krutnik as the "new romance," referring to the post-1989 renaissance of Hollywood romantic comedy.[34] The twin tendencies of neo-romantic comedies are signaled by the titles of two recent films, *Down with Love* (Peyton Reed, 2003) and *Knocked Up* (Judd Apatow, 2007). The first, echoing some sort of post-feminist slogan, implies the death of the romantic paradigm, which appears as if it can only survive as a nostalgic parody of itself. The second is marked by the strategies of farce, in which the body (its carnal pleasures and necessities) drives the plot towards the traditional conclusion of the romantic comedy: the coming together of the couple in an inevitable happy, if chastened, union. Whereas the first theme produces films that I shall characterize as "nostalgic neo-romantic comedies," the second theme delivers what I shall refer to as "farcical neo-romantic comedies."

Down with Love recounts the story of a successful career woman, an author (Barbara Novak played by Renée Zellweger) who has made her reputation by debunking popular myths about love for women, and by writing a sort of self-help book to assist women in overcoming their need for a romantic fix—of the type that inhabits, in multiple copies, popular bookstores around the world. She, of course, succumbs to the power of love in the form of a debonair playboy (Catcher Block played by Ewan McGregor) in a conclusion in which both are vanquished and victorious simultaneously. The film exploits the old topos of the "biter bit," exemplified by Benedick in Shakespeare's *Much Ado About Nothing*, which provided an archetype for subsequent romantic comedies, of which the character of Harry in *Something's Gotta Give* is yet another example. The "biter bit" appears in other contexts through the medieval and Renaissance period and was a commonplace of medieval moral literature, evoking a substantial literary legacy, particularly in the context of romance—here invoked nostalgically, and even ironically.[35]

In theme and style, *Down with Love* recalls the Rock Hudson and Doris Day sex comedies of the 1950s—with all that this implies in terms of irony.[36] As pointed out by Tamar Jeffers McDonald in her volume on romantic comedy, in these nostalgic neo-romantic comedies, which she calls "neo-traditional romantic comedies," and in which category *Down with Love* belongs, "sex" is frequently not an important issue—even if it does occur, the sex scene is not visually or erotically marked.[37] As is typical of the classical screwball comedy, we are rarely, if ever, invited to share in a voyeuristic, highly charged erotic exchange depicted visually on the screen. While contemporary romantic comedy heroines are not prudish in the way that their earlier counterparts were, even during the 1960s, erotic encounters are not the focus of their concerns. Similarly, while Erica and Harry (and also we assume Erica and Julian) have sex, it is the emotions evoked in Erica (and Harry) that are the focus of the film's interest. Finally, the reconciliation of Erica and Harry is not based on erotic attraction but rather on some unnamed bond that cannot be explained. The *London Times* commented: "As the female editor who sent me to see the film put it: 'What woman faced with a choice of Nicholson or Reeves would choose Nicholson? That's a no-brainer.' (er, been duped for once, have we, Nancy?)."[38] What draws Harry and Erica together is their mutual understanding. The romantic scene, which explains their attraction to each other, does not take place in the bedroom, but at an earlier moment in which Erica and Harry meet in the kitchen for late-night pancakes (both are insomniacs). At one point Erica queries Harry, wondering, "[i]f you hate me or if ... you're the only person who ever really got me." Harry responds: "I don't hate you." Their physical bonding is presented as a consequence of this under-standing—not as its cause.

Knocked Up, by way of contrast, presents a relationship that begins when a beautiful, talented young woman, Alison (Katherine Heigl), has a one-night stand (under the influence of alcohol) with a chubby, low achieving "slacker," Ben (Seth Rogan). The resulting pregnancy eventually forces the young man to face his responsibilities, bringing the couple together, more or less happily. Tamar Jeffers McDonald refers to this category of films, which includes titles such as *Along Came Polly* (John Hamburg, 2004), and *The 40 Year Old Virgin* (Judd Apatow, 2005), as "homme-coms," because, typically, they focus on the male protagonist and include farcical elements associated with gross-out films addressed to young male audiences.[39] Notwithstanding, she comments that "[n]arrative closure within this new groupings of films is only achieved by a capitulation to monogamy," attributing to the homme-com the same neo-tra-ditional tendencies that she sees in *When Harry Met Sally* (Rob Reiner, 1989) and its successors, such as *Sleepless in Seattle* (Nora Ephron, 1993), both starring Meg Ryan.[40]

From another perspective, David Denby posits *Knocked Up* as a recent spin on a variation of the romantic comedy that he identifies as the "slacker/striver" sub-genre.[41] In this sub-genre, the initial model provided by *High Fidelity* (Stephen Frears, 2000), a competent ambitious woman (the striver) is coupled with an inept, under-achieving but endearing man (the slacker). Like McDo-nald, Denby argues that these films do a disservice to the female protagonist, who is reduced to a flat, undeveloped "vehicle" for the male protagonist's education.[42] This perspective ignores the vitality of the striver heroine and her appeal to female viewers. Thus, *Knocked Up* arguably made Katherine Heigl (b. 1978) a romantic comedy star, the new "girl-next-door," who replaced Meg Ryan (b. 1961) and Julia Roberts (b. 1967) as the most significant female romantic comedy stars of the 1990s. Certainly, however, *Knocked Up*, like *Something's Gotta Give*, presents us with an exceptional heroine who, like Erica, succumbs to the charms of a man who is distinctly average, or even less than average, and who bears the burden of the narrative's farcical dimension, sug-gesting the validity of the striver/slacker pair as at least one paradigm for the couple within neo-feminism.

All these films, regardless of the tendency that they exhibit as nostalgic or farcical neo-romantic comedies, re-enact many features attributed to the comedy of remarriage of the 1930s and 1940s as described by Stanley Cavell.[43] In particular, the goal of the plot in these movies is to construct a couple who may unite within a context of productive equality with, however, this one caveat: in the neo-romantic comedy such a relationship is only possible for some women—women who meet a certain set of a criteria—beautiful, successful, hardworking—in every way exceptional and, as such, the ideal subject of capitalism as employee and, even more importantly, as consumer—and finally of the neo-feminist heroine. While the classical comedy of remarriage depends upon the education of the heroine (and to a lesser degree that of the hero) for its happy ending, the point of that education is not to single her out as exceptional, but to demonstrate how she is just like all other women. Indeed, the heroine of the classical screwball comedy may often suffer from the "tall poppy syndrome"—as is the case of Tracy Lord (Katharine Hepburn) in *Philadelphia Story* (George Cukor, 1940)—in which case her education consists of her realization that she is not "a goddess," but rather a common mortal among mortals.

In contradistinction, *Something's Gotta Give* offers us a neo-feminist heroine in Erica, as played by Diane Keaton, who, if not a goddess, is certainly a superwoman, and who can afford to be no less, should she wish to gain her happy ending. Like all striver heroines, Erica is competent and driven, the mistress of her fate, of very substantial homes, of an undeniable talent, admirable self-discipline and of an enviable bank account. Harry calls her "A Tower of Strength," who has developed a "killer combo" because "[y]ou use your strength to separate yourself from everyone, but it's thrilling when your defenses are down." Erica's very femininity, her attractiveness, depends paradoxically on her striver-derived strength. In many ways, then, the film unites the two tendencies of the neo-romantic comedy, with its self-consciously nostalgic themes and structure, its slacker protagonist, its striver heroine and its moments of coarse humor, suggesting how both forms are linked to the neo-feminist paradigm, which proclaims that only the girlish, successful woman has the capacity to surmount the obstacles that life will place in her path as she progresses towards happiness.

Something's Gotta Give addresses women over 30, too old for Harry and old enough to have been married and moved on and to have realized that marriage in one's youth is no guarantee of partnership in old age. Erica is the exception that proves that a woman may be girlish and marriageable ("nubile" in the original sense of the word) regardless of her age. In addition to her girlish looks, Erica is so exceptional in every other way that she is courted by a young doctor, Julian, played by the youth idol, Keanu Reeves. I would argue that, these other qualities notwithstanding, it is the "girlish" dimension that Keaton brings to this role that provides the necessary prosthetic that assists her in overcoming the disability of age. In contrast, as is the case with Harry, the man may be quite ordinary—even repugnant (according to the codes of women's magazines), which ties the film into the slacker/striver sub-genre as defined above, in which the ambitious, talented neo-feminist heroine is played against an inept and, if not unintelligent, immature hero. Harry represents the ways in which consumer culture permits and encourages a kind of prolonged adolescence, extending beyond middle age into old age, in which youth is constituted by a set of tastes and behaviors, or consumer choices.[44] This prolonged adolescence produces both the ordinary slacker male and the exceptional striver woman, the "Tower of Strength," worthy of equality with men.

This notion that only the exceptional woman is worthy of equality complements the general trends of neo-liberal culture, in which class and economic status, rather than race or gender, define identity and confer privilege. Here, Nancy Meyers' film deviates significantly from the slacker/striver genre, for while the film appears to support the romantic paradigm through its happy ending, it also seems unable to overcome its contradictions. Indeed, the film offers us two possible conclusions: a happy ending in which the couple unites and an alternative ending in which the hero dies. Erica as a successful Broadway playwright transforms her initial disappointment with love into a successful play. In "A Woman to Love," the title of Erica's play (which she steals from Harry), Harry as "Henry" dies at the end of the Second Act—as a farcical character whose episodes at the hospital are played to full comic effect through the "Dancing Henrys," a chorus of old men whose prosthetic buttocks protrude pathetically from their hospital gowns. Harry-as-Henry is punished, because, as Erica explains, "He made our heroine suffer."

Significantly, the affair on which Meyers based her script did not have a happy ending—except insofar, as was the case with Erica, she managed to transform it into a work of art, in this instance, a popular film. *People* reports: "Meyers sighs now at the thought of the romance that failed. 'But at least I got a hit movie out of it.'"[45] From this perspective, the film echoes traditional romances, in particular the female gothic, as a form of "loving with a vengeance" (to quote Tania Modleski's canonical work on women's romance) in which the heroine in one way or another triumphs over the hero through a narrative that requires him often to be in a debilitated state (as in the case of the nineteenth-century novel *Jane Eyre,* with its famously blind and maimed hero, Rochester) to succumb to love and marriage.[46] Nonetheless, the conclusion of this film is also about mutual education and equality, more in keeping with a Shakespearean model of romance than that promoted through the female gothic. Both the heroine and the hero must be brought low so that both can be redeemed through love, though Harry's humiliation seems more complete than Erica's.

In a certain sense, Harry, of course, does die as the result of his heart attack (or attack of the heart, more properly). The old Harry incapable of love is replaced by a new Harry for whom love, and the coupling that this entails, becomes a necessity. Through a double ritual of humiliation, the first through his farcical double, a great success on Broadway, and the second, as a result of his journey of expiation, Harry is reborn as "A Man to Love." First, of course, he must experience a final humiliation—during which moment, believing that Erica too has rejected him, he muses, "Look who gets to be the girl," as snow begins to fall. Through the experience of this position, the position to which he had relegated Erica earlier in the film, and the humiliation that it implies, Harry is redeemed through the logic of the film. He has suffered as did our heroine. He and Erica are now equals.

In its manipulation of the codes of gender to produce positions of parity between hero and heroine, the film calls upon the "me too" factor that often characterizes female friendship films such as *Romy and Michele's High School Reunion*.[47] Not coincidentally, Harry repeats the phrase "me too," throughout the film—at times inappropriately. When he "dumps" Erica, putting her in the position of, in her words, "the dumb girl," she says, "I just wish that it had lasted for more than a week." He responds, "Me too," which she characterizes as "a terrible thing to say." The first "me too" moment occurs at the beginning of their relationship, when they both discover, via e-mail, that they are insomniacs, the letters clearly typed out on Harry's computer screen. The bond between Erica and Harry is established on the basis of the recognition—not of difference—but of sameness. Like Romy and Michele, this is a "me too" couple—in which the identity is doubled—a me that is "two"—finally a feminine "me"—a return to the maternal bond of closeness that the masculine subject needs to escape in order to establish autonomy. The "me too" of Erica and Harry is established through similar habits (they both never sleep for more that four hours, for example), similar class status (they are both wealthy and talented) and finally similar problems (both need reading glasses). The glances that they inadvertently exchange signify their deep similarity, which is belied by the superficial differences between them. Neither masculine nor feminine, they are a "match"—a third sex—and finally ultimately "queer."

While the film works very hard to maintain the appearance of difference, female viewers in particular will be well aware of the kind of upkeep required by women of Diane Keaton's age (post-menopausal by her own admission) to maintain the appearance of femininity. Only assiduous dieting, exercise and visits to the hairdresser and beautician will create this feminine appearance. Without the work of maintenance, Keaton will revert to a hairy, pudgy figure—perhaps not quite as hairy as Harry, but close enough to bridge the appearance of difference. Increasingly as the body moves from middle age to old age, the physical and physiological signs of sexual difference diminish and the body loses its dimorphic qualities, which from a general biological perspective were never strongly marked in the human species. In the end, especially as they age, men and women do not appear "different." At the very least, they appear less and less different. The film, then, offers a fantasy in which sexual difference is maintained through the woman's participation in feminine consumer culture, while, paradoxically, she relinquishes her position as the girl. Conversely, the man must also be willing to take up the position of the girl, of the suppliant, of moral powerlessness.

Most improbably, the young doctor, Erica's ethical equal, must send Erica back to Harry, because he (the all-knowing doctor) understands that she (better than she herself) still loves Harry, and for some reason Erica concurs. She explains to Harry (and the viewer): "He said that when he saw me with you he knew that I was still in love with you." While this third act, and the happy reuniting of the couple restored in amity, corresponds to the conventions of the romantic comedy, the film, through the arbitrary nature of Erica's choice, and the film's double ending, makes us very aware that, in another genre, this ending would be quite different. Like *Down with Love*, the film calls into question the conventions of the genre and the paradigm of romance by making us aware of the artifice at work in the creation of these endings.

Of course, the final irony is that, just as in any other traditional romantic comedy, the couple unites to begin a life together—with the difference that this union will occur only in the twilight of their adult lives. Meyers explains: "It's not the beginning of their lives: they're not starting together, but they're going to end together."[48] The film, by depicting this successful outcome just after having sketched out an alternative pessimistic one (in Erica's stage play), reveals itself as inherently ambivalent. As the French title of the film suggests, "*Tout peut arriver*"—"anything can happen," even something so improbable as a happy marriage between a 50-year-old striver and a 63-year-old slacker. Here, then, we see the particularity of the nostalgia evoked by these films—which is that the couple themselves are continually pleasantly surprised, because, after all, anything can happen, even though it probably won't. Viewers are left both with a sense of the resilience of "love" and also with the conviction that for the contemporary woman the attainment of love is the exception rather than the rule.

While the film thus seems to suggest that romance is by and large the stuff of youth, with Erica and her story constituting the exception that proves the rule, research on the behavior of adults over 50 offers a very different picture. For example, Amanda Barusch, a pioneer in the area of gerontology, concludes in her 2007 study of older lovers that, as a group, older adults have vital and varied romantic experiences through their eighties.[49] The film's success appears to confirm Barusch's findings that romance occupies a central place in older adults' preoccupations, additionally suggesting that the public at large has an interest in thinking about romance as something that extends throughout their lives, rather than belonging exclusively to youth. While *Something's Gotta Give* did not reach the pinnacle achieved by *What Women Want*, it was nevertheless a box-office success, at $266,728,738, out-selling youth-oriented films such as *Stuck on You* (Bobby and Peter Farrelly, 2003), or *Love Don't Cost a Thing* (Troy Beyer, 2003), and occupying "the top spot at the weekend box office."[50]

From another perspective, *Something's Gotta Give* offers a new definition of marriage, or, rather, an old definition. According to anthropologist Helen Fisher, marital norms throughout human history accommodated multiple partners, divorce and even polygyny and polyandry, depending on the relative status of the individual—if we take the very long view. In cultures in which women held a high status, worked outside the home (as in foraging far afield from the base camp), accumulated and retained their own property, and in which geographic mobility was the norm, privileged women had a high degree of autonomy in choosing their partners, and even, though rarely, had more than one partner. Agricultural societies depended upon stable marriages; however, as in the case of earlier hunter-gatherer cultures, in our currently mobile culture, permanent marriages are not an advantage. Resources are no longer allocated at birth according to patrilineal systems of descent, and it is the mother rather than the father who retains jurisdiction over the child, regardless of her situation. Children are no longer an economic asset, for there are no farms for them to work—quite the contrary.[51]

In 2003 (the year in which *Something's Gotta Give* was released), the choice to have a child was based on notions of individual emotional self-fulfillment and male/female partnerships increasingly unstable. From Fisher's perspective: "We are shedding the agricultural tradition and, in some respects, returning to our nomadic roots."[52] While Fisher is not alone in observing new relationship patterns, her argument that these patterns echo what is "natural" to the human species in its fight to ensure its survival raises interesting questions about the romantic comedy as a philosophical incubator on the topic of marriage. For Fisher, humans are biologically driven to seek partners, to "pair-bond," but not necessarily according to the patterns dictated by Western culture in our recent agrarian past.

Something's Gotta Give as a neo-romantic comedy subscribes to a similar perspective. On the one hand, it recognizes the need and the desirability of the heterosexual couple. On the other, it affirms that its characteristics are no longer immutable or predictable. Only Zoe, Erica's sister, sounds a cautionary note. She is the voice of the traditional feminist: for Zoe, women remain the victims of men. In her words: "Single older women as a demographic category are about as fucked a group as one can get." Not to belabor the (no doubt intended) pun in the word "fucked," the film clearly proves her wrong, in the sense that it affirms the power of the successful older woman in the world of men—as long as she is willing to turn the men into girls, by taking a dominant role. In sidestepping the feminist by seemingly proving her wrong, the film allays the moral conscience of the post-feminist who has benefited from feminism's battles without having to bear the scars. Was feminism simply about advantaging the upper middle-class woman? This film seems to say "yes"—and that this should be sufficient. The prominence of consumer culture in the creating of this world of equity suggests another story in which the initial terms of feminism are replaced by neo-feminism, together with its emphasis on economic opportunism.

Typical feminist reactions to the film underline "the inexorable narrative drive toward the generationally appropriate heterosexual makeover that the film provides,"[53] as well as the manner in which the film "places definite constraints around what constitutes appropriate sexual relationship and gender identities," measuring the film's position against the standards of contemporary gender theory, which seeks to explode the normative legacy of patriarchy. At best, the feminist concedes that while films such as *Something's Gotta Give* exhibit an "almost compulsive need to show that these women come back into the family fold," "the 'older bird' chickflick" also constitutes "a welcome departure from earlier representations of older women's sexuality as deviant and toxic."[54] This perspective fails to recognize that the film is not a symptom of feminism's failures as much as a sign of the triumph of neo-feminism and its tenets, centered on self-cultivation and individual fulfillment. According to Eva Illouz, "the commodified language of individualist self-realization is, at present, the only language we understand well enough to open our relationships to a project of autonomy, equality, and emotional fulfillment."[55] Certainly, *Something's Gotta Give* subscribes to this view; while a question may be raised as to whether or not this is the "only language" available, there is no doubt that it is the only language spoken in Hollywood.

In 1962, in the opening chapter of *Sex and the Single Girl*, Helen Gurley Brown warned her readers that:

> A man can leave a woman at fifty (though it may cost him some dough) as surely as you can leave dishes in the sink. He can leave any time before that too, and so may you leave him when you find your football hero developing into the town drunk.[56]

Something's Gotta Give extends the logic of this remark: while a woman may lose her husband at 50, she may find another at 55; her mobility and her status as marriageable extended through her careful cultivation of the self. The logic advocated by *Something's Gotta Give* suggests the ways in which neo-feminism and its emphasis on self-fulfillment prevails over feminism by offering a pragmatic, functionalist system of behaviors whose efficiency overshadows the ethical concerns of the latter. Like Zoe, Erica's sister, feminism is preoccupied, in Zoe's words, with "the injustice of it all": Zoe protests against the inequity of a world that sees a 63-year-old man as an eligible bachelor while a woman 10 years his junior is considered ineligible, "out of the game." Erica's concerns are more practical, which are to ensure that neither she nor her daughter "miss out" on the meaningful (and fulfilling) aspects of life—the times of their lives. Erica is determined to enjoy, as she puts it at the beginning of the film, "this time of my life." To do so, she is willing to act like a man while looking like a girl, remaking the terms of gender.

Something's Gotta Give, then, is neither feminist nor anti-feminist. Rather, it testifies to the ways in which the neo-feminist subject reflects the ideals of neo-liberalism, in the words of Aihwa Ong, "as a technology of government" which "is a profoundly active way of rationalizing governing and self-governing in order to 'optimize.'" For Ong, neo-liberalism within the contexts of Asian politics may have an "active, interventionist aspect."[57] Within the context of *Something's Gotta Give*, neo-feminism functions similarly, in that it provides the feminine subject with a pragmatic agenda that allows her to optimize the advantages of her position in a largely indifferent, if not hostile, environment, to intervene in a dominant system of governmentality that privileges a masculine subject. By exploring how subjects such as older men and older women are incorporated into a neo-feminist discourse of girlishness within the romantic comedy, *Something's Gotta Give* moves us closer to an understanding of the power that this rhetoric holds over the imagination of women. While the neo-feminist position appears to disadvantage the "olds" by placing these last within a consumer-culture context in which the young girl represents the ideal of femininity, *Something's Gotta Give* demonstrates the resiliency of its discourse, which accommodates a range of identities, as long as the ideals of affluence and accomplishment are maintained, meeting the requirements of the neo-liberal state.

Conclusion
Post-Feminism and Neo-Feminism

The films analyzed in this volume as well as the ethos that they represent have been repeatedly characterized as post-feminist by contemporary scholars. Indeed, many of the traits that I have identified as associated with neo-feminism have been frequently described as post-feminist—that is to say, in some way the consequence of second-wave feminism, either as the outgrowth of theories about gender advanced in the period of second-wave feminism, or as a reaction to the values promoted by second-wave feminists.

As sociologist Rosalind Gill explains, post-feminism can be used alongside post-modernism to indicate an "epistemological break" and a "historical shift" in terms of the way that culture at large considers gender, moving from a biological determinist definition to culturally contingent definitions.[1] Neo-feminism clearly participates in these shifts, accepting, for example, lesbian sexuality, to the degree that the lesbian subject conforms to codes of self-presentation customarily associated with heteronormativity; however, it can also accommodate essentialist notions of gender identity grounded in motherhood, insofar as motherhood in the figure of the "yummy mummy" is understood as a choice that is made in terms of "mummy's" own self-fulfillment. Another significant definition, according to Gill, posits "post-feminism" as "part of a backlash against feminist goals and achievements."[2] While films like *Something's Gotta Give* (Nancy Meyers, 2003) may be seen to reacting against feminism—in particular through the inclusion of a feminist figure who seems irrelevant and outmoded—the director of the film sees herself as a feminist, albeit one, like Helen Gurley Brown herself, who fails to win the approval of more serious-minded women. Furthermore, the fact that neo-feminism appears to pre-date, or at least develop alongside, second-wave feminism suggests that it cannot be understood exclusively as a reaction against feminism.

Gill herself finds none of these perspectives convincing, arguing instead that post-feminism is largely "a new discursive phenomenon closely associated with neo-liberalism"—best understood as a "sensibility" that revolves around "a number of recurring and relatively stable themes, tropes and constructions" that include:

- "an obsessional preoccupation with the body"
- "the emphasis upon self surveillance, monitoring and discipline"
- "women presented as active and desiring subjects"
- "a focus upon individualism, choice and empowerment"
- "the dominance of a makeover paradigm"
- "the articulation or entanglement of feminist and anti-feminist ideas"
- "a resurgence in ideas of natural sexual difference"
- "a marked sexualization of culture"
- "an emphasis on commodification and the commodification of difference"
- "irony and knowingness."[3]

To a large degree, I am in sympathy with an analysis that posits current feminine culture as post-feminist or, perhaps more accurately, as exhibiting those traits that Gill ascribes to "a postfeminist sensibility." Indeed, many of the elements isolated by Gill correspond in a striking manner to the recurring motifs of the girly film as an expression of the neo-feminist paradigm. Though the notion of a "natural sexual difference" may be challenged through the ways in which directors like Nancy Meyers, most notably in *What Women Want* (2000), assume sexuality as the fungible manifestation of an endless play of difference, the degree to which these performances constitute exceptions to the norm leaves open the possibility of more essentialist perspectives, manifested in this film through an emphasis on motherhood and family. Importantly, Gill is particularly concerned with the way that the post-feminist sensibility is aligned with neo-liberalism. She argues that "the autonomous, calculating self-regulating subject of neo-liberalism bears a strong resemblance to the active, freely choosing, self-reinventing subject of postfeminism." She speculates that women, "required to work on and transform the self, to regulate every aspect of their conduct and to present their actions as freely chosen," represent neo-liberalism's "ideal subjects."[4]

Where I take issue with Gill is not in terms of her analysis of the characteristics of the dominant trends in feminine media culture, with which I largely agree (in particular, in terms of the ways that current feminine culture is intrinsically linked to the dominance of neo-liberalism) but with the way in which she tends to see post-feminism as a consequence of second-wave feminism. Rather than supporting an argument that contemporary feminine culture represents "an entanglement of feminist and anti-feminist ideas," the development of the girly films and feminine popular culture more broadly indicates that a dominant neo-feminist tendency, inaugurated by figures such as

Helen Gurley Brown in the 1960s, has incorporated aspects and dimensions of second-wave feminism, in particular certain rhetorical devices, to the extent that these are consonant with its own goal—that of the advancement of the individual feminine subject in her "pursuit of happiness" as a specifically American entitlement.

The notion of neo-feminism assists in explaining the difficulties that contemporary feminist thought encounters in its attempts to understand contemporary feminine culture. Media scholars such as Charlotte Brunsdon seem to suggest that the role of the feminist critic is to reject post-feminism in all its guises because the very term itself announces the impossibility of thinking about feminism today, which is the primary task of all feminists left standing.[5] Sarah Projansky, pointing out that post-feminist tendencies were apparent as early as the 1920s, finds it useful to understand post-feminism as "a cultural discourse—an attitude, a reaction formation, an always available hegemonic response to feminism—not entirely linked to any particular historical moment."[6] While there are elements in contemporary culture that might be understood as a backlash against feminism, girly films, as an expression of neo-feminism, do not situate themselves against feminism; rather, they are indifferent to the kinds of social and political concerns that set feminists apart from the general group of female strivers seeking to achieve the ideals of neo-liberalism. Thus, many feminist critiques of contemporary culture tend to underline its conflicted nature, producing an ambivalent and unresolved analysis that can neither reject nor affirm contemporary popular feminine culture, nor decipher its relations with feminism, in particular whether, in the words of Imelda Whelehan, "young women have moved beyond a need for such a gender specific politics." Whelehan herself confesses: "I remain in two minds about chick lit and this uncertainty might be discerned at the points I waver on both sides of the argument in this book."[7]

A further strand of feminist analysis of post-feminism is typically haunted by the specter of a second-wave feminism that failed to fulfill its promise to deliver a utopian existence to those who embraced its message; such analyses tend to produce a critique of contemporary feminine culture that frequently takes the form of a lament. Subtending the feminist lament is the lost dream of a feminism that was whole, unmarred by the dirty business of everyday life and by the bitter and sectarian debates that have marked feminist inquiry since its inception. While veteran feminist scholar Angela McRobbie explains that "it has not been my intention to suggest some kind of nostalgia for a sanctified past," she nonetheless defines this "lost" feminism as the shadow of a negative image of feminism propagated by popular media, in which feminism is portrayed as "as a hideous thing." This "feminism-that-never-was" [the "hideous thing" referred to above] is "different from the feminism-as-object-of-desire ... as something that is lost and becomes melancholically preserved."[8] For McRobbie, it is precisely this feminism-as-object-of-desire that haunts contemporary culture, constituting a defining facet of post-feminism.

Nowhere is this nostalgia more in evidence than in academia, where second-wave feminism fostered the development of a group of women scholars whose very authority derived from their feminist credentials, producing the current conundrum whereby feminist criticism appears to have outlived feminism itself. A clear example of this phenomenon is apparent in the various articles that comprise the recent volume *Interrogating Postfeminism: Gender and the Politics of Popular Culture* (Duke University Press, 2007), edited by Yvonne Tasker and Diane Negra, who comment, with regret and dismay, that "[p]ostfeminism in all its guises posits the contemporary as surpassing feminism, leaving it behind."[9] This position does not take into account that, during at least a major portion of second-wave feminism's history, neo-feminism, promoting the very sensibility to which Tasker and Negra object, has always maintained a strong and growing following beginning in the 1960s, if not earlier. Thus, in a widely discussed article written in 1992 for the *Washington Post*, entitled "The Death of Feminism," columnist Sally Quinn claimed that "many women believe that their needs are better understood by the Helen Gurley Browns of the world than the Germaine Greers."[10] The rise and dominance of the girly film in the form of the female event film suggest the continued pertinence of Quinn's remark.

Certainly, the bitterness of the twenty-first-century feminist is in striking contrast with Helen Gurley Brown's optimism. She proclaims in the 2003 edition of *Sex and the Single Girl*, "Something else kind of wonderful has happened to single women. You don't have to be beautiful anymore to be cherished."[11] The feminist media scholar, Diane Negra, echoing McRobbie, focuses on what she calls "the postfeminist melancholic," in which "the story of aging uncertainly but inexorably out of youth is marked by a deep and sustained melancholy."[12] Prefacing her comment with a request that we "[f]orgive" her "continuing to call women girls," Brown ripostes: "At around age 25 we often take on adult responsibilities—marry, have children, create homes for other people but I think the basic girl is still in there whooshing around—loving fun, being spontaneous, mainlining on enthusiasm."[13] The youthful and plucky Brown aspires to make girlishness attractive at the age of 80, in spite of the onerous regime of exercise, plastic surgery, dieting and other forms of self-improvement that she advocates: "[m]ercifully you can get more beautiful with incredible cosmetic and dermatological procedures these days and, of course, your body can be okay with the discipline of exercise and not cramming down chocolate-ripple cheesecake."[14] Negra, however, offers a more somber and pessimistic view of women's fate that is more closely aligned with the relative "humourlessness" attributed by writers of chick lit to second-wave feminism, according to Whelehan.[15] Whelehan, nonetheless, concludes that chick lit is an expression of the unresolved issues raised by feminism and of the anger that this inspires in contemporary women; she considers that the irony that characterizes these novels promotes "the anxious laugh at one's own expense; the humor that now rather ineffectively disguises the blood and the rage underpinning it."[16]

For feminists like Negra and McRobbie, and, to a lesser degree, Whelehan, the embracing of girlishness and pleasure evident in popular feminine culture among women too young to have read *Sex and the Single Girl* when it was initially published in 1962, is viewed as a repudiation of feminism. Angela McRobbie remarks: "It is as though this is the vengeance of the younger generation who had to put up with being chided by feminist teachers and academics at university for wanting the wrong things."[17] In defense of her position, McRobbie points to the proliferation of what she calls "female disorders," such as anorexia, promoted by the media and constituting a "return of the repressed," in consequence of feminism's unaddressed issues. In other words, for McRobbie, the clearly compulsive dieting that Brown advocates suggests the broader pathology to which women's bodies are routinely subjected in the post-feminist era. Through the impossible standards imposed and circulated by the media, the pathological becomes a social norm that offers the means of inscribing women's unresolved anxieties upon their own bodies in a form of a culturally sanctioned masochism. McRobbie goes so far as to claim that "[b]eing ... 'culturally intelligible' as a girl makes one ill."[18] Similarly, McRobbie indicts the fashion industry, fashion photography in particular, as instrumental in the promotion of "feminine disorders" by encouraging regimes of "pain, self-punishment and loss" with which "these images appear to be connected."[19] For McRobbie, women and girls are encouraged to misinterpret these discourses and the regimes of self-surveillance that they support "as enabling, and this is reinforced through an accompanying discourse which suggests that girls have never had it so good."[20]

It is difficult to disagree with McRobbie's summation of the pathologies associated with contemporary femininity, given the well-documented incidents, from anorexia to substance abuse, that the media circulate alongside the very images that support these pathologies.[21] Where I disagree with McRobbie, as with Gill, concerns the terms whereby she describes the etiology of this new feminine condition, which I regard not as a legacy of feminism, but, rather, of neo-feminism as a dimension of neo-liberalism. McRobbie identifies what she calls "the loss of a political love for 'womanhood' which feminism advocated and encouraged, which also allowed a certain suspension of the self in favor of 'the collective' or 'the communal'" as being at the heart of the new feminine condition; however, I would argue that we cannot describe as a "loss" something that was never there from the beginning. By thinking in terms of loss, feminists avoid the crucial question—the question asked by Sally Quinn—which concerns the reasons for why and how the perspectives advocated in magazines such as *Cosmopolitan* came to dominate the public imagination, to the extent of seemingly rendering irrelevant feminist analysis as inaugurated by the philosopher Simone de Beauvoir.

Though the publication of *The Second Sex* in English in 1953 arguably established the roots of what would come to flourish as second-wave feminism more than a decade later, de Beauvoir's contributions as an important and influential philosopher have only begun to be recognized in the last 10 years, during which her work has finally emerged from out of the shadow cast by her illustrious partner, Jean-Paul Sartre. Rigorously impersonal, the social and economic analysis advocated by Beauvoir was muddied by second-wave feminists themselves, like Betty Friedan, who focused on issues like "fulfillment," a tendency seized upon by neo-feminism as consonant with its own agenda.[22]

In 1963, Friedan exhorted:

> When society asks so little of women, every woman has to listen to her own inner voice to find her identity in a changing world. She must create, out of her own needs and abilities, a new life plan, fitting in the love and children and home that have defined femininity in the past with the work toward a greater purpose that shapes the future.[23]

While Friedan herself may have envisioned a utopian future and saw institutional reform as part of this "new life plan," the focus on individual women finding their "own inner voice" sat comfortably with the more pragmatic concerns voiced by Helen Gurley Brown: those of finding a job and keeping it. Yet the question persists: why was, and is, neo-feminism a dominant discourse in feminine culture?

The girly film suggests two possible answers. In the first instance, the structure of the girly film revolving around a woman at the center of her universe, in a direct line that descends from the woman's film of classical Hollywood,[24] underlines the importance of the woman and the feminine as a source of identification and pleasure for women audiences.[25] In *Feminism, Femininity and Popular Culture*, Joanne Hollows convincingly develops the thesis that feminist identity depended upon a rejection of feminine identity. Feminism, then, according to Hollows, must define itself against femininity.[26] With its focus on femininity as the primary site of identification, the girly film underlines the unwillingness of women to reject femininity and the ways in which a neo-feminist paradigm, unlike feminism, offers women a means of retaining "femininity," while evolving a definition of femininity that can respond to the social and economic shifts of the twentieth and twenty-first centuries. Neo-feminism did not require women to reject femininity; on the contrary, it suggested a mean of preserving and enhancing glamor as the sign of a new and revitalized feminine identity. A second dimension of the neo-feminist paradigm highlighted by the girly film that no doubt contributed to its success is the ways in which neo-feminism, unlike feminism itself, was compatible with the demands for synergy within Conglomerate Hollywood. The emphasis on consumer culture facilitated the circulation of the neo-feminist paradigm as one that supported an array of media industries from fashion to music. Feminism, in contrast, produced a discourse that was both hostile to, and critical of, consumer culture and its ancillary industries.

Joanne Hollows concludes *Feminism, Femininity and Popular Culture* with the following caveat: "Instead of popular culture being the object of a feminist 'make-over,' analyzing the popular could teach feminists how to 'make-over' feminism."[27] Certainly, examining popular culture may assist in understanding the potential role of feminism in the twenty-first century; however, an analysis of the girly film leads us away from the issues that formed the initial focus of second-wave feminism. For example, the object of Friedan's analysis was the middle-class housewife, who is portrayed as oppressed and unfulfilled. Though the girly film may include women who are married and supported by their husbands, as in the case of Charlotte in *Sex and the City: The Movie* (Michael Patrick King, 2008), her concerns are not depicted as distinct from those of other characters. Charlotte remains a girlish figure, regardless of her marital status, fulfilling Brown's injunction that a married woman retain her glamor in the same way as her single friends.

The oppression of the housewife is no longer a cultural concern, to the extent that Charlotte is seen to share, rather to stand in opposition to, the fate of her friends. Similarly, the characters on the popular *Desperate Housewives* (first aired on ABC in October 2004) play out narratives that replicate the themes of *Sex and the City* (HBO, 1998–2004) and even more pointedly those of *Sex and the City: The Movie*, with female friendship, relationship issues, career problems, fashion and appearance remaining significant concerns. The characters engage in "makeovers" and "do-overs" as a process of constant self-renovation, the sign of their girlishness, their ever "becoming," never realized womanhood. The darker implication of the characters' predicaments, noted by critics in *Sex and the City: The Movie*, are given expression in *Desperate Housewives*, through melodramatic devices, in particular a series of murders, that produce episodes that hover between comedy and tragedy, between farce and thriller, replicating the generic hybridity that characterizes the girly film itself. These contemporary narratives implicitly propose that the cultural moment that produced second-wave feminism and neo-feminism has passed, giving way to a messier world in which categories and norms may have shifted without resolving the larger dilemmas of contemporary existence. Contemporary popular forms suggest that it is not possible to consider the cartography of gender as somehow disconnected from a particular historical moment.

Neo-feminism and second-wave feminism were both responses to a single historical moment, a moment at which—as a result of a combination of factors, from an evolving economic structure to changing sexual mores—men and women began to develop different kinds of expectations about marriage and career; however, feminism itself may be seen to have had a much longer history, one which perhaps actually began with the Enlightenment, when the capacity for rational thought became increasingly the sign and pretext for humanity and, eventually, citizenship. One of the most important legacies of second-wave feminism has been the interrogation of the place occupied by the rational and the exploration of different kinds of epistemologies. Neo-feminism did not reason with women; it appealed to their emotions and feelings. By attempting to understand the emotions that drive the girly culture, it will become perhaps possible to think about the role that feminism might play in the twenty-first century. The appeal of neo-feminism cannot be divorced from the historical moment: neo-feminism and neo-liberalism are inextricably linked in terms of producing a subject who may disassociate herself from traditional notions of patriarchy and the family, but who remains convinced that her identity is largely defined in terms of her intimate relations with others. The challenge of the feminist in the twenty-first century is to imagine a sense of community in a culture in which identity and self are generated through individual achievement and fulfillment. Neo-feminism continues to attempt to adjudicate these tensions: between economic independence and the need for collective affirmation, whether through female friendship, some form of the heterosexual couple or children; between an ethical imperative and self-gratification; between self-discipline and self-mortification. In spite of its life-affirming rhetoric, however, the death-dealing practices of neo-feminism, expressed in the proliferation of the so-called "feminine" pathologies noted by McRobbie, cannot address the sources of the dissatisfactions that give rise to these tensions—sources that reside within the larger social field. A feminism that does not situate femininity as one dimension in the play of gender and identity within the broad terrain of neo-liberalism will continue to fail in its desire to make itself over in response to the new millennium.

Notes

Introduction

1. Diane Negra, *What a Girl Wants? Fantasizing the Reclamation of Self in Postfeminism* (London: Routledge, 2009), 5.
2. Rosalind Gill, *Gender and the Media* (Cambridge: Polity Press, 2007).
3. Imelda Whelehan, *Overloaded: Popular Culture and the Future of Feminism* (London: The Women's Press, 2000).
4. See chapter seven.
5. See chapter six.
6. Thomas Schatz, "New Hollywood, New Millennium," in *Film Theory and Contemporary Hollywood Movies*, ed. Warren Buckland (New York: Routledge, 2009), 19–46.

Chapter 1

1. The emphasis on "becoming" in feminist critical thought is, arguably, a product of the sustained and continued influence of Simone de Beauvoir's *The Second Sex* initially published in 1949, in which she coined the phrase, "One is not born, but rather becomes, a woman." Typical of this influence is the following comment by Penelope Deutscher, arguing that the feminist philosopher Luce Irigaray, in the tradition of de Beauvoir, posits that "women need 'a horizon of becoming' (or a field of infinite, open ended feminine identit[ies]) in the context of which a woman could situate herself." Simone de Beauvoir, *The Second Sex* (New York: Vintage Books, 1989), 267; Penelope Deutscher, "'The Only Diabolical Thing About Women ... ': Luce Irigaray on Divinity," *Hypatia* 9, no. 4 (Fall 1994): 100–01.
2. See Stuart Hall, "Introduction: Who Needs 'Identity'?" in *Questions of Cultural Identity*, ed. Stuart Hall and Paul du Gay (London: Sage, 1996), 1–17. For an example of this type of analysis, see Shelley Budgeon, *Choosing a Self: Young Women and the Individualization of Identity* (Westport, CT: Praeger, 2003). For a rigorously critical investigation of the concept and its implications for an understanding of contemporary feminine culture, see Camilla Griggers, *Becoming-Woman* (Minneapolis, MN: University of Minnesota Press, 1997).
3. For a complex discussion of the relations between capitalism and an unstable subjectivity or multiple-identities (defined as schizophrenia by these authors), see Gilles Deleuze and Félix Guattari, *Anti-Oedipus: Capitalism and Schizophrenia* (Minneapolis: University of Minnesota Press, 1983).
4. Robert Goldman, *Reading Ads Socially* (London: Routledge, 1992), 153.
5. For a discussion of the importance of "shopping" as a metaphor for contemporary feminine subjectivity, see Hilary Radner, *Shopping Around: Feminine Culture and the Pursuit of Pleasure* (New York: Routledge, 1995), in particular "Conclusion: Femininity: Do You Buy It?" 175–80.

6. The term "postfeminist girly film" was first coined by Charlotte Brunsdon to describe films such as *Working Girl* (Mike Nichols, 1988) and *Pretty Woman* (Garry Marshall, 1990). While my use of the term is indebted to Brunsdon, I do not entirely agree with Brunsdon's assessment of these films. In particular, I relate the genre to neo-feminism rather than post-feminism (as does Brunsdon). See Charlotte Brunsdon, "Post-feminism and Shopping Films," in *Screen Tastes: Soap Opera to Satellite Dishes* (London: Routledge, 1997), 81–102.

7. Hall, "Introduction," 4.

8. Hall, "Introduction," 1–17.

9. Hall, "Introduction," 8.

10. Dana P. Polan, "Brecht and the Politics of Self-Reflexive Cinema," *Jump Cut* 1 (1974), www.ejumpcut.org, accessed 18 April 2009.

11. For an example of an in-depth study of a discursive formation and its relations to a set of specific films, see Tony Bennett and Janet Woollacott, *Bond and Beyond: The Political Career of a Popular Hero* (New York: Methuen, 1987). For a more recent example of a text-based methodology grounded in historical context, see Alys Eve Weinbaum, Lynn M. Thomas, Priti Ramamurthy, Uta G. Poiger, Madeleine Y. Dong, and Tani E. Barlow, *The Modern Girl Around the World: Consumption, Modernity, and Globalization* (Durham, NC: Duke University Press, 2008).

12. See Celeste Hutchins and Christi Denton, "What is Neofeminism?" Tamera Ferro, "Utilitarianism = Neofeminism" and Danica Nuccitelli, "You are a Feminist ... ," in *Public Women, Public Words: A Documentary History of American Feminism*, vol. 3, *1960 to the Present*, ed. Dawn Keetley and John Pettegrew (Lanham, MD: Rowman & Littlefield, 2002), 496, 497–98; Sabrina P. Ramet, ed., *Gender Politics in the Western Balkans: Women and Society in Yugoslavia and the Yugoslav Successor States* (University Park: Pennsylvania State University Press, 1999); Margaret A. Simons, *Feminist Interpretations of Simone de Beauvoir* (University Park: Pennsylvania State University Press, 1995), 150, 153.

13. Ellen Morgan, "Humanbecoming: Form and Focus in the Neo-feminist Novel," in *Feminist Criticism: Essays on Theory, Poetry and Prose*, ed. Cheryl L. Brown and Karen Olson (Metuchen, NJ: Scarecrow Press, 1978), 272.

14. Kim A. Loudermilk, *Fictional Feminism: How American Bestsellers Affect the Movement for Women's Equality* (New York: Routledge, 2004), 157.

15. Loudermilk, *Fictional Feminism*, 149.

16. Margaret Atwood, *The Handmaid's Tale* (Toronto: McClelland and Stewart, 1985); John Updike, *The Witches of Eastwick* (New York: Knopf, 1984).

17. For a general introduction, see David Harvey, *A Brief History of Neoliberalism* (New York: Oxford University Press, 2005). For examples of influential analyses of gender within the context of neo-liberalism, see Valerie Walkerdine, "Reclassifying Upward Mobility: Femininity and the Neo-liberal Subject," *Gender and Education* 15, no. 3 (2003): 237–48; Beverley Skeggs, "Uneasy Alignments, Resourcing Respectable Subjectivity," *GLQ: A Journal of Lesbian and Gay Studies* 10, no. 2 (2004): 291–98.

18. Barbara Ehrenreich and Arlie Russell Hochschild, introduction to *Global Woman: Nannies, Maids, and Sex Workers in the New Economy*, ed. Barbara Ehrenreich and Arlie Russell Hochschild (London: Granta Books, 2003), 13.

19. Helen Gurley Brown, *Sex and the Single Girl* (New York: Random House, 1962). For a detailed account of Brown's career and its impact, see Jennifer Scanlon, *Bad Girls Go Everywhere: The Life of Helen Gurley Brown* (New York: Oxford University Press, 2009).

20. For a detailed analysis of nineteenth-century concepts of motherhood, see Eva Cherniavsky, *That Pale Mother Rising: Sentimental Discourses and the Imitation of Motherhood in 19th-Century America* (Bloomington: Indiana University Press, 1995). See also Sandra Matthews and Laura Wexler, *Pregnant Pictures* (New York: Routledge, 2000).

21. The phrase "the personal is political" is attributed to feminist activist, Carol Hanisch. See Carol Hanisch, "The Personal Is Political," 1969, carolhanisch.org, accessed 13 December 2009.

22. Imelda Whelehan, *The Feminist Bestseller: From Sex and the Single Girl to Sex and the City* (Basingstoke: Palgrave Macmillan, 2005), 31.

23. Desmond Morris, *Intimate Behaviour* (New York: Bantam Books, 1972), 105.

24. See "The Bridget Jones Economy—Singles and the City; How Young Singles Shape City Culture, Lifestyles and Economies," *Economist* (US), 22 December 2001; Kay Hymowitz, "World Bows to the New Girl Order," *Sunday Times* (London), 28 October 2007; Felicity Loughrey, "In the Bag: Can Single, Financially Independent Women Save the Economy," *Vogue* (Australia), January 2009. For a further discussion of the "New Girl Order," see chapter nine.

25. See Stephen Heath, *The Sexual Fix* (New York: Schocken, 1984).

26. See Hilary Radner, "Compulsory Sexuality and the Desiring Woman," *Sexualities* 11, nos. 1–2 (2008): 94–100, sexualities.sagepub.com, accessed 27 November 2009.

27. Sharon R. Ullman, *Sex Seen: The Emergence of Modern Sexuality in America* (Berkeley: University of California Press, 1997), 3.

28. Paul Robinson, *The Modernization of Sex: Havelock Ellis, Alfred Kinsey, William Masters, and Virginia Johnson* (New York: Harper & Row, 1976), 3.

29. Robinson, *Modernization of Sex*, 31–69.

30. Alfred C. Kinsey, Wardell B. Pomeroy, and Clyde E. Martin, *Sexual Behavior in the Human Male* (Philadelphia: W.B. Saunders, 1948); Alfred C. Kinsey, Wardell B. Pomeroy, Clyde E. Martin, and Paul H. Gebhard, *Sexual Behavior in the Human Female* (Philadelphia: W.B. Saunders, 1953).

31. For a discussion of the child in the 1950s, see Henry Jenkins, "The Sensuous Child: Benjamin Spock and the Sexual Revolution," in *The Children's Culture Reader*, ed. Henry Jenkins (New York: New York University Press, 1998), 209–30.

32. Richard von Krafft-Ebing, *Psychopathia Sexualis, with Especial Reference to the Antipathetic Sexual Instinct*, trans. Franklin S. Klaf (New York: Sent & Day, 1965), 8. (First published in German in 1887.)

33. Winston Graham, *Marnie* (New York: Carroll & Graf, 1961), 122.

34. The first Bond novel was *Casino Royale* (London: Jonathan Cape, 1953).

35. Bennett and Woollacott, *Bond and Beyond*, 116. See also Michael Denning, *Cover Stories: Narrative and Ideology in the British Spy Thriller* (London: Routledge, 1987).

36. Nora Ephron, *Wallflower at the Orgy* (New York: Bantam, 1970), 18.

37. Brown, *Sex and the Single Girl*; Betty Friedan, *The Feminine Mystique*, 1st ed. (New York: Dell, 1963). On the inauguration of second-wave feminism, see Barbara Ehrenreich, Elizabeth Hess, and Gloria Jacobs, *Re-making Love: The Feminization of Sex* (Garden City, NY: Anchor, 1986), 56.

38. Linda Gray Sexton, *Between Two Worlds: Young Women in Crisis* (New York: William Morrow, 1979), 18.

39. Sexton, *Between Two Worlds*, 25.

40. Betty Friedan, *The Feminine Mystique* (New York: Norton, 2001), 468–69.

41. Ehrenreich, Hess, and Jacobs, *Re-making Love*, 56.

42. Marjorie Hillis, *Live Alone and Like It* (New York: Sundial, 1936).

43. Alys Eve Weinbaum, Lynn M. Thomas, Priti Ramamurthy, Uta G. Poiger, Madeleine Y. Dong, and Tani E. Barlow, "The Modern Girl as Heuristic Device: Collaboration, Connective Comparison, Multidirectional Citation," in Weinbaum et al., *Modern Girl Around the World*, 1, 2.

44. Weinbaum et al., "Modern Girl as Heuristic Device," 5.

45. Weinbaum et al., "Modern Girl as Heuristic Device," 9.

46. Alys Eve Weinbaum, Lynn M. Thomas, Priti Ramamurthy, Uta G. Poiger, Madeleine Y. Dong, and Tani E. Barlow, "The Modern Girl Around the World: Cosmetics, Advertising and the Politics of Race and Style," in Weinbaum et al., *Modern Girl Around the World*, 25–54.

47. Weinbaum et al., "Modern Girl Around the World: Cosmetics," 35.

48. Brown, *Sex and the Single Girl*; Helen Gurley Brown, *Sex and the Office* (New York: Random House, 1964); "J," *The Way to Become the Sensuous Woman* (New York: Dell, 1969).

49. Brown, *Sex and the Single Girl*, 3.
50. Brown, *Sex and the Single Girl*, 105. See also "Helen Gurley Brown Papers, 1938–2001 [ongoing]," Sophia Smith Collection, Smith College, Northampton, MA.
51. Brown, *Sex and the Single Girl*, 3.
52. Brown, *Sex and the Single Girl*, 3.
53. Brown, *Sex and the Single Girl*, 104–18.
54. Brown, *Sex and the Single Girl*, 3.
55. Brown, *Sex and the Office*, 279.
56. Jessica Vandelay, "*Cosmopolitan Magazine*: Women's Best Friend," www.goarticles.com, 24 August 2009, accessed 13 December 2009. "company-profiles—COSMOPOLITAN," www.mandmglobal.com, 2 December 2009, accessed 13 December 2009.
57. Scanlon, *Bad Girls Go Everywhere*, 216, 217.
58. Scanlon, *Bad Girls Go Everywhere*, 218.
59. Scanlon, *Bad Girls Go Everywhere*, 144–51.
60. Helen Gurley Brown, *Having It All* (New York: Pocket Books, 1982), 303.
61. Brown, *Having It All*, 305.
62. William H. Masters and Virginia E. Johnson, *Human Sexual Response* (Boston: Little, Brown, 1966).
63. For a discussion of the history of pornography in mainstream cinema, see Linda Williams, *Screening Sex* (Durham, NC: Duke University Press, 2008). For a discussion of feminism and sex, see Lynne Segal, *Straight Sex: The Politics of Pleasure* (London: Virago, 1994). For a discussion of the representation of feminine sexuality on television, see Elana Levine, *Wallowing in Sex: The New Sexual Culture of 1970s American Television* (Durham, NC: Duke University Press, 2007). For a discussion of the representation of sexuality in the 1960s, see Hilary Radner and Moya Luckett, eds., *Swinging Single: Representing Sexuality in the 1960s* (Minneapolis: University of Minnesota Press, 1999).
64. Camilla Griggers, *Becoming-Woman*, xi.
65. See chapter nine for a more extended discussion of the New Girl Order.
66. Brown, *Sex and the Single Girl*, 114.
67. Richard Johnson, "How Cosmo Queen Got Booted," *New York Post*, 14 January 2009, www.nypost.com, accessed 23 April 2009.
68. Charlotte Hays, "The Secrets of Her Success," review of *Bad Girls Go Everywhere*, by Jennifer Scanlon, *Wall Street Journal*, 10 April 2009, online.wsj.com, accessed 12 April 2009.
69. Scanlon, *Bad Girls Go Everywhere*, 163–64.
70. Helen Gurley Brown, quoted in Scanlon, *Bad Girls Go Everywhere*, 161–62.
71. Hays, "Secrets of Her Success."
72. Laurie Ouellette, "Inventing the Cosmo Girl: Class Identity and Girl-Style American Dreams," *Media, Culture & Society* 21, no. 3 (1999): 363, 360.
73. Scanlon, *Bad Girls Go Everywhere*, 160.

Chapter 2

1. For all references to the film, see *Pretty Woman*, directed by Garry Marshall, 15th Anniversary Special Edition, DVD (1990; Burbank, CA: Touchstone Home Entertainment, 2005).
2. Richard Maltby, *Hollywood Cinema* (Malden, MA: Blackwell Publishing, 2003), 124.
3. For a further exploration of the representation of sexuality, see Hilary Radner and Moya Luckett, eds., *Swinging Single: Representing Sexuality in the 1960s* (Minneapolis: University of Minnesota Press, 1999), in particular, Moya Luckett, "Sensuous Women and Single Girls: Reclaiming the Female Body on 1960s Television," 277–96. See also Elana Levine, *Wallowing in Sex: The New Sexual Culture of 1970s America* (Durham, NC: Duke University Press, 2007).
4. Tamar Jeffers McDonald, *Romantic Comedy: Boy Meets Girl Meets Genre* (London: Wallflower, 2007), 55.

5. Molly Haskell, *From Reverence to Rape: The Treatment of Women in the Movies* (Chicago: University of Chicago Press, 1987), 323.

6. For a discussion of the female friendship film, see Karen Hollinger, *In the Company of Women: Contemporary Female Friendship Films* (Minneapolis: University of Minnesota Press, 1998).

7. Hollinger, *In the Company of Women*, 2.

8. Hollinger, *In the Company of Women*, 6.

9. For a comprehensive account of *loci communes*, or "commonplaces"—repeating figures found in medieval literature—see Ernst Robert Curtius, *European Literature and the Latin Middle Ages* (New York: Harper & Row, 1953).

10. For a discussion of women's magazines and advertising, see Hilary Radner, "The 'New Woman' and Her 'Self,'" and "Conclusion: 'Femininity: Do You Buy It?'" in *Shopping Around: Feminine Culture and the Pursuit of Pleasure* (New York: Routledge, 1995), 35–66, 175–80. For a discussion of television and feminism, see Susan J. Douglas, *Where the Girls Are: Growing Up Female with the Mass Media* (New York: Times Books, 1994); Bonnie Dow, *Prime-Time Feminism: Television, Media Culture and the Woman's Movement Since 1970* (Philadelphia: University of Pennsylvania Press, 1996).

11. Rachel Brownstein, *Becoming a Heroine: Reading About Women in Novels* (New York: Viking Press, 1982), xv.

12. Nancy K. Miller, *The Heroine's Text: Readings in the French and English Novel, 1722–1782* (New York: Columbia University Press, 1980), 149.

13. Garry Marshall, "Director's Commentary," *Pretty Woman*, DVD, directed by Garry Marshall.

14. Helen Gurley Brown, *Sex and the Single Girl* (New York: Random House, 1962).

15. Marshall, "Director's Commentary."

16. Press release for *Pretty Woman*, consulted Margaret Herrick Library, June 2009.

17. Marshall, "Director's Commentary."

18. eBay, cgi.ebay.com, accessed 4 May 2009.

19. For an extended discussion of the makeover in contemporary films for women, see Suzanne Ferriss, "Fashioning Femininity in the Makeover Flick," in *Chick Flicks: Contemporary Women at the Movies*, ed. Suzanne Ferriss and Mallory Young (New York: Routledge, 2008), 41–57. Ferriss argues for the centrality of the makeover, while concluding that ultimately women are not encouraged to view their appearance as crucial to their identity. While I am not as optimistic as Ferriss, I would agree that popular cinema's perspective on the makeover is paradoxical, emphasizing its importance while signaling that the heroine's intrinsic worth does not depend on it. For a broader exploration of the makeover in terms of its historical place in popular cinema, see Elizabeth A. Ford and Deborah C. Mitchell, *The Makeover in the Movies: Before and After in Hollywood Films, 1941–2002* (Jefferson, NC: McFarland, 2004).

20. Rachel Duplessis, *Writing Beyond the Ending: Narrative Strategies of Twentieth-Century Women Writers* (Bloomington: Indiana University Press, 1985), 200.

21. Dennis Delrogh, review of *Pretty Woman*, *LA Weekly*, 30 March 1990.

22. Henry Sheehan, review of *Pretty Woman*, *Reader*, 23 March 1990.

23. Sheila Benson, "'Pretty Woman': Roberts' Legs, a Cold Heart," *Los Angeles Times*, 23 March 1990.

24. Northrop Frye, *Anatomy of Criticism: Four Essays* (Princeton: Princeton University Press, 1957), 182–83. Frye explains that "[t]he action of the comedy begins ... in a world represented as a normal world, moves into the green world, goes into a metamorphosis there in which the comic resolution is achieved, and returns to the normal world. ... The green world has analogies not only to the fertile world of ritual, but to the dream world that we create out of our own desires. This dream world collides with the stumbling and blinded follies of the world of experience."

25. Marshall, "Director's Commentary."

26. Marshall, "Director's Commentary."

27. Marshall, "Director's Commentary."

28. Madonna's on-stage image and star persona extend and exaggerate many characteristics of the "Cosmo Girl"; the "campy" quality of her earlier incarnations suggests a complex and ironic relationship to the original single girl icon; however, her later evolution as star leaves those elements behind. See Cathy Schwichtenberg, *The Madonna Connection: Representational Politics, Subcultural Identities, and Cultural Theory* (Boulder, CO: Westview Press, 1993) for a discussion of Madonna as a feminist icon. I would argue that it is difficult to see Madonna as anything other than a neo-feminist icon, given her emphasis on self-empowerment.

29. Also Erica Todd, "'Big Mistake' or New Classic: The Response to *Pretty Woman* from Its Release to the Present" (BA Honours diss., University of Otago, 2006). See the discussion of *Pretty Woman* in chapter three on *Romy and Michele's High School Reunion* and its citation of the shopping sequence.

30. Barbara Klinger, "Once is Not Enough: The Functions and Pleasures of Repeat Viewings," in *Beyond the Multiplex: Cinema, New Technologies, and the Home* (Berkeley; Los Angeles; London: University of California Press, 2006), 144, 172.

31. Klinger, "Once is Not Enough," 172.

32. See chapter ten on *Something's Gotta Give* for a discussion of the older "girly" heroine.

Chapter 3

1. Garry Marshall, "Director's Commentary," *Pretty Woman*, directed by Garry Marshall, 15th Anniversary Special Edition, DVD (1990; Burbank, CA: Touchstone Home Entertainment, 2005).

2. Marshall, "Director's Commentary."

3. Karen Hollinger, *In the Company of Women: Contemporary Female Friendship Films* (Minneapolis: University of Minnesota Press, 1998). Female friendship films continue to be a vital genre; however, as in *The Sisterhood of the Traveling Pants* (Ken Kwapis, 2005) and *Bride Wars* (Gary Winick, 2009), there is often a "girly" dimension.

4. *Variety* (D), 27 May 1997.

5. *Variety* (D), 27 May 1997.

6. Review of *Romy and Michele's High School Reunion*, *Boxoffice*, July 1997; Review, *Los Angeles Times*, 25 April 1997.

7. Press release for *Romy and Michele's High School Reunion*, consulted Margaret Herrick Library, June 2009.

8. For all references to the film, see *Romy and Michele's High School Reunion*, directed by David Mirkin, DVD (1997; Burbank, California: Buena Vista Home Entertainment, 1997).

9. Press release for *Romy and Michele*.

10. Press release for *Romy and Michele*.

11. Jack Matthews, review of *Romy and Michele's High School Reunion*, *Los Angeles Times*, 25 April 1997.

12. Press release for *Romy and Michele*.

13. Candace Bushnell, *Sex and the City* (New York: Warner Books, 1997); Sophie Kinsella, *Confessions of a Shopaholic* (New York: Bantam Dell, 2003).

14. Press release for *Romy and Michele*.

15. Janet Maslin, "Being Smart Isn't, Like, Everything," *New York Times*, 25 April 1997.

16. Press release for *Romy and Michele*.

17. See Helen Fielding, *Bridget Jones's Diary* (London: Picador, 1996); Plum Sykes, *Bergdorf Blondes* (New York: Miramax Books/Hyperion, 2004) and *Débutante Divorcée* (New York: Miramax Books, 2006).

18. See the discussion of the use of the opera *La Traviata* in *Pretty Woman* in chapter one.

19. The concept, now widely circulated, was initially introduced in Angela McRobbie and Jenny Garber in "Girls and Subcultures: An Exploration," ed. Stuart Hall and Tony Jefferson, *Resistance Through Rituals: Subcultures in Post-War Britain* (London: Hutchinson, 1976), 209–22,

cited in David Muggleton, "From Classlessness to Clubculture: A Genealogy of Post-War British Youth Culture Analysis," *Young: Nordic Journal of Youth Research* 13, no. 2 (2005): 218–19.

20. Henry Jenkins, *Textual Poachers: Television Fans and Participatory Culture* (New York: Routledge, 1992).

21. For a discussion of the inherent contradictions in young females' use of urban space, see Mary E. Thomas, "Girls, Consumption Space and the Contradictions of Hanging Out in the City," *Social and Cultural Geography* 6, no. 4 (2005): 587–605.

22. Marcia G. Yerman, "The New Media Message for Women," www.huffingtonpost.com, 22 October 2008, accessed 18 December 2009.

23. For a discussion of the development of the "sell through market," and an example of how advertisers address the female "sell through" market, see Barbara Klinger, "The Contemporary Cinephile," in *Beyond the Multiplex: Cinema, New Technologies, and the Home* (Berkeley; Los Angeles; London: University of California Press, 2006), 58–62.

24. Erica Todd's work on *Pretty Woman*'s contemporary female audience confirms the importance of this scene for repeat viewers. See Erica Todd, "'Big Mistake' or New Classic: The Response to *Pretty Woman* from Its Release to the Present" (BA Honours diss., University of Otago, 2006).

25. Barbara Klinger, "Once is Not Enough: The Functions and Pleasures of Repeat Viewings," in *Beyond the Multiplex*, 170, 171.

26. See chapter six on *Maid in Manhattan*, for a further discussion of this scene in *Pretty Woman*.

27. Christine James, review of *Romy and Michele's High School Reunion*, boxoffice.com, 1 August 2008, accessed 19 December 2009.

28. For further discussion of the development of the fashion industry, see chapter eight.

29. Lisa Kudrow won an Emmy for her performance as "Phoebe," who in many ways resembles Michele, in the television program *Friends*.

30. Mary Celeste Kearney, "The Changing Face of Teen Television, or Why We All Love *Buffy*," in *Undead TV: Essays on* Buffy the Vampire Slayer, ed. Elana Levine and Lisa Parks (Durham, NC: Duke University Press, 2007), 23–26.

31. Kearney, "The Changing Face of Teen Television," 26.

32. See chapter eight on *The Devil Wears Prada* and chapter nine on *Sex and the City: The Movie*.

33. Kearney, "The Changing Face of Teen Television," 24.

34. Jennifer Scanlon, *Bad Girls Go Everywhere: The Life of Helen Gurley Brown* (New York: Oxford University Press, 2009), 184–85.

35. The concept of the "unruly woman" and its centrality to popularly feminine culture is attributed to Kathleen Rowe, developed in *The Unruly Woman: Gender and the Genres of Laughter* (Austin: University of Texas Press, 1995).

36. Karen Hollinger, "Theorizing Mainstream Female Spectatorship: The Case of the Popular Lesbian Film," *Cinema Journal* 37, no. 2 (Winter 1998): 7.

37. Chris Holmlund quoted in Karen Hollinger, "Theorizing Mainstream Female Spectatorship." See also Chris Straayer, "The Hypothetical Lesbian Heroine," *Jump Cut* 35 (April 1990): 50–58.

38. *Drama-Logue*, 24–30 April 1997.

39. The twins taken together as a trope, as both "different" and the "same," embody a widely discussed idea originating with feminist philosopher Luce Irigaray that a woman is not "one." Luce Irigaray, thus, claims in a frequently quoted passage: "A woman 'touches herself' all the time, and moreover no one can forbid her to do so, for her genitals are formed of two lips in continuous contact. Thus, within herself, she is already two—but not divisible into one(s)—that caress each other." Feminist theorist Diana Fuss explains: "Three words neatly summarize for Irigaray the significance of the two lips. 'Both at once.' Both at once signifies that a woman is simultaneously singular and double; she is 'already two—but not divisible into one(s),' or, put another way, she is 'neither one nor two.'" Luce Irigaray, *This Sex Which Is Not One*, trans. Catherine Porter with Carolyn Burke (Ithaca, NY: Cornell

University Press, 1985), 24; Diana Fuss, "'Essentially Speaking': Luce Irigaray's Language of Essence," *Hypatia* 3, no. 3 (1989): 65.

40. For a discussion of the double and castration, see Sigmund Freud, "The Uncanny," in *The Standard Edition of the Complete Psychological Works of Sigmund Freud*, ed. and trans. James Strachey, vol. XVII (London: Hogarth, 1953), 219–52.

41. Nancy Chodorow, *The Reproduction of Mothering: Psychoanalysis and the Sociology of Gender* (Berkeley: University of California Press, 1978).

42. For an explanation of this concept, see note 39 above.

43. Maslin, "Being Smart."

44. Maslin, "Being Smart."

45. Press release for *Romy and Michele*; Carla Hall, "MOVIES—'High School' Confidential," *Los Angeles Times*, 4 August 1996.

46. Hall, "MOVIES."

47. Betty Goodwin, "Keep It Short and Sweet," *Los Angeles Times*, 24 April 1997.

48. Goodwin, "Keep It Short and Sweet" Mona May, quoted in Goodwin, "Keep It Short and Sweet."

49. For a discussion of the fashion film and media synergies, see chapter eight.

50. For a discussion of promotional partners, see chapter nine.

Chapter 4

1. Melissa ("Missy") Stewart, "Production Designer's Commentary," *Legally Blonde*, directed by Robert Luketic, Special Edition, DVD (2001; Sydney, NSW: MGM Home Entertainment Group Australia, 2004).

2. *Romy and Michele's High School Reunion* was an unexpected success given its low budget; however, subsequent girly films did increasingly better at the box office culminating with films like *The Devil Wears Prada* (David Frankel, 2006) and *Confessions of a Shopaholic* (P.J. Hogan, 2009).

3. Theta Pavis-Weil, review of *Working Girl*, *Together* (UCLA), Winter 1989.

4. Nikki Finke, "Will Melanie Griffith's Role as Secretary Propel Her to Stardom," *Los Angeles Times*, 17 December 1988.

5. Andrea King, "Fox Marketing Staff Working Hard on Unique 'Girl' Promo," *Hollywood Reporter*, 8 December 1988.

6. Press release for *Legally Blonde*, consulted Margaret Herrick Library, June 2009.

7. *Los Angeles Times*, 9 July 2001.

8. Jill Feiwell, "'Blonde' has more Fun," *Variety* (D), 28 June 2001.

9. Press release for *Legally Blonde*, 1; B. Ruby Rich, "Catchers in the Wry," www.thenation. com, 23 August 2001, accessed 29 June 2009.

10. Press release for *Legally Blonde*, 7.

11. Press release for *Romy and Michele's High School Reunion*, consulted Margaret Herrick Library, June 2009.

12. Press release for *Legally Blonde*.

13. Press release for *Legally Blonde*.

14. David Rooney, "'Blonde' has more Fun," *Variety* (W), 7 May 2007.

15. For a discussion of the importance of media synergies to the girly film, see chapter seven.

16. Emanuel Levy, review of *Legally Blonde*, *Screen International*, 13 July 2001.

17. Kenneth Turan, review of *Legally Blonde*, *Los Angeles Times*, 13 July 2001.

18. Todd McCarthy, review of *Legally Blonde*, *Variety* (D), 9 July 2001.

19. Press release for *Legally Blonde*.

20. For a discussion of the fashion industry/Conglomerate Hollywood synergy, see chapters eight and nine.

21. See, for example, John Matsumoto, "You'll Need a Permission Slip for That," *Los Angeles Times*, 22 July 2001.

22. For further discussion of the marriage plot, see chapter two.

23. While much has been made of this source, in fact the film echoes a number of Austen's novels in which the heroine must be educated in order to cast off her first impressions and initial affections to find finally an appropriate husband—a narrative arc that is the staple of many tradition romances including format romances such as Mills and Boon or Harlequin. Notably in *Emma*, she falls in love with her guardian, who incarnates the double role of father and son, represented by two separate characters in the film *Clueless*.

24. Karen Joy Fowler, *The Jane Austen Book Club* (New York: Putnam, 2004).

25. A.O. Scott, review of *Legally Blonde*, *New York Times*, 13 July 2001.

26. Press release for *Legally Blonde*.

27. Sophie de Rakoff Carbonell, quoted in Greg Reifsteck, "Pretty in Pink and Rat Pack Chic," www.variety.com, 21 February 2002, accessed 9 December 2009.

28. Reifsteck, "Pretty in Pink."

29. Reifsteck, "Pretty in Pink."

30. Karen Levy, "Film to Fashion: *Legally Blonde*," *InStyle*, July 2001.

31. David Denby, "Girl Stuff," *The New Yorker*, 16 July 2001.

32. Denby, "Girl Stuff."

33. Denby, "Girl Stuff."

34. The view that business women owe their success, in part, to how they look is supported by women's magazines and popular manuals that instruct women in how to cultivate an appropriate appearance for the corporate world, in particular the widely circulated "Dress for Success" series starting in the 1970s. See, for example, John T. Malloy, *The Woman's Dress for Success Book* (Chicago: Follet Pub. Co., 1977).

35. Press release for *Legally Blonde*.

36. Press release for *Legally Blonde*.

37. Ginette Vincendeau, "Brigitte Bardot: the Old and the New; What Bardot Meant to 1950s France," in *Stars and Stardom in French Cinema* (London: Continuum, 2000), 89.

38. Vincendeau, "Brigitte Bardot," 88.

39. Vincendeau, "Brigitte Bardot," 88.

40. For a discussion of the changing conventions of costume in Hollywood film, see chapter eight.

41. For a discussion of fashion and bricolage, see Hilary Radner, *Making Do: Intersubjectivity, Film, Fashion and Bricolage* (Dunedin: University of Otago, 2005), Inaugural Professorial Lecture no.1. For a discussion of the expanded market for fashion, see chapter eight.

42. Mona May, the costume designer for *Romy and Michele*, filled the same role for the production of *Clueless*.

43. "See That Girl: She Can Jingle," *Hollywood Reporter*, 21 January 1991.

44. Elizabeth Sporkin, "Style Watch," *People*, 30 April 1990.

45. "How Long Will This Be Going On?" *Los Angeles Times*, 27 March 1992. In the course of focus group studies, a young researcher reported that, in 2006, young shoppers were still making the connection between *Pretty Woman* and a "come-back" for "polka dots." See Erica Todd, "'Big Mistake' or New Classic: The Response to *Pretty Woman* from Its Release to the Present" (BA Honours diss., University of Otago, 2006).

46. See chapters seven, eight and nine.

47. Amy Taubin,"Stocks and the Bonds That Tie," *Village Voice*, 12 April 1990.

48. Janet Maslin, "High-Polling Boy Meets Streetwalking Girl" *New York Times*, 23 March 1990.

49. Scott, review.

50. Denby, "Girl Stuff," 86.

51. Levy, review.

52. *Pretty Woman* delivered a domestic gross of $178,406,268, *Legally Blonde* $96,520,674 and *Romy and Michele's High School Reunion*, $29,235,353.

53. For a discussion of "Me too" culture, see chapter three.

54. Stewart, "Production Designer's Commentary."

Chapter 5

1. "Nuyorica," "Nuyorico" or "Nuyorican" is a colloquial expression referring to a Puerto Rican female or male born in New York.
2. *Hollywood Reporter*, 26 November 2002.
3. Press release for *Maid in Manhattan*, 4, consulted Margaret Herrick Library, June 2009.
4. Anne Thompson, "In Turnaround," nymag.com, 23 November 2003, accessed 6 October 2009; Cover story, *W Magazine*, October 2003; Dana Kennedy, "Homegirl, Working Woman, Empire Builder," *New York Times*, 3 November 2002.
5. Sandy M. Fernandez, "Jenny's Image on the Block," *Washington Post*, 21 May 2005.
6. For a discussion of Lopez's star persona in the context of "choice feminism," see Alan Dodd and Martin Fradley, "'I believe that if I haven't found my Prince Charming already that I will; or that he will find me, if he hasn't already': Jennifer Lopez, Romantic Comedy and Contemporary Stardom," in *Falling in Love Again: Romantic Comedy in Contemporary Cinema*, ed. Stacey Abbott and Deborah Jermyn (London: I.B. Tauris, 2009), 190–207. For a discussion of Sarah Jessica Parker's star persona, see chapter nine.
7. D. Soyini Madison, "*Pretty Woman* through the Triple Lens of Black Feminist Spectatorship," in *From "Mouse" to "Mermaid": The Politics of Film, Gender, and Culture*, ed. Elizabeth Bell, Lynda Haas, and Laura Sells (Bloomington: Indiana University Press, 1995), 230.
8. Zorianna Kit, "'Chambermaid' in Hughes' Diary," *Hollywood Reporter*, 20 February 2001; Ginia Bellafante, "My Big Fat Palace Wedding," *New York Times*, 8 December 2002.
9. *Variety* (D), 2 December 2002.
10. See, for example, Stephen Knadler, "'Blanca from the Block': Whiteness and the Transnational Latina Body," *Genders OnLine Journal* 41 (2005), www.genders.org, accessed 7 September 2009.
11. Bellafante, "My Big Fat Palace Wedding."
12. Bellafante, "My Big Fat Palace Wedding."
13. For a discussion of the marriage plot, see chapter two.
14. Kennedy, "Homegirl."
15. Laura M. Holson, "When Jenny Dumped Benny," *New York Times*, 14 July 2003.
16. Dodd and Fradley, "'I believe,'" 191.
17. Fernandez, "Jenny's Image on the Block."
18. Jennifer Lopez, interview by James Lipton, *Inside the Actors Studio: Jennifer Lopez*, Bravo, 10 October 2004.
19. Press release for *Angel Eyes* (2001), consulted Margaret Herrick Library, June 2009; David Ciminelli, "Lopez Poised for Superstardom with Singing and Acting Career," *Variety* (D), 5 March 2002.
20. Zorianna Kit, "Col Makes Bet on Lopez Star Power," *Hollywood Reporter*, 11 April 2002.
21. Deirdre Mendoza, "Heavy Hitters," *Variety* (D), 15 May 2002.
22. Baz Dreisinger, "J.Lo's Ethnic Sleight-of-hand," *Los Angeles Times*, 22 December 2002.
23. Richard Dyer, *Stars* (London: British Film Institute, 1979), 30.
24. Dyer, *Stars*, 30.
25. From the 1924 Pledge of Allegiance, the oath of loyalty to the Republic of the United States of America.
26. Michelle Tauber, "Livin' La Vida Lopez," *People*, 27 May 2002.
27. For discussion of Lopez's media persona in the late 1990s, see Mary C. Beltrán, "The Hollywood Latina Body as Site of Social Struggle: Media Constructions of Stardom and Jennifer Lopez's 'Cross-over Butt,'" *Quarterly Review of Film and Video* 19 (2002): 71–86.
28. Stuart Elliott, "Banc One Uses Promotional Tie-ins to a Movie about Selena to Reach out to the Hispanic Market," *New York Times*, 21 March 1997.
29. Luisita López Torregrosa, "Latino Culture Whirls onto Center Stage; Even as They Capture the Spotlight, Performers Question Their Identity," *New York Times*, 26 March 1998, E1, E6.
30. Taylor Hackford, quoted in R. Serge Denisoff and George Plasketes, "Synergy in 1980s Film and Music: Formula for Success or Industry Mythology?" *Film History* 4 (1990): 265.

31. See chapter seven for a discussion of Conglomerate Hollywood.
32. Bernard Weinraub, "Hispanic Film Audience Grows Fastest," *New York Times*, 11 March 1998.
33. Stephen M. Silverman, "J.Lo Enters Movie Salary Statosphere," *People*, 31 October 2001, www.people.com, accessed 7 December 2009.
34. Lea Goldman and Kiri Blakeley, "In Pictures: The Richest 20 Women in Entertainment," *Forbes*, 17 January 2007, www.forbes.com, accessed 8 December 2009.
35. John P. McManus, "The Waif is Over," *American Demographics*, 1 July 2003.
36. For a discussion of Lopez's body type and its significance, see Beltrán, "Hollywood Latina Body," 71–86. Lopez was reported as a "five-foot-six, 120-pound" woman, "five-foot-six," and as "5'6", 125 lbs.," while randomdetox.com claims that the "[h]eight and weight of Jennifer Lopez is 5"6, and 145 lbs," perhaps reflecting a recent pregnancy. "Dinner by J.Lo," *Us Weekly*, 13 May 2002; Michael Lewittes and Gabriel Snyder, "J.Lo and Ben Surprise! Surprise!" *Us Weekly*, 12 August 2002; autumn_x_chill.livejournal.com, 18 March 2009, accessed 8 December 2009; www.randomdetox.com, 30 November 2008, accessed 8 December 2009. In spite of these variations, all reported weights and heights suggest above average height and less than average weight.
37. Lopez's high fashion clothing line "Sweetface" closed production in spring 2009. Lopez's diffusion line, JLO, closed U.S. sales in 2007, while remaining available in 40 countries. See Suzanne Heibel, "Jennifer Lopez's 'Sweetface' Clothing Line Comes to an End," www.hispanicbusiness.com, 26 June 2009, accessed 27 June 2009. See also Julee Kaplan, "Jennifer Lopez Exits Apparel in the U.S.," *Women's Wear Daily*, 24 June 2009.
38. In its Latino Power 50 list issued in 2007, *Hollywood Reporter* places the Mexican actress Salma Hayek at number four, as against Lopez's number 10. Reporting these results, Latin Gossip affirmed that Lopez "has more clout on camera and behind the scenes than any other Latino—or Latina—in Hollywood." "THR's Latino Power 50," www.latingossip.com, accessed 12 October 2009.
39. Beltrán, "Hollywood Latina Body," 74. See entire article for a discussion of Lopez as a crossover star and her relations to other Latina stars.
40. For a comprehensive discussion, see Clara E. Rodriquez, ed., *Latin Looks: Images of Latinas and Latinos in the U.S. Media* (Boulder, CO: Westview, 1997).
41. Dodd and Fradley, "'I believe,'" 192.
42. *Instyle Magazine*, September 2009.
43. "From Here to Divinity," *Entertainment Weekly*, 9 October 1998.
44. Helen Gurley Brown, text of television show 24 July 1991, quoted in Jennifer Scanlon, *Bad Girls Go Everywhere: The Life of Helen Gurley Brown* (New York: Oxford University Press, 2009), 180.
45. Holson, "When Jenny Dumped Benny."
46. Justin Oppelaar, "Lopez Puts J.Lo Stamp on Signatures," www.variety.com, 16 June 2002, accessed 27 June 2009.
47. Holson, "When Jenny Dumped Benny." Lopez and Medina renewed their relationship several years later. In 2009, he worked for both Lopez and her current husband, Marc Anthony. Paula Froelich, "Benny Bounced," *New York Post*, 15 March 2009.
48. Michael Lewittes, "J.Lo's New Feud," *Us Weekly*, 21 July 2003.
49. Josh Tyrangiel, "Jennifer Lopez," www.time.com, 13 August 2005, accessed 30 September 2009.
50. *Parade*, 7 December 2003.
51. "When Stars Love the Lowly," *MailOnline*, www.dailymail.co.uk, 19 April 2004, accessed 18 December 2009; Liz Smith, "Two Mr. Wrongs for Lopez," *Los Angeles Times*, 13 June 2002.
52. Brian Orloff, "Jen Garner: Ben a 'Sweet' Dad—Just Don't Let Him Do Hair," *People*, www.people.com, 21 April 2009, accessed 8 December 2009.
53. *Hollywood Reporter*, 6 March 2002.

Chapter 6

1. See chapter five. For references to the film, see *Maid in Manhattan*, directed by Wayne Wang, DVD (2002; Culver City, CA: Columbia TriStar Home Entertainment, 2003).

2. "Perspectives," *Newsweek*, 17 February 2003.
3. Reported in Gregory D. Smithers, "Barack Obama and Race in the United States: A History of the Future," *Australasian Journal of American Studies* 28, no. 1 (July 2009): 9. Determining (accept through self-identification) what precisely constitutes an inter-racial marriage is difficult; however the figures probably do represent general trends in American thinking.
4. Lucy Kaylin, "The Goddess," *GQ*, December 2002.
5. Lawrence Donegan, "Spinning Jenny," *Observer* (London), 14 September 2003.
6. Richard Dyer, *Stars* (London: British Film Institute, 1979), 30.
7. Christopher Tookey, review of *Maid in Manhattan*, *MailOnline*, www.dailymail.co.uk, 7 March 2003, accessed 20 September 2009.
8. "Ben Affleck stronca J.Lo," blog.leiweb.it, 11 July 2009, accessed 20 September 2009; "Ben Affleck revient sur son histoire d'amour avec Jennifer Lopez," www.voici.fr, 24 July 2009, accessed 20 September 2009; "Affleck: 'Lopez Was Bad for My Career,'" www.hollywood.com, 9 July 2009, accessed 20 September 2009.
9. Sandy M. Fernandez, "Jenny's Image on the Block," *Washington Post*, 21 May 2005.
10. Donegan, "Spinning Jenny."
11. David Ciminelli, "Lopez Poised for Superstardom with Singing and Acting Career," *Variety* (D), 5 March 2002.
12. *Us Weekly*, 12 August 2002, 40.
13. Stephen M. Silverman, "J.Lo and Ben's Jewels of Engagement," *People*, 6 November 2002, www.people.com, accessed 27 September 2009.
14. Isobel Fox, "Stars Behaving Badly," *MailOnline*, www.dailymail.co.uk, 3 March 2003, accessed 20 September 2009. For another example of Lopez's depiction as a diva, see Michael Lewittes, "Saying No to J.Lo," *Us Weekly*, 1 April 2002. See also Donegan, "Spinning Jenny."
15. Dyer, *Stars*, 49.
16. David Carr, "Paparazzi Cash In on a Magazine Dogfight," *New York Times*, 4 November 2002.
17. Carr, "Paparazzi Cash In," *New York Times*, 4 November 2002. See also "Pictures of J.Lo, Affleck Trigger a Bidding War," *Los Angeles Times*, 6 August 2002.
18. See, for example, *People*, 6 October 2003.
19. Mara Reinstein, "Born in the Bronx: Made in Manhattan," *Us Weekly*, 23 December 2002.
20. "Star's Enormous Entourage is a London Traffic Stopper," *London Times*, 27 February 2003.
21. Mike Sager, "What does It Feel like to be Jennifer Lopez?" *Esquire*, August 2003, 60.
22. Jennifer Lopez, interview by James Lipton, *Inside the Actors Studio: Jennifer Lopez*, Bravo, 10 October 2004; Colin Paterson, "How Low can J-Lo Go?" *Guardian*, 16 November 2002.
23. "Hands-on Connie," *People*, 4 November 2002.
24. Lopez, interview by James Lipton.
25. Tookey, review.
26. Dana Kennedy, "Homegirl, Working Woman, Empire Builder," *New York Times*, 3 November 2002.
27. Jo Berry and Angie Errigo, *Chick Flicks: Movies Women Love* (London: Orion Books, 2004), 32.
28. Stephen Knadler, "'Blanca from the Block': Whiteness and the Transnational Latina Body," *Genders OnLine Journal* 41 (2005): www.genders.org, accessed 7 September 2009.
29. Smithers, "Barack Obama and Race," 5.
30. *ABC News Classics: Helen Gurley Brown*, DVD, ABC News, 2007.
31. Prov. 24:16.
32. Jill Gerston, "Fashion Focus: Jennifer Lopez," *Biography Magazine*, July 2003.
33. Jeanine Basinger, *A Woman's View: How Hollywood Spoke to Women, 1930–1960* (Hanover, NH: Wesleyan University Press, 1993), 8. See chapter two for a discussion of the concept of the "Green World."
34. A stolen diamond necklace plays a crucial role in an earlier Lopez film, *Blood and Wine* (Bob Rafelson, 1996).
35. *People*, 17 November 2003; Boydie Beener, "I Want That! Jennifer Lopez in Dolce & Gabbana," www.stylelist.com, 6 October 2008, accessed 12 December 2009.

36. Annie Flanzraich, "R-Jeneration: Perfect for Prom," *Las Vegas Review-Journal*, 6 May 2003, www.reviewjournal.com, accessed 5 October 2009.

37. *Entertainment Today*, 13 December 2002; Gerston, "Fashion Focus"; "Famous Celebrities and Their Diamond Engagement Rings," www.abazias.com, 16 April 2009, accessed 6 October 2009.

38. Karen S. Schneider, "What a Difference a Year Makes," www.people.com, 4 August 2003, accessed 29 December 2009.

39. Lauren Weisberger, *The Devil Wears Prada* (New York: Doubleday, 2003); *Chasing Harry Winston* (New York: Simon & Schuster, 2008).

40. Tresanna Hassanally, "Harry Winston: Jeweler to the Stars," *Hilary Magazine*, hilary.com, 11 October 2008, accessed 22 September 2009; Cecily Hall, "Glitz Factor," www.wwd.com, 28 May 2009, accessed 1 June 2009; Ed Dinger, "Harry Winston Diamond Corporation," www.answers.com, accessed 6 October 2009. In some cases, the lending of jewelry to stars is reported as a 1980s phenomenon.

41. Maura Spiegel, quoted in Michael Montgomery, "Hollywood's Diamonds," americanradioworks.publicradio.org, accessed 22 September 2009.

42. Maura Spiegel, "Hollywood Loves Diamonds," in *The Nature of Diamonds*, ed. George E. Harlow (Cambridge: Cambridge University Press in association with the American Museum of Natural History, 1998), 202.

43. George E. Harlow, "Diamonds in the Twentieth Century," in *The Nature of Diamonds*, ed. George E. Harlow (Cambridge: Cambridge University Press in association with the American Museum of Natural History, 1998), 208.

44. Spiegel, "Hollywood Loves Diamonds," 199.

45. Hall, "Glitz Factor"; "Pretty Nice," *Los Angeles Times*, 20 April 1990.

46. Terry Pristin, "New Partners Hope to Expand Harry Winston," *New York Times*, 22 December 2000; Dinger, "Harry Winston Diamond Corporation."

47. Libby Golden, "Who is Chasing Harry Winston?" *NYC Pavement Pieces*, 22 February, pavementpieces.com, accessed 27 June 2009.

48. Carl DiOrio, "'Maid' in the Shade," *Variety* (D), 16 December 2002.

49. Sarah Jane Rowland, "Fashion Films," www.mixitup.co.nz, accessed 6 October 2009.

Chapter 7

1. For a discussion of the aging woman as neo-feminist heroine, see chapter ten.

2. These included the following parent companies who controlled Hollywood through "ownership of the traditional major studios": TimeWarner (Warner Brothers), Disney, News Corp (20th Century Fox), Sony (Columbia), Viacom (Paramount), GE (Universal). Thomas Schatz, "New Hollywood, New Millennium," in *Film Theory and Contemporary Hollywood Movies*, ed. Warren Buckland (New York: Routledge, 2009), 20.

3. Schatz, "New Hollywood," 20; Michael Allen, *Contemporary US Cinema* (Harlow: Longman, 2003), 35–61.

4. Anne Thompson, "In Turnaround," nymag.com, 23 November 2003, accessed 10 December 2009.

5. Laura M. Holson, "Chief of Sony Pictures Plans to Step Down," *New York Times*, 7 August 2003; Schatz, "New Hollywood," 21.

6. Schatz, "New Hollywood," 26.

7. Wendy Mitchell, "In Focus: The Makings of a Mega-hit," www.screendaily.com, 7 November 2008, accessed 30 December 2009.

8. *Variety* (W), 9 June 2008.

9. Borys Kit, "Hollywood Sitting Pretty in 'Pink Lit,'" *Hollywood Reporter*, 26 August 2003.

10. Amy Silverman, "Legally Brown," *Phoenix New Times*, 30 October 2003, www.phoenixnewtimes.com, accessed 17 October 2003.

11. For a discussion of the term and of contemporary novels for women typically categorized as "chick lit," see Suzanne Ferriss and Mallory Young, eds., *Chick Lit: The New Woman's Fiction*

(New York: Routledge, 2006). For a discussion of its place in the history of twentieth-century popular literature for women, see Imelda Whelehan, *The Feminist Bestseller: From* Sex *and the Single Girl to* Sex and the City (Basingstoke: Palgrave Macmillan, 2005).

12. For a discussion of chick lit as a genre, see Whelehan, *Feminist Bestseller*, and Ferriss and Young, *Chick Lit.*

13. Kathy Lette, *How to Kill Your Husband (and Other Handy Household Hints)* (London: Simon & Schuster, 2006).

14. While many "chick-lit" novels are written in the first person, this is not always the case as in the more recent novels of Candace Bushnell.

15. Maggie Alderson, *Handbags and Gladrags: A Novel* (New York: Berkley Books, 2005), 81, 111, 371.

16. Whelehan, *Feminist Bestseller*, 219.

17. Whelehan, *Feminist Bestseller*, 177–80.

18. Mitchell, "In Focus."

19. Mitchell, "In Focus."

20. Whelehan, *Feminist Bestseller*, 175.

21. Richard Simpson, "Renee Zellweger: 'Putting on weight again for Bridget Jones 3 might kill me,'" *Mail Online*, www.dailymail.co.uk, 13 December 2007, accessed 20 October 2009; Kevin Conley, "The Indiscreet Charm of Charlize Theron," *Vogue*, September 2009, www.vogue.com, accessed 20 October 2009.

22. Suzanne Ferriss, "Narrative and Cinematic Doubleness: *Pride and Prejudice* and *Bridget Jones's Diary*," in *Chick Lit: The New Woman's Fiction*, ed. Suzanne Ferriss and Mallory Young (New York: Routledge, 2006), 83.

23. Whelehan, *Feminist Bestseller*, 176.

24. Whelehan, *Feminist Bestseller*, 176.

25. Sophie Kinsella, *Shopaholic Ties the Knot* (New York: Delta Trade Paperbacks, 2003).

26. See Whelehan, *Feminist Bestseller*, 162, 206–07. For an alternative reading of these characters, see Joke Hermes "'Ally McBeal', 'Sex and the City' and the Tragic Success of Feminism," in *Feminism in Popular Culture*, ed. Joanne Hollows and Rachel Moseley (Oxford: Berg, 2006), 79–95.

27. Whelehan, *Feminist Bestseller*, 207. See also Angela McRobbie, *The Aftermath of Feminism: Gender, Culture and Social Change* (London: Sage, 2009), 20–22.

28. Diane Negra, *What a Girl Wants: Fantasizing the Reclamation of Self in Postfeminism* (London: Routledge, 2009), 61. Suzanne Ferriss and Mallory Young make a similar claim in the introduction to their edited volume, positing Helen Fielding's *Bridget Jones's Diary* as the "single urtext" at "the origins of chick lit." Suzanne Ferriss and Mallory Young, introduction to *Chick Lit: The New Woman's Fiction*, ed. Suzanne Ferriss and Mallory Young (New York: Routledge, 2006), 4.

29. For a discussion of the Cosmo Girl, see the introduction to this volume.

30. Candace Bushnell, *Lipstick Jungle* (London: Little, Brown, 2005), 339.

31. Bushnell, *Lipstick Jungle*, 340.

32. Whelehan, *Feminist Bestseller*, 177.

33. See chapters five and six.

34. Whelehan, *Feminist Bestseller*, 27.

35. Tom King, "Hollywood Journal," *Wall Street Journal*, 22 December 2002.

36. Leslie Camhi, "Terms of Endearment," *Village Voice*, 16 April 2002.

37. Mike Goodridge, "My Big Fat Sleeper Smash," *Screen International*, 30 August 2002.

38. Colin Brown, "A Tale of Two Torontos," *Screen International*, 6 September 2009.

39. Stephen Kinzer, "An Indie Movie Is Outlasting the Blockbusters," *New York Times*, 29 August 2002.

40. *Screen International*, 6 September 2002.

41. Goodridge, "My Big Fat Sleeper Smash."

42. Claudia Eller, "Jilters Regret Missing Wedding," *Los Angeles Times*, 14 September 2002; Rick Lyman, "A Big Fat (and Profitable) Cinderella Story; 'Greek Wedding' Courts a Prince Named Oscar," *New York Times*, 28 November 2002.

43. King, "Hollywood Journal."
44. Lyman, "Big Fat (and Profitable) Cinderella Story"; Kinzer, "Indie Movie is Outlasting the Blockbusters."
45. Dave McNary, "O'Seas Flies with Batpic," *Variety* (D), 2 September 2008.
46. Thomas G. Schatz, e-mail message to author, 24 June 2009.
47. *Variety* (W), 6 April 2009.
48. Ella Taylor, "Thank You for the Music," *LA Weekly*, 18 July 2008.
49. Andy Klein, "*Brideshead* and Bride's Dad," *LA City Beat*, 24 July 2008.
50. "The 'Mamma' Mix," *Los Angeles Times*, 24 July 2008.
51. Ali Jaafar, "Globe-trotting 'Mamma' has Multinational Appeal," *Variety* (W), 14 July 2008; Mitchell, "In Focus."
52. Christina Lane, *Feminist Hollywood: From* Born in Flames *to* Point Break (Detroit: Wayne State University Press, 2000), 33.
53. Diane Garrett, "Chick Pic Clicks," *Variety* (W), 9 June 2008.
54. Meryl Streep, quoted in Peter Travers, "Meryl Streep," *Rolling Stone*, 15 November 2007.
55. Schatz, "New Hollywood," 20.
56. Schatz, e-mail message to author, 24 June 2009.
57. Nikki Finke, "Warner's Robinov Bitchslaps Film Women: Gloria Allred Calls for Warner's Boycott," www.dealine.com, 5 October 2007, accessed 18 October 2009.
58. Tad Friend, "Call Me," *The New Yorker*, 12 October 2009, 96.

Chapter 8

1. Peter M. Nichols, "Home Video; 'Pretty Woman,' Then and Now," *New York Times*, 28 January 2000.
2. Wendy Mitchell, "Making a Mega-hit: The Key Ingredients," *Screen International*, 7 November 2008.
3. Press release for *Legally Blonde*, 9, consulted Margaret Herrick Library, June 2009.
4. Sarah Jane Rowland, "Fashion Films," www.mixitup.co.nz, accessed 2 September 2009; Nana, "*Confessions of a Shopaholic* Countdown: The Best Fashion Flicks of all Time," www.flypaper.bluefy.com, 9 February 2009, accessed 2 November 2009. For references to *The Devil Wears Prada*, see *The Devil Wears Prada*, directed by David Frankel, DVD (2006; Moore Park, Australia: Fox Studios Australia, 2007).
5. For a discussion of fashion in classical Hollywood, see Sarah Berry, *Screen Style: Fashion and Femininity in 1930s Hollywood* (Minneapolis: University of Minnesota Press, 2000).
6. For a discussion of the evolution of the fashion industry and its relations to film, see Hilary Radner, "Migration and Immigration: French Fashion and American Film," in *France/Hollywood Échanges cinématographiques et identités nationales*, ed. Martin Barnier and Raphaëlle Moine (Paris: L'Harmattan, 2002), 203–23.
7. Deborah Nadoolman Landis, *Dressed: A Century of Hollywood Costume Design* (New York: Collins Design, 2007), 372.
8. Deborah Nadoolman Landis, quoted in Michelle Lee, *Fashion Victim: Our Love–Hate Relationship with Dressing, Shopping, and the Cost of Style* (New York: Broadway Books, 2003), 117.
9. Rowland, "Fashion Films."
10. Stella Bruzzi and Pamela Church Gibson, "'Fashion is the fifth character': Fashion, Costume and Character in *Sex and the City*," in *Reading "Sex and the City,"* ed. Kim Akass and Janet McCabe (London: I.B. Tauris, 2004), 123.
11. Bruzzi and Gibson, "'Fashion is the fifth character,'" 123.
12. Stella Bruzzi, *Undressing Cinema: Clothing and Identity in the Movies* (London: Routledge, 1997), 34.
13. Jeffrey Kurland, quoted in Deborah Nadoolman Landis, *50 Designers/50 Costumes: Concept to Character* (Beverly Hills, CA: Academy of Motion Picture Arts and Sciences, 2004), 2.

14. Patricia A. Cunningham, Heather Mangine, and Andrew Reilly, "Television and Fashion in the 1980s," in *Twentieth-century American Fashion*, ed. Linda Welters and Patricia A. Cunningham (Oxford: Berg, 2005), 210.

15. Cunningham, Mangine, and Reilly, "Television and Fashion in the 1980s," 209–28; Richard Zoglin, "Cool Cops, Hot Show," www.time.com, 16 September 1985, accessed 25 October 2009.

16. For a description of Klensch's approach to clothing, see Elsa Klensch with Beryl Meyer, *Style* (New York: Berkley Publishing Group, 1995).

17. For example, see Amanda D. Lotz, "Postfeminist Television Criticism: Rehabilitating Critical Terms and Identifying Postfeminist Attributes," *Feminist Media Studies* 1, no. 1 (2001): 105–21; Jane Arthurs, "*Sex and the City* and Consumer Culture: Remediating Postfeminist Drama," *Feminist Media Studies* 3, no. 1 (2003): 83–98; Jane Gerhard, "*Sex and the City*: Carrie Bradshaw's Queer Postfeminism," *Feminist Media Studies* 5, no. 1 (2005): 37–49; Stephen Gennaro, "*Sex and the City*: Perpetual Adolescence Gendered Feminine," *Nebula* 4, no. 1 (2007): 246–75; Rosalind Gill, "Postfeminist Romance," in *Gender and the Media* (Cambridge: Polity Press, 2007), 218–48; Deborah Jermyn, *Sex and the City* (Detroit: Wayne State University Press, 2009).

18. Christina Binkley, "The 'Sex' Effect: Empowering to Some, Trashy to Others," *Wall Street Journal*, 29 May 2008.

19. Serena French, "The $1 Million Wardrobe of 'The Devil Wears Prada,'" *New York Post*, 21 June 2006; boxoffice.mojo.com, accessed 7 September 2009.

20. French, "$1 Million Wardrobe."

21. Time Warner also owned HBO, which produced *Sex and the City*; Warner Brothers produced *Sex and the City: The Movie* through its subsidiary, New Line.

22. James Barron with Linda Lee, "Boldface Names," *New York Times*, 18 October 2002.

23. Associated Press, "New Magazine from Time Inc.," *New York Times*, 19 May 1994.

24. "Reviews: *InStyle Instant Style: Your Season-by-Season Guide for Work and Weekend*," *Publishers Weekly*, 16 October 2006.

25. Rachel Tiplady, "Zara: Taking the Lead in Fast-Fashion," www.businessweek.com, 4 April 2006, accessed 2 November 2009.

26. David Carr, "Contemplating Time Warner without Time," *New York Times*, 18 September 2006.

27. Geraldine Fabrikant, "*Vogue* Tries a More Relaxed Look," *New York Times*, 31 October 1988.

28. Anna Wintour, quoted in Jerry Oppenheimer, *Front Row: Anna Wintour, the Cool Life and Hot Times of Vogue's Editor-in-chief* (New York: St. Martin's Press, 2005), 288.

29. Fabrikant, "*Vogue* Tries a More Relaxed Look."

30. Oppenheimer, *Front Row*, 322.

31. Emili Vesilind, "Hollywood Style—Unscripted—Actress Sienna Miller Steps into a New Role: Fashion Designer," *Los Angeles Times*, 30 September 2007.

32. Andrew Harmon, "Mining LA Style for William Rast," *Los Angeles Times*, 15 March 2009.

33. Maureen Orth, *The Importance of Being Famous: Behind the Scenes of the Celebrity-Industrial Complex* (New York: Henry Holt, 2004), 19.

34. Leisa Barnett, "The Field of M&S," www.vogue.co.uk, 21 May 2008, accessed 4 November 2009.

35. Oppenheimer, *Front Row*, 328.

36. Borys Kit, "Hollywood Sitting Pretty in 'Pink Lit,'" *Hollywood Reporter*, 26 August 2003.

37. Anne Thompson, "Exec with Character Does Films with Same," *Hollywood Reporter*, 30 June 2006. For a discussion of male-centered romantic comedies, see Tamar Jeffers McDonald, "Hommecom: Engendering Change in Contemporary Romantic Comedy," in *Falling in Love Again: Romantic Comedy in Contemporary Cinema*, ed. Stacey Abbott and Deborah Jermyn (London: I.B. Tauris, 2009), 146–57.

38. Thompson, "Exec with Character Does Films with Same."

39. Anne Thompson, "Elizabeth Gabler Guides Fox 2000," www.variety.com, 8 January 2009, accessed 3 November 2009.
40. Nicole Laporte and Gabriel Snyder, "Auds Dance with 'The Devil,'" *Variety* (W), 10 July 2006.
41. Thompson, "Elizabeth Gabler Guides Fox 2000."
42. Peter Chernin and Bill Mechanic, quoted in Thompson, "Exec with Character Does Films with Same."
43. Thompson, "Exec with Character Does Films with Same."
44. Roger Armbrust, "NY Lawmakers Fight Runaways," *BackStage*, 20 August 2004, www.all business.com, accessed 15 November 2009.
45. Sarah Jessica Parker, quoted in Ron Simon, "*Sex and the City*," in *The Essential HBO Reader*, ed. Gary R. Edgerton and Jeffrey P. Jones (Lexington: University Press of Kentucky, 2008), 196; Simon, "*Sex and the City*," 196.
46. Arthurs, "*Sex and the City* and Consumer Culture," 90.
47. David Denby, "Dressed to Kill," *New Yorker*, 10 July 2006, 90.
48. Thompson, "Exec with Character Does Films with Same."
49. Janet Maslin, "Elegant Magazine, Avalanche of Dirt," review of *The Devil Wears Prada*, by Lauren Weisberger, *New York Times*, 14 April 2003.
50. Oppenheimer, *Front Row*, 348.
51. Rachel Syme, "Lauren Weisberger Exorcises the Devil," *Page Six Magazine*, 15 June 2008.
52. Kate Betts, "*The Devil Wears Prada*: Anna Dearest," *New York Times*, 13 April 2003.
53. A.O. Scott, "Sadistic, Manipulative and So Very Stylish," *New York Times*, 30 June 2006.
54. David Edelstein, "Gods and Monsters," *New York Magazine*, 25 June 2006.
55. David Edelstein, "Summer of Streep," *New York Magazine*, 6 August 2006.
56. Denby, "Dressed to Kill," 90.
57. *Birmingham Post*, 20 September 2006.
58. Karen Hollinger, "'Magic Meryl': Meryl Streep," in *The Actress: Hollywood Acting and the Female Star* (New York and London: Routledge, 2006), 80. Hollinger deems Streep's status as an actress to be the single most important influence on her public and onscreen persona. See Hollinger, "'Magic Meryl,'" 71–99.
59. Cher, quoted in Robert Hofler, "Meryl Streep as Actor and Coach," *Variety* (D), 11 April 2008.
60. Hollinger, "'Magic Meryl,'" 86.
61. Belinda Luscombe, "7 Myths about Meryl," *Time*, 11 June 2006.
62. David Frankel, quoted in Diana Jordan, "Fashion Statement," *Costco Connection*, December 2006, 33.
63. David Frankel, quoted in Jordan, "Fashion Statement," 33.
64. David Frankel, quoted in Jordan, "Fashion Statement," 33.
65. David Frankel, quoted in "The Directors," *Variety* (D), 6 December 2006.
66. Luscombe, "7 Myths about Meryl," 57.
67. French, "$1 Million Wardrobe."
68. Azadeh Ensha, "Meryl Wears Patricia," *Advocate*, 18 July 2006.
69. Stuart Levine, "The Contenders," www.variety.com, 16 November 2006, accessed 15 November 2009.
70. Ruth La Ferla, "The Duds of 'The Devil Wears Prada,'" *New York Times*, 29 June 2006.
71. Mimi Avins, "With 'Devil' It's all in the Details," *Los Angeles Times*, 18 June 2006.
72. *USA Weekend*, 6 October 2006.
73. Denby, "Dressed to Kill," 90.
74. Jan Lisa Huttner, "Jan Chats with Aline Brosh Mckenna," www.films42.com, 7 September 2006, accessed 5 November 2009.
75. Scott, "Sadistic, Manipulative and So Very Stylish."
76. Sidney Toledano, quoted in Tomoko Okawa, "Licensing Practices at Maison Christian Dior," in *Producing Fashion: Commerce, Culture, and Consumers*, ed. Regina Lee Blaszczyk (Philadelphia: University of Pennsylvania Press, 2008), 107.
77. Laporte and Snyder, "Auds Dance with 'The Devil.'"

Chapter 9

1. Michael Cieply and Bill Carter, "'Sex' and the Box Office: Gal Pals Knock Indy Jones from the Top Spot," *New York Times*, 2 June 2008.
2. Josh Friedman, "'Sex and the City' Won't Keep Audiences Away From 'Indiana,'" *Los Angeles Times*, 30 May 2008.
3. Ainnet 4rom NYC!, "Thiz is the best Song ever," best_of_youtube, www.hiphopmusic.com, 11 June 2008, accessed 16 November 2009.
4. "Fergie—'Labels or Love' Lyrics," justjared.buzznet.com, 23 April 2003, accessed 16 November 2009.
5. For references to *Sex and the City: The Movie*, see *Sex and the City: The Movie*, directed by Michael Patrick King, Extended Cut, Two-disc Special Edition (2008; Burbank, CA: Warner Home Video, 2008).
6. I am indebted to Peter Stapleton for this observation and other observations about the use of music in this film.
7. R. Serge Denisoff and George Plasketes, "Synergy in 1980s Film and Music: Formula for Success or Industry Mythology?" *Film History* 4 (1990): 257.
8. Ron Givens, "Tracking Pretty Woman," *Entertainment Weekly*, 23 March 1990, www.ew.com, accessed 18 November 2009.
9. Givens, "Tracking Pretty Woman."
10. Diane Garrett, "Broad Appeal: Studio Touts Group 'Sex,'" *Variety* (D), 28 May 2008.
11. Chris Carlisle, quoted in Stuart Elliott, "'Sex and the City' and Its Lasting Female Appeal," *New York Times*, 17 March 2008.
12. Elliott, "'Sex and the City.'"
13. For a discussion of the role of the fashion designer, see chapter eight.
14. Elliott, "'Sex and the City.'"
15. John Melfi, quoted in Elliott, "'Sex and the City.'"
16. For a discussion of the importance of style to contemporary culture, see chapter eight.
17. Katie Baker, "Attack of the Clones," *Newsweek*, 19 May 2008.
18. Jennifer Soong, "Michael Patrick King Talks about *Sex*," www.moviemaker.com, 30 May 2008, accessed 6 November 2009.
19. Chris Lee and John Horn, "'Sex' Appeal," *Los Angeles Times*, 15 May 2008.
20. Friedman, "'Sex and the City.'"
21. Lee and Horn, "'Sex' Appeal."
22. Randee Dawn, "In Their Shoes," *Hollywood Reporter*, 23 April 2008.
23. Dawn, "In Their Shoes."
24. Garrett, "Broad Appeal."
25. Pamela McClintock and Dave McNary, "B.O. Gets Sexy: Frame Shows Feminine Side," *Variety* (D), 30 May 2008.
26. Lauren A.E. Schuker, "A Film with Underage Fans Faces Marketing Issues," *Wall Street Journal*, 30 May 2008.
27. Schuker, "Film with Underage Fans."
28. Schuker, "Film with Underage Fans."
29. Shelley Zalis, quoted in Schuker, "Film with Underage Fans."
30. Schuker, "Film with Underage Fans."
31. David Edelstein, "Give It to Me One More Time," *New York Magazine*, 24 May 2008.
32. See chapter three for a discussion of prolonged adolescence and its significance to the neo-feminist paradigm.
33. For example, see *Hello!*, 9 October 2007.
34. Quoted in *The Holiday* (Nancy Meyers, 2006). The original *Newsweek* quote referred to women "over 40." See *Newsweek*, 5 June 2006, and *Newsweek*, 2 June 1986.
35. Liz Smith, *Los Angeles Times*, 10 July 2004.
36. Friedman, "'Sex and the City.'"

37. Lee and Horn, "'Sex' Appeal."
38. John Melfi, quoted in Dawn, "In Their Shoes"; Katherine Oliver, quoted in Dawn, "In Their Shoes."
39. John Melfi, quoted in Dawn, "In Their Shoes"; Katherine Oliver, quoted in Dawn, "In Their Shoes."
40. See chapter eight for a discussion of the role of the fashion designer and fashion more generally.
41. Fern Mallis, quoted in Diane Clehane, "Gotham's Fashion Elite Dress up for 'Sex,'" *Variety* (D), 22 April 2008.
42. Dawn, "In Their Shoes."
43. *Hello!*, 16 October 2006.
44. Emili Vesilind, "Dressing 'Sex' again," *Los Angeles Times*, 4 November 2007.
45. Dawn, "In Their Shoes."
46. Dawn, "In Their Shoes."
47. Melena Ryzik, "More 'Sex' and the City is Happy about It," *New York Times*, 25 November 2007.
48. Cieply and Carter, "'Sex' and the Box Office."
49. John Melfi, quoted in Clehane, "Gotham's Fashion Elite."
50. For a developed discussion of Parker's star persona, see Deborah Jermyn, "'Bringing out the * in You': SJP, Carrie Bradshaw and the Evolution of Television Stardom," in *Framing Celebrity: New Directions in Celebrity Culture*, ed. Su Holmes and Sean Redmond (London: Routledge, 2006), 67–85.
51. Geraldine Fabrikant, "From a Start on Welfare to Riches in the City," *New York Times*, 30 July 2000.
52. Emily Nussbaum, "Sarah Jessica Parker Would Like a Few Words with Carrie Bradshaw," *New York Magazine*, 4 May 2008.
53. Ryzik, "More 'Sex.'"
54. Plum Sykes, "Rebel Romance," *Vogue*, June 2008, 127.
55. Liz Smith, *Los Angeles Times*, 10 August 2000.
56. For a discussion of stars and "ordinariness," see Richard Dyer, *Stars* (London: British Film Institute, 1979), 49–50.
57. Julia Baird, "Girls Gone Mild," *Newsweek*, 26 May 2008.
58. See chapter eight for a discussion of Anna Wintour's inaugural *Vogue* cover.
59. Booth Moore, "One Manolo Too Many," *Los Angeles Times*, 25 May 2008.
60. "Interview by Scoop," *People*, 25 February 2003.
61. Moore, "One Manolo Too Many."
62. Fabrikant, "From a Start on Welfare."
63. See chapters five and six.
64. Christine Geraghty, "Re-examining Stardom: Questions of Texts, Bodies and Performance," in *Reinventing Film Studies*, ed. Christine Gledhill and Linda Williams (London: Arnold, 2000), 187.
65. See chapter eight for a discussion on Meryl Streep.
66. Geraghty, "Re-examining Stardom," 187.
67. See chapter eight for a discussion of Field.
68. "Council Tips to Parker, the Queen of Accessories," *Los Angeles Times*, 4 January 2002.
69. See Maureen Orth, *The Importance of Being Famous: Behind the Scenes of the Celebrity-Industrial Complex* (New York: Henry Holt, 2004).
70. André Leon Tally, quoted in Clehane, "Gotham's Fashion Elite."
71. See chapters five and six.
72. *Hello!* (London), 9 October 2007.
73. Samantha McIntyre, "Stylewatch: Sex Sells ... Again!" *People*, 16 June 2008.
74. Diane Garrett, "Chick Pic Clicks," *Variety* (W), 9 June 2008.
75. Lisa Rosen, "Well-Heeled Audience," *Los Angeles Times*, 31 May 2008.
76. Dan Fellman, quoted in McClintock and McNary, "B.O. Gets Sexy."
77. Pamela McClintock, "Ladies Have Their Way with Indiana Jones," *Variety* (D), 2 June 2008.

78. Ginia Bellafante, "Back to the City, for More than Just Sex," *New York Times*, 4 May 2008.
79. Eric Wilson, "10 Years Later, Carrie Coordinated," *New York Times*, 1 June 2008.
80. Anthony Lane, "Carrie: 'Sex and the City,'" *New Yorker*, 9–16 June 2008.
81. Carina Chocano, "An Inviting Return," *Los Angeles Times*, 30 May 2008.
82. Ella Taylor, "Cheap *Sex*," *Village Voice*, 28 May 2008.
83. "Frumpy and Boring," styledlife.excite.co.uk, 24 June 2008, accessed 15 November 2008.
84. Rosen, "Well-Heeled Audience."
85. Baird, "Girls Gone Mild."
86. Bellafante, "Back to the City."
87. "The Bridget Jones Economy—Singles and The City; How Young Singles Shape City Culture, Lifestyles and Economies," *Economist* (U.S.), 22 December 2001.
88. "Bridget Jones Economy."
89. Kay S. Hymowitz, "The New Girl Order," *City Journal*, Autumn 2007, www.city-journal.org, accessed 23 March 2009. See chapter one. See also Alys Eve Weinbaum, Lynn M. Thomas, Priti Ramamurthy, Uta G. Poiger, Madeleine Y. Dong, and Tani E. Barlow, *The Modern Girl around the World: Consumption, Modernity, and Globalization* (Durham, NC: Duke University Press, 2008).
90. Cieply and Carter, "'Sex' and the Box Office."
91. Ann Hornaday, "Women & Film," *Washington Post*, 25 October 2009.
92. Samuel E. Craig, e-mail message to author, 9 December 2009.
93. Linda Obst, quoted in Hornaday, "Women & Film."

Chapter 10

1. Michael Allen, *Contemporary US Cinema* (Harlow: Longman, 2003), 113.
2. Allen, *Contemporary US Cinema*, 114.
3. The exception is *Something's Gotta Give* (2003). I discuss the reception of this film by feminists later in this chapter.
4. Margy Rochlin, "Out on Her Own Now, and Feeling Liberated," *New York Times*, 10 December 2000.
5. Peter Knegt, "B.O. of the '00s: The Top Grossing Female Helmed Films," www.indiewire.com, 4 December 2009, accessed 12 December 2009.
6. For a discussion of the new hybridized comedy and the woman's film, see Hilary Radner, "*Le Divorce*: Romance, Separation and Reconciliation," in *Falling in Love again: Romantic Comedy in Contemporary Cinema*, ed. Stacey Abbott and Deborah Jermyn (London: I.B. Tauris, 2009), 208–21.
7. For references to *Something's Gotta Give*, see *Something's Gotta Give*, directed by Nancy Meyers, DVD (2003; Pyrmont, Australia: Warner Home Video, 2004).
8. For a more detailed discussion of Jane Fonda and the concept of serial authenticity, see Hilary Radner, "Speaking the Body," in *Shopping around: Feminine Culture and the Pursuit of Pleasure* (New York: Routledge, 1995), 147–48.
9. Amy Taubin, "Desperate Men and Twisted Sisters," *The Village Voice*, 22 February 2000.
10. Carina Chocano, "It's Best to Let Keaton Be Keaton," *Los Angeles Times*, 20 January 2008.
11. Nancy Griffin, "Diane Keaton Meets Both Her Matches," *New York Times*, 14 December 2003.
12. Liz Smith, review of *Something's Gotta Give*, *Los Angeles Times*, 1 October 2003. Sadie Wearing argues that Erica's initial "untouchability" is represented by the turtlenecks she wears at the opening of the film, which give way to "'feminine' pastels" and "V-necks" after Harry cuts through her off-white turtleneck sweater in the seduction scene. Though Erica wears "V-necks" more frequently as the film progresses, her first notable "V-neck" is the LBD that she wears on her first date with Julian, significantly before Harry seduces her. Her color palate does not change and she continues to favor turtlenecks throughout the film. For example, she sports a grey turtleneck at the moment at which she finishes her new play based on her affair with Harry in the film's third act. The turtleneck is a signature look for

Keaton herself—though here it is modified to reflect the "cleaner" esthetic of Nancy Meyers. See Sadie Wearing, "Subjects of Rejuvenation: Aging in Postfeminist Culture," in *Interrogating Postfeminism: Gender and the Politics of Popular Culture*, ed. Yvonne Tasker and Diane Negra (Durham, NC: Duke University Press, 2007), 301. See also Hugh Hart, "Let's Talk—Diane Keaton," *San Francisco Chronicle*, 11 December 2005.

13. Griffin, "Diane Keaton Meets Both Her Matches."
14. "The Veterans," *Variety* (D), 19 December 2003. *Baby Boom* also starred Keaton.
15. "Production Notes," Press release for *Something's Gotta Give*, consulted Margaret Herrick Library, March 2008.
16. Zachary Pincus-Roth, "Preem's 'Gotta' Warm up," *Variety* (W), 8 December 2003.
17. Tom Carson, "Phoning It In," *GQ*, April 2004.
18. "Playboy Interview: Jack Nicholson," *Playboy*, January 2004.
19. Gaby Wood, "The Two Jacks," *Observer Review*, 19 January 2003.
20. *Los Angeles Times*, 3 November 2003.
21. Griffin, "Diane Keaton Meets Both Her Matches."
22. Molly Haskell, quoted in Wood, "Two Jacks."
23. Griffin, "Diane Keaton Meets Both Her Matches."
24. For a discussion of the role of the makeover in contemporary "chick flicks," see Suzanne Ferriss, "Fashioning Femininity in the Makeover Flick," in *Chick Flicks: Contemporary Women at the Movies*, ed. Suzanne Ferriss and Mallory Young (New York: Routledge, 2008), 41–57.
25. Scott Foundas, "*Something's Gotta Give*," *Variety* (D), 5 December 2003.
26. Griffin, "Diane Keaton Meets Both Her Matches." See also *Architectural Digest*, November 2003, March 2006 and July 2007.
27. Kirk Honeycutt, "'Something's Gotta Give,'" *Hollywood Reporter*, 5 December 2003.
28. "Discoveries by Designers: Editors Present Designers' Sources," *Architectural Digest*, March 2006.
29. See *Architectural Digest*, November 2003, March 2006, and July 2007. Mary Ann Doane in her discussion of the women's films of classical Hollywood emphasizes the function of "the film frame" as "a kind of display window and spectatorship consequently as a form of window-shopping." See Mary Ann Doane, *The Desire to Desire: The Woman's Film of the 1940s* (Bloomington: Indiana University Press, 1987), 27. The role of consumer culture in films like *Something's Gotta Give*, while not unrelated to the strategies of classical Hollywood, marks a heightening and refinement of this tendency as well as a significant ontological deepening in terms of its ability to define the self.
30. Press release, 6.
31. Nancy Collins, "Set Design: *Something's Gotta Give*, Setting the Scene for Romance in the Hamptons," *Architectural Digest*, July 2007.
32. For a fuller discussion of makeover television programming, see Dana Heller, ed., *Makeover Television: Realities Remodelled* (London: I.B. Tauris, 2007).
33. For a description of the screwball romantic comedy in classical Hollywood, see Thomas Schatz, *Hollywood Genres: Formulas, Filmmaking, and the Studio System* (New York: Random House, 1981), 150–85.
34. Frank Krutnik, "Conforming Passions? Contemporary Romantic Comedy," in *Genre and Contemporary Hollywood*, ed. Steve Neale (London: British Film Institute, 2002), 130–47.
35. For a fuller description of the "biter bit," see Julia Briggs, "Shakespeare's Bed-Tricks," *Essays in Criticism* XLIV, no. 4 (1994): 293–314.
36. Tamar Jeffers McDonald, *Romantic Comedy: Boy Meets Girl Meets Genre* (London: Wallflower Press, 2007), 95.
37. McDonald, *Romantic Comedy*, 87, 97.
38. "In Praise of Younger Love," *London Times*, 3 February 2004.
39. *The Sweetest Thing* (Roger Kumble, 2002) and *Dirty Love* (John Mallory Asher, 2005), are, arguably, farcical neo-romantic comedies with a female protagonist; however, the box office successes in this category, such as *There's Something about Mary* (Bobby and Peter Farrelly, 1998), routinely revolve around a male protagonist.

40. Tamar Jeffers McDonald, "'Hommecom: Engendering Change in Contemporary Romantic Comedy," in *Falling in Love Again: Romantic Comedy in Contemporary Cinema*, ed. Stacey Abbott and Deborah Jermyn (London: I.B. Tauris, 2009), 158.

41. David Denby, "A Fine Romance: The New Comedy of the Sexes," *New Yorker*, 23 July 2007, 58–65.

42. Denby, "Fine Romance," 59.

43. Stanley Cavell, *Pursuits of Happiness: The Hollywood Comedy of Remarriage* (Cambridge, MA: Harvard University Press, 1981).

44. For a discussion of the concept of prolonged adolescence, see chapter three.

45. Tom Gliatto, "Aging Gratefully," *People Magazine*, 9 February 2004.

46. Tania Modleski, *Loving With a Vengeance: Mass-Produced Fantasies for Women* (Hamden, CT: Archon Books, 1982).

47. See chapter three.

48. Christy Grosz, "Love Story," *Hollywood Reporter*, 6 December 2003.

49. Amanda Barusch, *Love Stories of Later Life: A Narrative Approach to Understanding Romance* (New York: Oxford University Press, 2008).

50. Carl DiOrio, "Old's Gold at Box Office," *Variety* (D), 15 December 2003.

51. Helen E. Fisher, *Anatomy of Love: The Natural History of Monogamy, Adultery, and Divorce* (New York: Norton, 1992).

52. Fisher, *Anatomy of Love*, 310.

53. Wearing, "Subjects of Rejuvenation," 301.

54. Margaret Tally, "*Something's Gotta Give*: Hollywood, Female Sexuality, and the 'Older Bird' Chick Flick," in *Chick Flicks: Contemporary Women at the Movies*, ed. Suzanne Ferriss and Mallory Young (New York: Routledge, 2008), 130.

55. Eva Illouz, *Consuming the Romantic Utopia: Love and the Cultural Contradictions of Capitalism* (Berkeley: University of California Press, 1997), 295.

56. Helen Gurley Brown, *Sex and the Single Girl* (New York: Random House, 1962), 5.

57. Aihwa Ong, *Neoliberalism as Exception: Mutations in Citizenship and Sovereignty* (Durham, NC: Duke University Press, 2006), 3.

Conclusion

1. Rosalind Gill, *Gender and the Media* (Cambridge: Polity Press, 2007), 250, 251.

2. Gill, *Gender and the Media*, 253.

3. Gill, *Gender and the Media*, 254–68.

4. Rosalind Gill, "Postfeminist Media Culture, Elements of a Sensibility," *European Journal of Cultural Studies* 10, no. 2 (2007): 147–66, http://eprints.lse.ac.uk/2449/, accessed 19 December 2009.

5. Charlotte Brunsdon, "Feminism, Postfeminism, Martha, Martha and Nigella," *Cinema Journal* 44, no. 2 (2005): 110–16.

6. Sarah Projansky, "The Postfeminist Context: Popular Redefinitions of Feminism, 1980–Present," in *Watching Rape: Film and Television in Postfeminist Culture* (New York: New York University Press, 2001), 88.

7. Imelda Whelehan, *The Feminist Bestseller: From* Sex and the Single Girl *to* Sex and the City (Basingstoke: Palgrave Macmillan, 2005), 218.

8. Angela McRobbie, *The Aftermath of Feminism: Gender, Culture and Social Change* (London: Sage, 2009), 94. McRobbie is using "melancholia" in a strict Freudian sense, in which a lost object is introjected as a cathected phantasy.

9. Yvonne Tasker and Diane Negra, "Introduction: Feminist Politics and Postfeminist Culture," in *Interrogating Postfeminism: Gender and the Politics of Popular Culture* (Durham, NC: Duke University Press, 2007), 11.

10. Sally Quinn, "The Death of Feminism," *Washington Post Weekly Edition*, 27 January–2 February 1992.

11. Helen Gurley Brown, *Sex and the Single Girl* (Fort Lee, NJ: Barricade Books, 2003), xii.
12. Diane Negra, *What a Girl Wants? Fantasizing the Reclamation of Self in Postfeminism* (London: Routledge, 2009), 77.
13. Brown, *Sex and the Single Girl*, xii.
14. Brown, *Sex and the Single Girl*, xiii.
15. Whelehan, *Feminist Bestseller*, 218.
16. Whelehan, *Feminist Bestseller*, 218.
17. McRobbie, *Aftermath of Feminism*, 21.
18. McRobbie, *Aftermath of Feminism*, 97.
19. McRobbie, *Aftermath of Feminism*, 99.
20. McRobbie, *Aftermath of Feminism*, 98.
21. Angela McRobbie, "Illegible Rage," [chapter 4] in *Aftermath of Feminism*, 94–123. See especially 96–97.
22. Betty Friedan, *The Feminine Mystique* (New York: Norton, 1997).
23. Friedan, *Feminine Mystique*, 463–64.
24. For a discussion of the woman's film of classical Hollywood, see Jeanine Basinger, *A Woman's View: How Hollywood Spoke to Women, 1930–1960* (Hanover, NH: Wesleyan University Press, 1993).
25. For a discussion of the pleasure in femininity encouraged by classical Hollywood films for women, see Basinger, *Woman's View.*
26. Joanne Hollows, *Feminism, Femininity, and Popular Culture* (Manchester: Manchester University Press, 2000).
27. Hollows, *Feminism, Femininity, and Popular Culture*, 203.

Index